The Global Human Problem

American University Studies

Series VII
Theology and Religion

Vol. 48

PETER LANG
New York • Bern • Frankfurt am Main • Paris

Emmanuel K. Twesigye

The Global Human Problem

Ignorance, Hate, Injustice and Violence

PETER LANG
New York • Bern • Frankfurt am Main • Paris

Library of Congress Cataloging-in-Publication Data

Twesigye, Emmanuel K.
   The global human problem : ignorance, hate,
injustice & violence / Emmanuel K. Twesigye.
     p. cm. — (American university studies. Series
VII, Theology and religion ; vol. 48)
   Bibliography: p.
   Includes index.
   1. Man (Christian theology) 2. Sociology, Christian.
3. Languages — Religious aspects — Christianity.
4. Moral education. I. Title. II. Series.
BT701.2.T83   1989   233—dc19   88-12717
ISBN 0-8204-0753-4   CIP
ISSN 0740-0446

CIP-Titelaufnahme der Deutschen Bibliothek

Twesigye, Emmanuel K.:
The global human problem : ignorance, hate,
injustice and violence / Emmanuel K. Twesigye.
— New York; Bern; Frankfurt am Main; Paris:
Lang, 1988.
(American University Studies: Ser. 7,
  Theology and Religion; Vol. 48)
  ISBN 0-8204-0753-4

NE: American University Studies / 07

Printed by Weihert-Druck GmbH, Darmstadt, West Germany

TO

MY DEAR WIFE BEATRICE

AND

JOY, GRACE, GLORIA AND PEACE

OUR BELOVED CHILDREN

and
all other God's Children
everywhere

With

Unconditional Love and Thanksgiving

THE TABLE OF

CONTENTS

PREFACE

This book has been deliberately and painstakingly written in straightfoward, everyday, ordinary language so that it can be more easily read by a wide reading audience. Consequently, hard academic language has been softened, exclusive professional jargon and tedious footnotes have been entirely eliminated in order to make the book flow more naturally and smoothly.

However, the academic integrity, depth and scholarly scope of the material have been preserved. As a result, the task of this book has been almost double for me, since I had to simplify and translate the contents of this book from my first draft that was conceived and written in a hard, academic and professional language.

I have found out the hard way that it is easier for me to write and communicate with my fellow professional philosophers and theologians than the undergraduate students and the general public for whom this book has been primarily conceived and written.

Nevertheless, the book is scholarly and deep enough to be used as a main or supplementary textbook for college introductory courses in Ethics, Applied or Moral Theology, Philosophy, Religion, Peace Studies, Sociology, International Studies, Political Science and Education. I have kept in mind the intellectual needs and difficulty level of the courses, as I write this book.

Being a university professor myself, and having also taught these introductory level as well as more advanced courses in these areas, I am confident that this book will prove to be valuable for the college professors and teachers in these areas since there is a lack of good books and easy reading material that is educationally sound.

Consequently, this book represents Christian, moral, ethical and academic efforts at looking at our present multi-dimensional world and the pluralistic complex nature and the role of the human being in it.

The human being is viewed as the special creature and concrete representative of the abstract God in creation. He is also correlatively viewed as God's steward whose moral obligation and duty is to become the custodian of God's creation and not its polluter and destroyer.

This work was in part inspired by the United Church of Christ's great commitment and exemplary Christian concern for both public Christian education and global justice as the material in the appendix the role of the Church in teaching about justice and human equality, will clearly illustrate. In addition, my involvement in the Tennessee Governor's School for International Studies as a professor for "Creative Global Solving" provided further impetus for research and writing. Nevertheless, this book would not have taken this stand on violence and war, if I had not come very close to execution in Uganda during Idi Amin's repressive rule.

However, in order to understand the basic philosophy and real theological inspiration behind this book, one has to read my more academic and difficult book entitled, Common Ground: Christianity, African Religion and Philosophy, New York: Peter Lang, 1987. Its central thesis is that the unconditional love for the neighbor is the only divine and moral requirement for God's supernatural salvation, and that wherever it occurs, God's salvation also simultaneously takes place, since these two are inseparable coextensive correlatives.

The Bible quotations in this book are taken from the Good News Bible: Today's English Version. Occasionally, I do my own translations from the Greek because of the need for more accuracy and better contemporary english rendering. The Good News Bible was found the most preferable version because of my overriding intention to keep the language of this book plain, simple and contemporary; yet without losing or sacrificing the essential academic depth, and professional value of the material contained in the book.

The elimination of the footnotes has been made necessary for easy flow and smooth reading of the book. However, this omission of footnotes has been judiciously compensated for by the addition of four extensive appendices.

I am deeply grateful to the United Church Board for Homeland Ministries (UCBHM) for granting me permission to include the "Biblical Essay" with instructions for workshop which originally came from Margaret Shafer of the National Council of the Churches of Christ (NCCC) Education in Society Unit, with a cover letter from Dr. Nannete M. Roberts. It is an excellent essay and the instructions for teaching and workshop are most helpful for Churches and Sunday Schools and college or university religious settings.

I am also grateful to Dr. Henry Ponder who allowed me to use his speech to a freshmen class. It is a great example of how educators can legitimately become the advocates for good personal moral values. He even tackled the sensitive moral questions of drugs and teenage pregnancies, whereas some embarrassed parents and ministers in the Black Church, try to avoid them.

I am also very pleased to include Mr. Malcolm Dean's paper on the problem of "Moral Values and Crime in the Inner City Black Community." He is a freshman at Fisk University and he wrote the paper for one of my classes which he was required to take as a general college requirement for all entering Fisk University students. It shows that he is very much aware of the moral problems in his community, and that there are constructive ways to change and improve them.

Last, but not least, I am grateful to Miss Shana Barnes and Ms. Ida Watts for their great diligence in typing the final manuscript, Beatrice Twesigye my kind wife for her invaluable assistance with proof-reading and suggesting some important changes and corrections. This assistance is, particularly, appreciated since it was an additional responsibility to her regular chores of taking care of four young children.

I hope that this book will make a difference to the people who will read it carefully, reflect on its contents, and subsequently act in unconditional love, concern, goodwill and beneficent justice in God's name to change world and bring it into conformity with God's primordial will and goodness in creation.

Thank you for reading carefully this important material and I hope that after some contemplation, that you will also think of joining in the moral crusade to restore God's world to its essential primordial goodness, harmony, and peaceful coexistence with all its diverse inhabitants of which we, as human beings or the "homo sapiens," are probably the most intelligent, and correlatively, the most dangerous.

PROFESSOR EMMANUEL K. TWESIGYE, PhD
Chairman
Department of Religion & Philosophy
Fisk University
Nashville, Tennessee, USA

INTRODUCTION

Each human being is created by the Almighty God the Creator in order to become an intelligent, thinking, creative, moral agent as God's own concrete representation and ambassador in God's world of creation, both living and non-living. The Bible expresses this special human nature and its supernatural abstract qualities in terms of "God's image," whereas Greek philosophy calls this nature rational and political.

As a result, the human being's nature is essentially both divine and wordly, it is both rational and irrational, it is both spiritual and material, it is both humane and beastly, and it is both divine and human. The best example of this duality of human nature in one human being is Jesus the Christ, who in orthodox, Christianity, is considered to be both truly God and truly human.

This being the case, then unlike other creatures, human beings are God's unique and most special creatures in that they are most open to God of all creatures because they share in God's own divine nature while still open to and sharing the nature of the other earthly animals, particularly, the primates from whom God elected and chose them out of gratuitous and purposive redemptive grace and advanced them into the fullness of biological brain capacity and its corresponding full mental capity and its abilities for higher intelligence, learning memory, thinking, understanding, judgment, choice and moral decisions.

Subsequently, to be a normal human being is to possess fully these specialized and abstract mental powers and thinking, learning, knowing and decision-making skills. As a result, to be fully human also means to

2

learn, acquire and possess correct knowledge, make moral judgment and decisions by it, and live in accordance to this knowledge and truth. When this happens, then the person is truly God's moral agent and the decisions made according to correct knowledge and truth are also said to be moral, virtuous and good. And they are always godly, perfect and just, since they are impartial and in accordance with the truth and truth being of God and pure perfection.

However, in most cases human beings are ignorant of the truth, and do not possess correct knowledge due to the very nature of the human finite mind, and its inability to apprehend and comprehend the whole which is the real and correlatively, the truth. Instead, the human mind, essentially concentrates on the fragments of knowledge which the mind can easily apprehend and process. Unfortunately, the finite human mind tends also to treat and process the fragmentary bits of knowledge as the definitive whole, reality, the whole truth and infallible totality of knowledge on the subject in themselves.

Consequently, any moral and other practical decisions, whether educational, socio-economic, political or medical based on such partial knowledge which is unknowingly treated as the whole truth, are bound to error, and subsequently, cause more harm than good to human beings and the community.

Nevertheless, human beings constantly make important global decisions on the basis of limited fragmentary knowledge which in ignorance is treated as the whole truth. As a consequence, the world is full of evil due to human moral imperfections, ignorance, poor judgment, serious errors, and carelessness and accidents.

Consequently, if the world today is observed or said to be evil, polluted, and desert, it is not because God made it that way. The world today, is in many respects what it is, because in the name of God, we have made it what it has now become.

In other words, God created us in his/her own image, entrusted us with his/her creation as his or her intel-

ligent, creative, moral and physical representatives
and stewards, and instead, we became greedy, immoral
and rebelled against God. As a result, we too, also
became the ruthless masters, exploiters and destroyers
of ourselves, one another and God's creation. As a
consequence, we have transgressed against God, ourselves and the rest of creation, which we have abused,
injured and tragically marked with our own sins of
aggression, exploitation, pollution, vandalism and
destruction.

In short, the society and the environment are the
external expressions of the human being. And as such,
both bear the testimony to the social and moral values,
immorality, imperfection, sin, ignorance, and also
positively the sense of beauty and goodness.

However, whereas moral imperfection, ignorance, prejudice, hate, strife, conflict, and war, were prevalent
in the past and were tolerated by society, today, these
kinds of moral evils and imperfections cannot be tolerated. This is necessarily the case because in the past,
these vices, conflicts and wars were generally local
problems except for the last two World Wars which ended
tragically with the destruction of Hiroshima and Naga-
saki, the two Japanese cities with the unforgettable
deadly hydrogen bomb holocaust explosions.

Whereas the lesson of those cities may easily be
forgotten by the simple-minded, immoral warmongers,
prejudiced and racist politicians, fundamentalist com-
munist-hating Christians and the ignorant masses, those
who understand of the global danger of a nuclear warfare, the environmentalists, those who love God and
Christ's teaching of unconditional love for all human
beings, and everyone of goodwill, should all unite to
protest against the foolish suicidal nuclear arms race
and nuclear arsenals that endanger and threaten the
existence of the global freedom, human moral and physical well-being, everywhere, and ultimately, the very
survival and continued exsistence of life itself on
this unique and fragile planet.

Conseqently, the human being today is called upon to

become more ethical and morally responsible more than ever before in the recent or remote past. This is necessarily the inevitable truth and moral human requisite for every human being today, because human beings now possess the scientific knowledge, powerful nuclear military technology and capability to inflict quick indiscriminate massive harm on others, and even to destroy the whole life and the very planet itself. Consequently, the human being today, has the moral imperative to become more moral, loving, humane, careful, tolerant, less violent and more peace loving if the human species and the whole of life on this planet are to continue to survive and thrive.

Whereas, most of us are in full agreement with Socrates when he says that nobody can make another person more moral and virtuous, nor corrupt a truly perfect person, we must also remember that Socrates also says that there cannot be virtue and resposible human moral values without the acquisition and possession of correct knowledge of what is true and what is false, what is right and what is wrong and what is good and what is bad, that a genuine moral judgment and sound moral decision can be made. In addition, a good and positive moral role model is essential for the young to imitate, since all the young learn moral values by hearing the words and observing the actions of their own parents, other adults and their own peers, regardless of whether they are good or bad. Consequently, parents are viewed as the primary moral educators, and more influential role models for their own children.

However, churches and the media are requested to provide reinforcement for good moral education started at home by the parents and caring relatives, such as older siblings and grandparents. But these influential institutions are also challenged to provide good moral role models where they are absent in the homes, and the public mass media, especially the television, is challenged to come up with more educational programs for the children and young viewers; and to remove rampant sex and violence from young viewers' programs, especially violent cartoons, such as Bugs Bunny, the Incredible Hulk, Road Runner; and Bluto and Popeye who are ever violently competing, fighting and deceiving each other.

The mass media, just like the rest of the human institutions, has got to take its moral responsibility seriously, and try to influence both the young and the old members of our society in responsible ways of living together in harmony, despite competing differences and divergent personal or group interests.

Therefore, no moral and responsible society should ever teach its young that violence and cheating are harmless as long as one finally wins. Instead, the young should be taught that the means are as important as the end, and that greed, cheating, fraud, falsehood, and selfishness and fighting or all kinds of violence are wrong and moral evils which should not be indulged in by all civilized, well-educated, well-mannered, polite, honest, courageous, loving and peace seeking people.

Conversely, parents and the society should by their own words and example teach their children to extoll the moral virtues of courage, justice, truth, charity, compassion, caring, honesty, temperance and nonviolence, as the moral requisites for a civilized, humane and good life, in a harmonious, moral, caring, loving, forgiving, peaceful and happy human community both local and global.

Chapter One

THE HUMAN BEING

AS A MYSTERY

The greatest mystery still remaining to be probed on this earth by great scholars both in the sciences and the humanities is the human being himself or herself. We have studied everything on this planet and we have probed space, other planets, and galaxies for both knowledge and extraterrestrial life, and we have quite well succeeded in our humanistic quest and scientific research, thus enhancing both our own knowledge and the general improvement of the material quality of human life which advances in modern science and technology have made possible.

For instance, the advances in modern aerodynamics and space science have made it possible for human beings to go into space, walk on the moon, and work and build laboratories to manufacture better quality chemicals and medicines in the "zero gravity" conditions of outer space. Whereas this has constituted good utilization of the heavens for the benefit and betterment of human kind on earth "below," other human forces have been at work to extend the human evil of warfare, deadly nuclear arms race, and destruction into this hallowed space, lovingly known by many as "heaven."

This kind of modern scientific or technological advance that has revolutionized the medical technology, medicine, mass food production, better housing, clear water, and better transportation systems, all of which

have improved the material quality of our lives by
extending the life span from mid 40's to mid 70's just
within a few decades, has to be commended and supported.

Unfortunately, it is this advanced modern technology
in science which has also brought about the deadly
threat of nuclear arms race and a possible threat of
their being used with the subsequent global catastro-
phic destruction, either in the fiery nuclear explosions or the aftermath massive global radiation contamination, deadly toxic smoke, and radiative dust-
storms which might combine with thick clouds of smoke
emitted by billions of burning buildings and green
vegetation set ablaze by nuclear explosions.

Why should we as human beings commit this kind of
horrible suicide? Or why should a few individuals or
even nations be allowed to destroy us and all life on
this unique planet? What is there to be gained by going
to war in which mutual destruction and no winner is
assured? Or one should ask why should some intelligent
and responsible people go to war at all? Is warfare and
hatred a survival of animality in humanity or a survival of sin in a child of God?

Indeed, these and many other questions should be
asked by us and all intelligent human beings, everywhere, regardless of creed, ideology, level of technology, or economic development because our own existence
and survival as human beings on this delicate globe we
all inhabit and lovingly call home, is in this modern
era of nuclear arms, instant video telecommunication,
supersonic air travel, dwindling natural economic resources, environmental pollution, international trade,
and international politics. Strife is a mutual or a
collective global community affair, and not an isolated
affair to be left to the individual nation's whims.

Our globe has become our Noah's Ark, and therefore,
we cannot let anyone puncture a hole by a nuclear
explosion or drill a hole in his or her own corner
either in ignorance or a suicide attempt, for to let
such people carry out their own will and illogical

decisions is tantamount to our own reluctant suicide and sure destruction by our failure to restrain the illogical, paranoid, suicidal, bigoted, careless, insane, and irresponsible members of our global community.

Therefore, the people of the Third World should be as concerned about what happens or does not happen in Washington, D.C. and Moscow as the people in the West, for they too are citizens and an integral part of the global community. Subsequently, if there is a massive nuclear explosion in the Northern hemisphere, winds will carry nuclear radioactive dust and pollution to their developing people in the other hemisphere.

Consequently, no one should be complacent when the fate of the globe and the life on it are at stake. This is more so when we realize that it is our very own life and that of our posterity at stake and not merely that of some strangers or "Communists" in the Soviet Union that one has never met nor will ever meet.

Even then, the thought that if one is a stranger then it is alright for him or her to be killed is very inhumane and obnoxious. In addition, in some cases the strangers could also be us, and therefore, we have to be careful what we say to be right when it comes to murder, homicide or genocide.

For instance, would you shoot or stab a communist if you met one on the street in New York or London? If not, why would you say it is alright to build an intercontinental nuclear missle specifically designed to kill indiscriminately and targeted at Moscow with its millions of inhabitants, both young and old, communist and noncommunist, tourist and citizen, friend and foe, just because the leaders have disagreed on some technicality in bilateral relations or have failed to agree on what portion of the globe or its wealth should belong to whom and by what means it should be acquired without rousing the public outcry or denouncements by the nonaligned nations and the more courageous or economically independent of the allies.

Today, the world is in more danger of being destroyed

than ever before. The destruction of the earth, although foretold in the Bible (Mk. 13:24-33; Mth. 5:18,
10:23; Lk. 16:17), is almost more imminent than God
the great Cosmic Creator would have wanted. We know
this because one of the major signs that Jesus gave
that would have to be fulfilled before his second
return and the destruction of this world in fiery
judgement or hell for the sinners was that the Gospel
would have to be preached to every person in the world
(Mk. 13:32; Mtt. 24:14) and to all nations. But according to David Barret's recent mammoth statistical data,
Christianity in all its different thousands of Churches
only accounts for just a third of the total population
and was on the decline and not the increase. In addition, millions of people in Islamic countries, Communist, Hindu, and Buddhist India and Japan had never
heard of Christ presented as a beneficently loving,
world and personal Redeemer (or Savior).

In which case, we can claim from this Christian
perspective that we are not acting on God's behalf if
we destroy the world and those not yet converted in a
fiery nuclear holocaust. It is quite clear and beneficial that instead of seeking to destroy those we call
atheistic "communists," we should seek to convert them
to Christ and his way of loving the neighbor, as well
as the enemy (Matt. 5:43-48):

> You have heard that it was said, "You shall love
> your neighbor and hate your enemy." But I say to
> you, Love your enemies and pray for those who
> persecute you, so that you may be sons of your
> Father who is in heaven; for he makes his sun to
> rise on the evil and on the good, and sends rain on
> the just and the unjust....."

It is, therefore, quite clear from this passage that
Jesus does not want us to send nuclear bombs and missiles to rain destructive fire on those we deem to be
evil or unjust, but rather to neutralize their evil
with good deeds of unconditional love and prayer for

their conversion, reformation and deliverance from evil
and its oppression. In the case of arms race and war,
it is evident that we have ignored Christ's teaching
and Commandment that we should love God and love our
neighbor as we love ourselves.

Therefore, Christians, whether in politics or government, have the rare opportunity to become the world's
leader of peace as they become exponents of disarmament
and not war-mongers either by supporting great military
spending budgets or war activities themselves both in
rhetoric or real action. Christians have a divine mandate to act in this world as peace-makers and global
community builders and to do otherwise is to repudiate
God's unconditioned redemptive love in Christ that was
expressed to this world on the cruel and painful cross.
We too, as Christians are called to bear our own crosses as we faithfully follow Christ's teaching and example.

Therefore, we are not to crucify other people on
crosses in the name of Christ; but rather, we should be
willing to bear our own crosses, and even to be cruci-
fied on them by the world if that will perfect God's
salvation for the world which was ushered into the
world incognito, but definitely humanely in Christ.

As a result, if God had even to sacrifice his only
"Begotten Son" in order to save this world, surely we
who are Christians cannot stand still and let people
like President Ronald Reagan endanger its very own
existence by their ideological and military crusade
against communism. God acted in love in Christ in
order to save this world; we too have to act in love
for our fellow human being so as to save them from
evil, hatred, oppression, cruelty, warfare and self-
destruction. Subsequently, love calls us to oppose the
nuclear arms race, and the militarization of oceans and
space.

In the final analysis, the love we express to our
neighbor and the goodwill we extend in peace to all
human beings, are directly returned to us in the same
or greater measure, and as such, the love and peace we

extend to our neighbors around the globe are extended to ourselves in reflected manner, just as the boomerang goes out and eventually returns to its thrower.

By the same analogy, we will also receive what we extend to others around us; if it is evil that we express to others, it will also be generously recipro- cated with greater evil. Therefore, as Christians, let us sow the seeds of love and peace on this ever "shrinking globe" and pray that God will bless it to yield the traits of love and global peace which we desperately need today.

Subsequently, what humanity needs today is not more knowledge and more technology, but more love, more human caring, and more peace nationally and interna- tionally on a global level. This is extremely important for mere knowledge and nuclear technology, without human love and care to direct and safeguard its humani- tarian usage, will soon prove tragic and suicidal for humanity and this planet.

But since the greatest good and value of any knowl- edge, skill, science and technology is the enhancement of survival and well-being of the human being, it seems that in the recent advances made in the sciences and technology, the necessary moral teaching required to govern ethical usage has lagged far behind the scienti- fic breakthroughs so that technology has tended to master the inventor of the human being rather than the human being staying in control.

The results have been tragic. Industrial waste has been allowed to pollute our water supply by polluting the air, clouds, rivers, lakes, and oceans. Acid rain has killed off essential vegetation and if not halted, we face a deadly global environmental crisis. Some man- made chemicals have even eaten holes in the ozone layer, leaving us exposed to the sun's cancer-causing radioative rays. Nevertheless, driven by greed for profit and economic success, industries continue to manufacture these chemicals and we buy them even when we know the great harm caused on a global scale.

Therefore, at this point, one should stop and pose a

vital question about our nature as human beings. What kind of creature or being is the human being? In traditional terms, the infinite question has always been put as follows: "What is 'Man'?"

What is a Human Being?

The historic question of "What is man?" or "What is a human being?" has always been asked by each individual, thinking human being, regardless of era, technological and economic level of development, creed, ideology, race, color, nationality, gender and socio-economic status. As soon as a person implicitly or explicitly asks questions like: "Who am I?" "Where did I come from?" "What is my future?" "Why am I here?" and "Is death the end?" that person is not just only searching for his or her ultimate origins and destiny, but also asking if human life has any special meaning.

These questions which Paul Tillich correctly characterized as the human existential questions of ultimate concern, thus requiring religious and philosophical answers dealing with the existential meaning of the human nature and finite human life in the presence of an eternal, loving, Creator God who gives meaning to human life as its ultimate source, grounding, and final destiny. In this Judeo-Christian understanding, the human being is a special creature or creation of God living in the world created by God and the final future resting place of the human being, also being God.

This understanding of the human being is certanly the one supported by the Bible. For instance, in Genesis 1:26-27, we read that God created humankind (Adam) and that both male and female were created in God's image to have dominion over the rest of God's creation as God's own representatives and stewards.

In this creation account, as well as the second one found in Genesis 2:4 and 4:2, the human being is a special creation or creature of God created in two natures. The first nature is creaturely and beastly.

It is symbolized by dust and the body. The second
nature is a divine; and it is symbolized by God's
image, mind, spirit, soul (and in the New Testament it
is symbolized by unconditional love).

Accordingly, in the biblical second creation account,
we read that God breathed into Adam's body which was
made of dust, and subsequently, Adam became a living
soul (Gen. 2:7). It is also to be noted that Adam became a living soul even when he still possessed the
physical body costituted of dust to which it was destined to return at death.

This divine spirit which is said to have been breathed into the human being by God, is a good symbol for
the divine qualities which are found in the human
being. There is great truth in this in that God and the
human being share certain qualities, such as spirit,
intelligence, knowledge, justice, love, sense of holiness, creativity, and an awareness of order and beauty.
However, unlike God, the human being remains finite,
temporal, material and as such, subject to the corro-
sion of time, death and decay just like the rest of
God's creation.

Furthermore, we who are Christians also believe that
God has, in Christ, become a human being by the virtue
of the Incarnation. If this is true, then it also
follows that in Christ, human beings have also become
one with God or become God. The Eastern Orthodox
Churches have exactly taught this doctrine and the
Christian Mystical tradition has historically taught
that human beings can become divinized or deified into
union with God through the various rigorous ascetic
stages of self-purification, purgation, and divinization.

In the second biblical account of the creation of
humankind, we also find that our human nature is still
not as pure as God had either originally created it or
had intended it to be. This defect in our nature is
explained in terms of human sin, or more specifically,
disobedience against God's guiding moral law or commandments as divinely proposed direction for human life

and the subsequent human self-autonomy, self-centeredness, selfishness, greed, envy, hatred and murder (Gen.
3-4). This observation is true regardless of whether we
believe in a literal creation of adult and fully developed human beings by God or whether we believe in a
slow divine process of human creation through the scientifically reconstructed evolution. In both cases,
human beings are said and known to be imperfect.

Human moral imperfection is taught by all religions,
along with the various creation accounts of which many
greatly vary from those found in the book of Genesis
while others may even sound almost similar to those in
Genesis. In all cases, the human problem is that of
disobedience against God's given moral law for human
life. And the results of this sin, generally, include
loss of love for the neighbor, hatred, strife and
murder or death.

This means that even if God had intended for us to
live together happily in a community, by our own sin
and disobedience to God, we would have invented a way
to kill off those we dislike and thus disrupt both
peace and communal harmony and defy God-given immortality for all human beings. The high number of crimes
involving bodily harm and homicide is ample evidence
that human beings do not generally desire a good, happy
and long life for all members of their own kind. Some
governments, even try to eliminate those people they
regard as a danger to their national security and/or to
their fellow citizens.

Thus, unjust state capital punishment and clandestine
killings of opponents by secret police agents can a-
mount to a form of state terrorism for many of her
citizens; thus a negation of the state's very reason
for being there, namely, to protect the life and property of her citizens. This remains true whether the
citizen is law abiding or not.

Therefore, criminals are still human beings with
constitutional rights to life and state protection of
that life and their property. The fact that states have
abused their powers is evidence that human sin and

imperfection have infiltrated all human institutions, including politics, government, the judiciary system, police departments and even the Church. In short, wherever human beings are found, also expect to find human imperfection and sin in terms of corruption, defective products, envy, malice, plots, gossip, hatred, strife, and murder.

This is why dangerous nuclear weapons in the hands of such imperfect creatures as the ones described above pose a great danger not just to the nation possessing them and its antagonists, but to the whole world. For instance; imagine a quietly insane President who wants to commit suicide, and in doing so, takes down the whole world with him! He could do great global damage with nuclear weapons in such a short time before those around him realize that he is mentally ill, and therefore, not to be obeyed.

However, a general or tactical commander of a nuclear missile submarine could become mentally unbalanced and set off nuclear missiles in paranoia, just as guns in the hands of the insane have left us with periodic mass murders in public places. Nuclear weapons in the hands of many imperfect human beings or governments are also going to leave this planet in a tragic shambles and quiet, desolate smoking ruins where once life was loud and vibrant.

It is not amazing, therefore, that because of the evil inherent in the human being, the first great attraction for any new technology and invention is the possible value of the new technology is its perceived great killing capacity. The killing power is not sought to kill off dangerous animals but fellow human beings. The greater the killing power at a long distance, the greater the value is placed on such an item.

One is sometimes forced to wonder about what kind of great advancement we as human beings would have made if investments put in human killing (strategic) weapons had, instead been made in agriculture or medical research. The world and humanity would have been better off this way than at the present moment when some governments spend a greater portion of the national budgets making or buying deadly arms than on either education on social welfare. The priority here seems to be killing human beings rather than either saving or serving them.

When Aristotle defined the human being as a "political animal," I am sure that what he had in mind was a human being who was more of a result of the socialization or humanization process of a civilized human organization or community that is willfully established for the purpose of collective, peaceful, self-governing, and non-deadly power struggle and dominance for either the strongest or the most war-like. Indeed, before Aristotle, Plato had advanced the idea of a philosopher-king in order to ensure that the political leader was knowledgeable in the common good and would not abuse his important office for self-gratification, oppression of his opponents, or to inflict harm and evil on the people he ruled through ignorance and bad decisions.

For Plato, as for Socrates, a good person was one who was virtuous and virtue itself was considered to be a product of correct knowledge, wisdom and self-discipline aimed at life in accordance to one's knowledge. Subsequently, whereas for the Bible, the human moral problem is that of sin of disobedience to God's moral law and the cure is repentance and obedience to God; for Socrates and Plato, human evil is due to human ignorance and lack of the knowledge of the good. Therefore, for both Socrates and Plato, good moral education was the prescribed cure for human evil.

As a philosopher and an educator, I do agree with both Socrates and Plato that good moral education will enable many people to become more aware of the importance of their decisions and choices, and therefore, also to increase the awareness of the responsiblity which goes along with decisions and choices.

However, as a Christian, I am also aware that mere good education alone does not have the power to transform human nature from an evil one to a good one. This is necessarily true because this human fundamental transformation calls for a supernatural transformation of the human being which can only be effected by holy, loving Creator and Redemptive God can effect this kind of total transformation from a lost sinner into a redeemed child of God, which constitutes a secondary act of creation, in as much as redemption is restoration of the human being to the original divinely intended state of wholeness and holiness.

Accordingly, this divinization process by which God redeems and restores the sinner to himself or herself, is also commonly known in Evangelical churches as being "born again" or "being saved," since only God can save or redeem human beings.

The Unique Human Features
and Characteristics

There is no question that the human being is regarded
to be special by all people irrespective of era, creed,
ideology, level of technological development, race,
color, and education. This is a well documented factor
from the ancient Egyptian and Babylonian civilizations
through the Bible and Greek civilizations up to the
present time. Human beings have always thought of themselves as being unique children or creatures of God
with special divine, endowed gifts in order to become
masters of the creation on God's behalf. We have already examined this claim in relationship to the book
of Genesis.

However, the other human unique features are empirical and can be observed objectively and studied scientifically by any able scholar. For instance, whereas
human beings are biologically classified as mammals
belonging to the rest of the "animal kingdom" on earth
and from which we are supposed to have originally
evolved, we are physically, socially, intellectually,
spiritually, morally, linguistically, and culturally
quite different from them. This is an obvious observation which cannot be refuted by any thinking and sane
human being.

This dual nature of the human being as both a divine
and an animal or beastly being has plagued human civilization with savage vandalism, senseless warfare,
crime and violence of all kinds, including that in
intimate relationships, family spats, and entertainment. Whereas today we enjoy rough games, such as
wrestling, boxing, American football, and bull-fight-
ing, the ancient Romans enjoyed deadly games of gladi-
ators and during the eras of Christian persecution,
crowds came to be entertained by watching unarmed
Christian men and women being thrown into the arena to
fight hungry lions with bare hands. Sadistically, the

crowds shouted with delight as the hungry animals ferociously tore the poor defenseless men and women to pieces, one after the other.

This kind of human delight in cruelty, beastly actions, savage games for mere entertainment, and deadly warfare for the sake of asserting exclusive territorial rights or dominance is a clear case of the animality still surviving in the human being. Sometimes, it is even difficult to tell whether the human being is less savage and beastly than the wild beasts themselves which rarely kill off their own kind in a jungle war for mates, territory and food. Animals probably know better how to follow the natural laws more than the human beings for among these natural laws are included the idea of animals of one kind flocking together and not killing each other in order to ensure a peaceful animal community conducive to mutual protection and survival.

However, survival and community constitute the first law of nature. As a result, some animals live in well organized communities in order to ensure their survival whereas the less social ones live alone, also to ensure their own survival ability, by themselves, especially when food is scarce.

Nevertheless, in each case, one's survival is closely tied in together with the survival of one's own species. For instance, if there is an elephant hunter who hunts elephants for their expensive tusks, the safety of each elephant lies either in the death of the hunter or his/her stopping to hunt either through a change of heart or legal intervention.

Subsequently, in the presence of the enemy, bull elephants try to protect the herd, and try to ensure their own species' survival by charging and eliminating the enemy, even at the cost of their own lives. Whereas this may also be true for most groups of people, unfortunately, the enemy is always perceived to be the other people.

As a result, unlike the other animals, human beings have tended to view one another with great suspicion, envy and intolerance. Human beings have tended not to view each other as members of the same species, but rather, they have preferred to view themselves in terms of families, tribes or ethnic groups, regions, states, nations, races and colors.

Subsequently, there have been feuds at each of those human classification levels. There have been family feuds, tribal wars, regional civil wars, international wars, race and color prejudice, strife, conflicts, and violence. Therefore, what we need is to bridge and heal all these unnecessary human divisions, strife, and conflicts so as to create a new positive global human self-identity as the "Humankind and Global Citizens."

This global awareness and international human identity would naturally neutralize the narrow local loyalties of tribe, region, and nation by focusing the local attention to the wider international scene. This would also mean that to ensure the survival of my own offspring, I would also have to ensure the survival of the planet itself and its delicate ecological balances and the environment. This is a justified shift and concern because of the modern technological new shift from a local community to a global community in activity and scope. This means that for any one to survive, all have to survive and the planet has to survive as well for modern technology has turned and shrunk the previous expansive world into "a human global community."

Consequently, each individual life has become internationally linked to all human lives, and therefore, whatever affects one now affects all, and when there is a contagious disease on one part of the globe today, the next day it will have traveled to the other half of the globe. Therefore, individuals, like nations, are now more linked together more than ever before, making it impossible for one group of people to survive alone without the other. This is why to love our neighbor is to love ourselves and to ensure our own survival.

Hopefully, gone forever, are the days when "primitive" and ignorant tribal groups thought of themselves as the total humanity, the very chosen children of God living at the very center of the universe. We do not find such exclusive tribal claims only in the Bible (Gen. 12:1-3), but also in other tribal Creation and Election Myths such as those found among the African people, particularly, among the "Bantu" (People).

This kind of exclusive claim to humanity of one group of people at the exclusion of others, particularly, the strangers and foreigners, has been the background to "tribalism" in modern African and political instablity prevailing there whereas in the West, it has led to wars, such as the Second World War, which was directly linked to Hitler and his ethnocentric and racist Nazi Party. In the USA, Northern Ireland, Lebanon, Israel, and South Africa, there are still ethnic and racial armed conflicts which flare up now and again.

The ruthless repression of the Black people who are the in South Africa by a minority White group is the clearest contemporary example of this racial problem. The problem becomes even more complex when the dominant group claims that it is because of God's election or gracious choice that it happens to be the privileged group in power, endowed with the special gift of beauty, and the white color as evidence of this divine choice for royalty and governing of the majority who happen to be Black (and also to be considered ugly because of black skin, kinky hair, thick lips, and flat noses). The recent facist-like trends in South Africa remind us of Hitler and the way he sent millions of Jews to the gas chambers as the world kept silent. This time, the world has no excuse not to intervene when the Afrikaaners are systematically exterminating the Black people.

The Black people's extermination process is currently underway, and we have all the evidence, but why do we wait? What are we still waiting for? A major mass black massacre? How many people have to be killed before the world can respond? Will the world ever respond honestly to such black mass murders, or like the ancient Romans, will we still love to sit before our television sets and enjoy the entertainment of the grueling scenes of unarmed masses of Black men, women, and children being mowed down by the machine gun bullets fired by White police officers from the safety of armoured personnel carriers?

The innate beast inside us, seems not to have changed since the ancient Roman days, though the nature of cruel games, the technology of weapons, and the arena contestants have changed, human beings themselves have not changed and still enjoy to see war games, real wars, and the suffering of others. This is always enjoyable as long as those suffering are always the others and not ourselves or our close friends and family members.

Therefore, sadism seems to be one of the unfortunate, unique major characteristics of the human being, and unless we find a constructive and effective way to counteract it, it can lead the very extinction of the human species through some fatal, stupid mistake; such as using a nuclear weapon to inflict pain and punishment on a group of people of one's intense dislike or fear. This can also happen in times of international disagreement, strife, and armed conflict.

However, the miscalculation can lead to unexpected counter retaliations and mutual destruction at a higher level, never taken into account before the onset of the conflicts. This is how minor wars have in the past led into greater wars and how international wars have started in minor diplomatic disagreements which have kept on growing into a full military hurricane. This also illustrates the capricious nature of the human being and how futile it is for human social scientists to try to predict all future human behavior, both individual and corporate.

The Unique Physical Features
of the Human Being

The human being has a very unique and characteristic feature of being bipedal and upright in posture. This upright posture is very advantageous because it frees the hands to do work. Definitely, this is one of the main distinguishing features between the human being and the rest of the animals; most especially, the primates that so closely resemble the human beings.

The other primates may occasionally walk on two legs and even use their hands to manipulate tools, but unlike the human being, the usual posture of these creatures is walking on four legs or using their long, strong arms to swing from branch to branch and from tree to tree. Whereas we are better at walking, these primates are better runners and tree climbers, for their own life and survival require it when it is mere sport for us.

In addition, the human thumb is very mobile compared to that of other primates. This again enables the human being to utilize the hand better and more efficiently, and thus, to undertake and successfully accomplish very fine tasks that require agility in terms of hand co-ordination such as writing, curving, painting, making or using small hand-held tools like the surgeon's scalpel, or the seamstress' needle.

Another interesting and unique physical feature of the human being that is regularly utilized by scientists in the study of pre-history and its extinct ancient creatures is the size of the head and its structure. Human heads are very distinctive. They are very large compared to any other animal of our size, including the large apes. Our brain's size is also much larger, so the head structure is important as a means of enabling us to have more brains in a very safe protective set of bones well fused together to form a protective armour around the delicate brain.

This protective round structure around the brain

which we usually call the skull is a human unique physical feature. And it can be used to study and identify an ethnic group, race, and age of a human remain or fossil. The human upright posture also helps in ensuring that the head is safer and better situated high up on the top of the human body, not as mere symbol of its priviliged position, but also to enable better view for the eyes and hearing and balance sensory input for the ears.

Since the human being is bipedal and upright in posture, in order to remain well balanced on the two feet, the head with its two ears has to be where it is in order to sense and correct the problems of balance since this is an activity performed by the ears and the brain. Moreover, the human upright posture, with the eyes located close to the top of the head, has a great advantage which most animals envy in that the human being can see much further from this position than from a lower position in which other primates often find themselves when walking on four legs.

Subsequently, most animals try to stand on their hind legs so as to see more clearly above the tall grass. And in some cases, even some animals climb trees or high ground so as to survey carefully the territory around them for enemies or food which they cannot do from under the grass or lower ground. Some animals like monkeys and other primates have been known to keep one of them on guard high up in a tree or on higher ground while others remain on the ground feeding until it is their turn to keep watch.

This is also true of some human beings during wartime. Therefore, in this respect, the animals and human beings desire the same things; namely, better vision, security, and advance warning when there is trouble or danger coming.

Animals are better than human beings at using natural instincts and senses to "smell or sense trouble" coming. The animals have keener senses of smell, taste, hearing, and sight. For instance, we keep watch dogs to hear and see what we cannot hear or see. With our modern powerful telescopes, binoculars, and smoke detectors, we can very easily compensate for this deficit. However, we can never carry these gadgets around with us everywhere and at all times!

Moreover, whereas the animals have sharper teeth and can run faster than us, we have invented easy ways to catch them and kill them. Guns and traps are more efficient today than ever before; subsequently, the human being, though small in size, has almost caused the extinction of many species of wild life by his/her careless hunting habits, uncontrolled commercial development of the environment where animals lived, and the subsequent careless pollution of water, air, and the land with industrial toxic waste, both in liquid and gas forms.

This is the kind of embarrassing ecological imbalance and environmental crisis brought about by us in the name of technology and progress. Furthermore, it is now self-evident that wherever animals have destroyed their own environment by both overpopulation and overgrazing, they have also perished along with their environment. Consequently, it can be said that, we are no exception to this natural law of ecological balance and mutual coexistence or symbiosis.

Whereas it is true, that unlike the other animals, our advanced technology allows us to dominate and shape our own enviroment to our own particular taste, it remains also true that we are still creatures of our environment, and therefore, subject to the natural laws that govern all natural life of which we are an integral part. Moreover, there is a limit to how far we can go without destroying our own environment, and subsequently, causing our own destruction, along with it since our own existence is essentially dependent on our physical and biological environment.

I am not in any way suggesting that we return to the prescientific era when the human being behaved like the rest of the animals around him or her, and therefore, logically sought to live in harmony with nature and the given surrounding environment by making adjustments to

the weather and the local conditions, whereas today, we
seek to adapt the environment to our needs and tastes,
rather than adapting ourselves to its ways.

This is why the human being is found on every continent, regardless of weather, though characteristically
hairless on most of the body, unlike the other mammals
which are entirely covered with thick coats of fur to
protect them from the elements as well as the other
hazards of living in the jungle, such as insect bites,
scratches and cuts. Being hairless on most of the body
seems to be a unique, expensive feature of the human
being. It is an expensive feature in that most of the
earning of "civilized people" in our society seem to go
for either expensive clothes or lavish food!

Indeed, this natural nakedness of the human being
seems to be one of the great driving sources for human
inventions, moral codes, social etiquette, religious
inspiration, love, romance, elaborate dressing, and
housing arrangments, including "bathroom taboos," some
being for the "ladies" and others for "gentlemen." The
idea behind being that in a public place, if anyone has
to see the other naked, it should be a member of the
same gender. The implication and underlying understanding, in this case, is that public nakedness is bad and
should not be tolerated among people of different gender. Again, one has got to go further than this and
speculate that in some people's mind nudity can only
mean sexual immorality, and therefore, sin.

However, what is often forgotten is that sin is not
in the exposure of the genitals, but rather in the
human mind of those either exposing themselves or looking at this natural body area. For instance, when we
are born we are naked and it does not seem to bother
either God or those present at birth that both the
mother and the baby are exposed. Why is this the case,
we might ask? Is it because the attention of those
present is not focused on the genitalia for its sexual
appeal but as an organ of child birth?

I have been to some parts of tribal Africa where
western dress is still frowned upon. In this hot tropi-
cal climate, in the absence of air conditioners, it

makes great sense to have on minimum clothing! After all, does not the popular biblical account of human creation in the book of Genesis tell us that when God first created human beings, they were naked, sinless and without shame? (Gen. 2: 21-26; 3:4-11.)

However, I was the one embarrassed to see young women's pointed breasts heaving up and down as these young women indifferently walked about doing their daily work! If I found these attractive naked breasts both seductive and provocative, it was because I was from another culture and it would not have been the slightest fault of these African tribal girls. They do not regard exposed breasts as sexual exposure or an invitation to sexual activity. Indeed, the evidence is that they are still expected to be virgin when they get married. Disaster still befalls those not found virgin and great shame is felt by their families for not having kept their daughter virtuous.

Ironically, being fully clothed may be a sign of wealth and a certain socio-economic status, but it has nothing to do with sexual morality! This is because clothing can be quickly discarded by intending to engage in sexual intercourse. Yet, we still condemn with great zeal those "tribesmen" who insist on going either naked or with scanty clothing! Isn't this a form of protection of our own sexual lewdness and guilt on others who may be completely innocent?

Unfortunately, this seems also to be the other unique trait of the human being; namely, that we deny the evil in us and project it on those we dislike. As a consequence, we often hate and persecute other people for what we hate in ourselves but see in them. For instance, we very often find it easy to blame others for the bad we do, whereas taking all credit for the good we do, even that done by others! Subsequently, both fraud and plagiarism are also uniquely human characteristics.

The Intellectual Uniqueness
of the Human Being

We have already seen that the human being has a distinctively and characteristically large, round head protectively housing a very large brain. The huge brain is one of the greatest unique features of the human being, distinguishing humans from non-humans by the virtue of enabling the humans to possess a much higher and greater intellectual cability for abstract thinking, memory, freedom, moral responsibility, and self-transcedence.

This human intellectual power enables the human being to possess an infinite curiosity for knowledge, higher abilities of thinking or data collection, a scientific analysis for cause and other relationships, great capacity for memory which serves as data storage for both processed and unprocessed data; and systematic storage for later retrieval when needed in analysing and solving a new problem.

This distinctive human intellectual characteristic is so basic in understanding the human being that great skeptic philosophers like the great French philospher Rene Descartes was able to prove his own existence and that of God, merely on the basis of thinking. His great proof for his own existence and indirectly that of all human beings was: "I think, therefore, I am" (Cogito ergo sum).

Subsequently, Descartes' understanding of thinking includes human self-awareness or self-consciousness, reason or logic, and understanding. If this is the case, then as far as we know, human beings are the only true thinkers or rational beings.

However, this does not mean that animals completely lack any form of intelligence and limited capacity for correct data processing, decision, and memory. On the contrary, the animals, particularly, the higher primates, such as baboons, monkeys, chimpanzees and gorillas, seem to exhibit some human-like forms of intelligence and even behavior.

Nevertheless, this is at a very rudimentary and limited level. In addition, there is no evidence so far that these animals are getting more intelligent in terms of brain structural change and increase. Since thinking is a complex functional structure of the brain, as well as being also a result of good education, it seems unlikely that even if we gave these animals the best of the human education, they would become human. Sure enough, a few animals have been trained for human entertainment and to act in the circus, but apart from this sophisticated training and conditioning, these animals remain mere tamed beasts. For instance, they can neither think nor speak. If they did, then they would truly become human, regardless of their physical form or looks.

Thinking and creativity are major qualities in themselves. For instance, in traditional Christian theology and philosophy, God is known as the Creator and Omniscient. This is also true in most world religions, particularly in Judeo-Christianity, Islam, and the African Traditional Religion. Saint Thomas probably speaks for most Christians when he defines and describes God as "pure intellect," "the Omniscient," and "the Omnipotent."

If this Thomistic characterization of God is correct and true to God†s essence and reality, then it follows that the human intellectual activity and the essentially correlated thinking processes, the acquisition of knowledge and subsequent mental or skilled creativity, are divine attributes found in the human being. In other words, by an intellectual activity, the human being participates in God's divinity and God's own transcendental, eternal dimension, traditionally and variously known as "spirit" or "mind."

This takes us back to the biblical book of Genesis, which states that God made human beings, both male and female, in "his" own image (Gen. 1:27), or that God breathed his life-giving breath into Adam and "he became a living soul" (Gen. 2:7). In this biblical understanding, the divine quality God imparted to the human being that makes the human being more God-like or God's image, is the intellect or the soul. No other creature is referred to as "God's image" apart from the human being who was endowed with the divine breath or spirit for his/her uniqueness of being, special position and responsibility in God's creation.

Unfortunately, according to the Bible, it is also this divine quality found in the human being in the form of intellect, thinking, and creativity that led to the human being's disobedience and rebellion against God's moral and natural laws in favor of unrestricted human independence and experimental search for more empirical and moral knowledge so as "to be like God"; to know the good and the bad and also to gain the secret to eternal life, and therefore, to live forever, just like God.

This is the kind of spirit still driving us on to do more experiments and conduct more research to unlock more of the secrets of life, and therefore, live longer and better lives. We are still searching for eternal life. Unfortunately, Adam's disobedience and forbidden experiments only brought in the cognitive awareness and discovery of the reality of human finitude and the definitive reality of human death rather than that of divinity and eternal life.

Adam's disobedience and experiments brought in empirical knowledge but the knowledge was of human nature and its limited achievements, duration, and temporal, composite constitution dissolved into its original constitutive elements by time, and ultimately by death. As a result, death was viewed as the human being's chief enemy. Subsequently, all major religions focus on this human weakness and despair in the face of the unescapable radical threat of death, and try to look for ways to either escape it or overcome it with God's help.

Consequently, in most religious teachings, God's free saving grace is required if most human beings are to be transformed, redeemed, spared or saved from the eternal destruction of death. Christianity is a classic example with its doctrines of Christ's atonement by his own innocent death on the cross on behalf of all sinners in the world or all human beings and the hope for a general resurrection of all those who have died, with those who will be judged morally upright, going to live eternally with God in heaven, whereas the wicked ones go to live in eternal punishment known as "hell."

However, this characterization of human freedom, infinite curiosity and search for knowledge as the possible venue for human sin and rebellion against God's natural and moral laws does not mean that we should discard science and technology in order to live in conformity with natural laws. It simply means that we should not destroy the natural foundation of human society; the ecological balance and the natural environment on which both animal and plant live, which are themselves non-human since our life depends on theirs for food, rain, and the air we breathe. An example of mutual co-existence is an expanding desert in Africa because of deforestation and the consequent drought and human starvation due to lack of water and food. Even animals have died for lack of both water and adequate grass or food to eat.

This African drought and famine is directly linked to human sin and disobedience against God's moral and natural laws governing correct interaction between the human being and the rest of nature. For instance, in Africa, the Traditional Religion taught was that one had to pray to God (as the God of the forest) for permission to cut down a big tree.

This African respect for the environment and caution dealing with it, was due the fact that the African Religion teaches that big trees are the temples of God and the departed ancestral spirits, and therefore, they are sacred to both God and the ancestors, particularly, since most big trees surrounding the homestead happened also to be planted over the ancestral tombs or protected the family burial grounds.

However, when the Western Christian Missionaries arrived in Africa, they condemned the African Traditional Religion and its doctrines, especially, the teaching on the environment; namely, that huge trees were the temples of God and the ancestral spirits. In this crusade against the African Traditional Religion which was summarily dismissed and condemned as paganism, some Christian Missionaries are even known to have killed some of these venerated and revered trees in the presence of their disbelieving African converts in order to demonstrate to them the folly of the African beliefs!

The Christian converts soon learned convincingly from their Western Christian Missionary teachers to cut down trees indiscriminately for timber and firewood, demanded to ship to the West by the new urban and missionary centers. Soon, the trees in most countries were gone. But alas! To the African horror and God's vengeance for disobedience and rebellion, the vital soil fertility, rain, and food had also gone and vanished, along with the vanishing trees and forests!

Consequently, for the Traditional African Religion adherents, this was taken as proof that God and the ancestral spirits live in forests and big trees and since the Christians had disrespectfully cut down these forests and big trees indiscriminately, God and the angry ancestors were now punishing the whole continent by inflicting punishment on the disobedient people in terms of unprecedented, prolonged years of drought, the drying up of streams and water-holes, shortage of human and animal food, and subsequently, unprecedented mass starvation and deaths of both human beings and wild life.

Therefore, human thinking, technology, and rational knowledge have not brought about good consequences, but in many cases have brought about death, rather than enhanced and improved human life as promised. Subsequently, human reason and intellect, unaided by God's eternal vision and wisdom, are bound to endure short-sightedness always present in all human knowledge due to human finitude and inabilty to see the whole in terms of past, present, and future. Since only the eternal God is able to scan the eternal stretch at a single glance in all these dimensions of knowledge in terms of past, present, and future contingent events, then only God can possess all the knowledge of all events both past, present, and still yet to occur.

Consequently, human knowledge is always partial and imperfect. This is as true in the humanities as it is true in the sciences. Even scientific knowledge is partial and relative to change and improvement, as we learn more about ourselves, the observers and the phenomena or nature we observe.

New theories replace the antiquated ones and new truths are revealed which have always been present but hidden from us largely due to our natural intellectual limitations and imperfection of both our present scientific theories and research instruments. And the more we know, the more we realize how little we know and how much more there is still to know. Here, a good analogy would probably be that we are like small children playing with water buckets at the beach of the infinite sea of knowledge. Or, that if we only came down each day, we would have the whole sea contained in our water buckets!

What is probably the most surprising and perplexing mystery about us human beings is that although we have sent probes into outer space, made trips to outer space to walk on the moon or work in the shuttle or space laboratories, and although we have made a plane that goes around the world without stopping or refueling on the way, we still have not yet learned enough about ourselves as human beings nor have we learned to live together in mutual respect and peace.

Most regretably, as essentially and intrisically moral, intelligent and rational beings, we still live irrational lives and do stupid things together or individually which do not show any evidence of rationality or wisdom, which we claim to possess as our chief "trade-mark" or characteristic as human beings. What then, is wrong with us?

This very puzzling question will take us to the very next question, namely, that of the human being's moral problem which is, subsequently discussed in the next section below.

The Human Being's
Moral Dilemma

Since the human being is essentially an intelligent, free, thinking creature, possessing knowledge, including the knowledge of what is right and what is wrong, and the knowledge of what is good and what is evil, subsequently, the human being is by functional definition, "a thinking, free moral agent in the world." That is, the human being possesses an "a apriori" intrinsic freedom and an intellectual capacity to choose to act and live according to what he or she knows to be good and right moral principles; that is, to act and live in accordance with the knowledge of the good or to act and live in a very contrary manner to what he or she knows to be right and good for lack of goodwill, courage and moral integrity.

The human being is unique in this respect. Whereas other animals are primarily governed by their natural instincts, particularly, the instinct of security and survival, including correct food, mating behavior, protection of the offspring, and interaction with others, the human being is largely governed by culturally established moral codes of behavior and actions. In addition, the human being has a moral understanding of what is right and wrong. This is the basis for some individual's deviation from what is otherwise, culturally and traditionally, taught as either morally correct or the reverse.

Whereas social norms and moral codes are in many literate societies written down in a legal code and used to enforce the desirable moral behavior in a given society, the moral interpretation of that code may vary from person to person depending on family background, education, personal moral stand, and personal conscience. This was the case with the Mosaic Law. It was originally written down by Moses whose code was made up of the Ten Commandments given to the Jewish people in

God's holy name. But the code itself later expanded until it was stretched to about 613 commandments. This in turn was expanded by the Rabbis as the Jewish moral teachers until it filled many volumes of the Talmud and the Mishnar.

However, this did not prevent Jesus and the prophets from denouncing these religious moral teachers as hypocrites and dangerous blind guides of the masses. Jesus condemned the religiously zealous Pharisees as unspiritual and immoral because they failed to see the divine love and holiness behind the Mosaic code which they observed. They just observed the "letter of the law" and failed in God's redemptive love that was the grounding of this moral law.

Subsequently, they made a terrible burden for the common or ordinary people, and the masses failed to see God's moral love acting in the principles of the moral law in order to guide them, protect and save them from pain, guilt, and anguish of moral evil, sin, and injustice.

Because human beings are intelligent, free, knowledgeable, and moral agents and creatures, they are also able to suffer mental or spiritual pain, when they knowingly do what is wrong, instead of doing what is right and good. This defiant act of knowingly doing evil is very common among humans. But it is an immoral evil condemned by both society and religion. In religion, this immoral evil deed or act is referred to as sin. And sin or evil deeds hurt the perpetrator, the target, and ultimately, injure the whole society by disrupting social networks, order, and harmony.

This is one of the main reasons why society has to formulate, codify, and enforce social moral norms and moral laws, if it has to continue to exist as a society and not a mere collection of autonomous individuals and groups of people with nothing in common and without the bond or common restraint of the common good or law and order. Such a collection of people is not a society or community, but rather, a mere destructive mob and anarchy.

The human being's cost for doing evil or committing
sin is guilt and in some cases, immediate physical harm
does result, such as a fine, jail sentence, deadly
venereal diseases in cases of sexual sin, death (in
cases of drugs), broken families, divorces, loss of job
and property, and the like. Each evil deed has a tendency to produce an evil effect in return whereas the
good deed also "begets a good yield." And because there
are more evil doers in the world than those who do good
deeds, the world itself appears to be evil. But the
world itself is not evil since it was created by a
good-loving God.

However, human beings, with their great capacity for
both doing good and evil, and their freedom to choose
being otherwise grounded in selfishness or self-interest and self-centeredness, subsequently, the human
beings more often choose to do evil more than good;
thus causing imbalances in the world. This is not God's
fault or failure to create a more perfect and better
world. Rather, it is full evidence that the human
being's actions are morally free and have real consequences in the society and in the world at large; that
these are actions for which the human beings should
accept and take full responsibility for.

The saying that what we reap is what we sow seems to
be very appropriate here. If a farmer sows wheat he or
she reaps wheat and if he/she sows corn, he or she also
reaps corn, and not rice or beans. Likewise, if human
beings sow the seeds of moral evil, similarly, they
reap evil and when they sow seeds of goodness and
righteousness, they likewise, reap the joyful fruits of
goodness and righteousness that bring us joy and happiness together with those connected with us, such as
friends, colleagues, neighbors, and relatives. In the
very same way that evil spreads quickly to eat away and
damage society like cancer in a human body, similarly,
good deeds and moral integrity, act to bring the doers
and the society all the fruits of joy and happiness
that result from doing good deeds.

Therefore, it is encouraging to learn from the Bible

that although the wicked and evil-doers have always
abounded in the world and far outnumbering the morally
upright, it has been always through the dedicated work
of those few saints and obedient children and servants
of God that the world has been always redeemed from
evil and transformed. For instance, the biblical story
of Noah's faithfulness in a land full of sin, corruption, and evil is one such great story. We also have
the story of Lot in Sodom and Gomorrah, and how God
promised to spare the evil city if a few holy people
would be found in it.

We also have the examples of prophets and saints who
worked to transform and redeem for God the people of
their own age. Gautama Siddhartha in India who came to
be known as Buddha, Socrates the Greek moral philosopher, Abraham, Moses, King David, John the Baptist,
Jesus, and Muhammad of the Middle East are such good
examples of non-Christian saints and prophets whose
personal holiness, moral uprightness, courage, exemplary life and moral teaching have served to change,
reshape and transform the world morally, religiously,
socially, and politically.

For instance, the West is built on the Judeo-Christian moral principles originating basically from Africa
and is based on the moral principles taught by the
Prophet Muhammad, the founder of Islam. It is also true
that most of Eastern Europe is also based on the doctrine of Karl Marx and Frederick Engels.

It focuses on their disillusionment for religion and
its moral teachings of love for the neighbor which they
emphatically reflected and repudiated as the opium of
the people, utilized by the rich powerful ruling group
to keep the poor, exploited, working masses obedient in
hopes of a reward in heaven rather than this present
life in which they were being oppressed and exploited
by the ruling rich elite class that owned the means of
production and the religio-political machinery power
and its coercive force to enforce their economic and
political will on the helpless poor masses.

However, even these Marxists had to come up with a

practical form of moral code for their society, even when they had done away with the idea of God and religion, the two foundations of most moral codes. This observation is of great importance for it reveals how deeply moral the human being basically is. The Marxist experiment proves that human values and sense of morality are not mere results of human religious sentiments and illusory beliefs in a non-existent God, but rather, they do show that human beings are, by essential nature, moral beings or agents just because they possess the intellect, knowledge, and the capacity to judge between right and wrong, good and evil.

Religion is not necessarily the basis for this moral judgement, but sound reason and correct knowledge. Religion can enhance human moral sensitivity but some religions have been known to teach that which is ethically questionable and even evil so that religion by itself cannot always be taken as a reliable and correct moral guide. For instance, the biblical book of Joshua seems to praise as ethical and holy what we would condemn today as genocide.

Similarly, the Mosaic doctrine of "tooth for a tooth and an eye for an eye" does not seem ethical to most of us. We also find in the Mosaic law unjustifiable numerous cases where punishment is stoning or being burned alive. Fortunately, Jesus saw this problem and reversed the Mosaic Law of retaliation to "love your neighbor" and "forgive those who wrong you," including one's enemies.

However, Islam, Judaism, and some fundamentalist Christian groups still insist on savage revenge and retaliation as proper responses to evil or to being wronged. What is clear here is that only in the good deed can good come out and that evil will produce evil and violence will only cause more violence and not peace. Those who are defeated in the war soon regroup to reorganize themselves for a more effective reversal of the humiliation suffered in the war when they were defeated.

Subsequently, peace obtained by war or other forms of

violence has to be maintained through continued violence or threat of violence if it is to endure. This is
currently the case in Northern Ireland, Israel, Lebanon, and South Africa. In these cases, police or military coercion and violence are required if "peace" has
to endure. The conquered people never give up the
military struggle to regain their lost freedom, unless
there is either mutual shared political and economic
power or the conquered get exterminated, like most of
the warlike, as the American Indians were during the
wars of conquest and settlement of the continent.

Christianity itself has had its own bad record of
violence and bloodshed. For instance, the ill-advised
crusades were Christian military attempts at exterminating the Muslims in order to free Jerusalem from
them. This was no better than the Islamic Jihad of
which we now repudiate as state-sponsored terrorism.

The infamous inquisition was another Christian moral
and religious authoritarianism, which in reality, a-
mounted to a Christian reign of terror. In this era,
freedom of scientific research and academic expression
were severely curbed by the church and the State. For
instance, Galileo was forced to recant his scientific
findings unless he wanted to die!

Therefore, there is a great danger when we allow
religion to dictate moral absolute values and to regulate what can be learned or researched into. Indeed, it
was because of Christianity's failure to address the
moral, social, and economic problems created by the
industrial revolution in Europe that Marx and Engels
became disillusioned with all religions as mere opium
of the oppressed poor masses. Indeed, Marxism has of-
fered a great challenge to Christianity to become more
constructive and practical in its own ethical teachings.

For instance, whereas Jesus taught mainly the poor
and the outcast, he also healed their diseases free of
charge and fed them when they were hungry. He never
sent them away ill and hungry. This example in itself
is very revolutionary. Yet, Christian churches spend

most of their time today ministering to the rich and less time is given to the poor, for they do not give the money that supports the Church ministry, or pay the pastor's middle class income stipend! It is still true in the church that whoever pays the minister's salary "calls the tune" or sets the minister's agenda! This is tragic but that is the case.

Jesus never got paid by his poor audience. But today, the minister, like anyone else, has to live by his occupation, and that means that some churches have to become business-like in order to afford and support a minister. Subsequently, the role of the Church has become very mundane and some ministers' concerns have become church business and making "big money" than taking care of the poor or speaking out on behalf of the voiceless and the oppressed.

In some cases, this would displease the minister's rich congregation members who are doing the exploitation and the oppression, and subsequently, there is more temptation to keep quiet so as not to be fired. To these kinds of worldly, money-loving ministers, Jesus would have probably said:

Hypocrites! Lovers of money more than God's work which you so profess to love and do! Go away from my sight. Go into the eternal punishment prepared for the Devil and his followers who cleverly disguised themselves as the children of God, but in honesty, they were greedy, ravenous wolves in sheep's clothing. You can fool human beings, but you cannot fool God. Hypocrites, you will truly get what you deserve.

It is by now probably clear to the reader that what is basically wrong with the human being is sin and moral evil. This problem is so great that there is no easy solution or simple cure for it. If there had been an easy cure for the human moral crisis the world would not be in such a mess as it is in right now.

Philosophers have prescribed various ethical remedies

and theologians have prescribed various confessional rites and absolutions, but all of them seem to have failed to work for the majority of the evil-doers and sinners. Judiciary systems have also tried various laws and punishments in order to deter crime and restrain evil-doers or reform them. But the jails have, instead, become filled, mostly, with the poor who cannot afford the high cost of hiring competent attorneys to defend them. Ironically, the jails have sadly become evil schools for producing more sophisticated criminal behavior, and as such, they have become a failure, if viewed as a form of punishment meant to deter crime or reform criminals.

The reformation of the criminals has largely failed to work, and yet we cannot sentence to death people for annoying common petty crimes, such as pickpocketing, fraud, theft, and burglaries. It is also known that a prison sentence or even a death penalty does not effectively deter crime. So, what do we do about chronic evil-doers and habitual criminals?

The Human Moral Obligation to Prevent Crime
and Other Forms of Evil

Most of us know that we have a moral obligation to do good and to stop others from harming us and our society through doing evil or committing crime. This obligation extends from our immediate neighbor to our leaders, such as President Ronald Reagan. However, the problem arises when an ethical individual knows that some powerful leader or person is planning evil, such as building a powerful nuclear bomb so as to blast the communist Soviets or other people.

Consequently, we have a major moral dilemma. The dilemma or the moral problem can, then, be simply stated as follows: how does one individual who may be morally upright and correct stop the President from doing evil who may be supported by a naive majority but surrounded by greedy and evil influential advisers? This is the kind of situation where democracy can become a source of great harm. Democracy becomes evil when the voting masses are either ignorant of the good or when they are themselves corrupt and morally evil. This was the case with Hitler's fascist Germany.

Nevertheless, one can still validly ask about what the few morally upright could do in this kind of state of affairs. For instance, should the upright try to kill an evil ruler like Hitler or Idi Amin in their moral efforts to get rid of an evil regime or ruler supported by an ignorant or an evil majority? In other words, is it moral to use violence to get rid of violence and evil to get rid of the evil through evil?

Undoubtedly, this is a great ethical question with no single definitive answer, but the morally upright cannot afford to keep quiet or do nothing when evil is being done and masses of innocent people are getting killed. In this case, the lesser evil should be done even by those who hate evil in order to stop a greater evil from happening. This should be the guiding moral principle in matters of this nature and other similar ones involving the taking of a human life, such as the death penalty and abortion.

Nevertheless, the present and future human moral condition remains a great problem to arouse the concern and action of all morally upright men and women, everywhere, regardless of creed, ideology, color, or race. This is because of the world's moral crisis which urgently requires a united global effective remedy if the human species and the world are to continue to survive in a meaningful existence and relationship.

One is even led almost to despair when one realizes that the great nation's leaders are also very easily capable of great evil, ignorance, bigotry, corruption and wrong doing. This accounts for most coups in the Third World, and particularly, Africa. Men like Idi Amin and Bokassa have been accused of great felonious crimes while they were self-declared life presidents of their impoverished, and mismanaged African nations; namely, Uganda and the Central African Republic, respectively.

Unfortunately, the super powers are no exception. In USA, President Nixon was impeached, on moral grounds, out of office, to which he had been just re-elected for the second time with a great majority. Currently, President Ronald Reagan's office is also under investigation for illegal activities committed during its handling of foreign affairs.

For instance, it is alleged that whereas President Reagan told the American people and allies that it is wrong to negotiate with international terrorists and Arab kidnappers, he was secretly dealing and negotiating with these offenders in order to free the American hostages kidnapped and held by Muslim Arabs in Lebanon in protest against the aggressive American military policy and intervention in the Middle East and support for Israel. Meanwhile, in South Africa, Botha is becoming more belligerent in dealing with the black majority population and its bid for political power and more equitable distribution of the nation's economic natural resources.

The evil perpetrated by hateful, power-seeking, immoral national leaders, such as Hitler and Idi Amin, the deposed former president of Uganda, leaves us wondering to whether Plato was not right and prophetic when he declared that there will not be peace on earth until more philosophers became rulers and rulers became philosophers. By a Philosopher King, Plato had in mind a person who was the most educated, knowledgeable, virtuous, just, and skilled in ruling.

This kind of national leader was in essence more of a national moral teacher, example, and guide. The closest recent examples that come to mind are India's Mahatma Gandhi, and Tanzania's former President Julius Nyerere who is known to his people as "Mwalimu" (Teacher).

Both of these national leaders were nationalists who brought independence to their respective colonized nations. Interestingly, Gandhi refused to become the first President of independent India and also refused to immerse himself in the materialism and luxury which the departing colonial British left behind in the newly independent Indian nation. This was great evidence that he fought for Indian independence, primarily on moral grounds, namely, that it is just and moral for the right for nations to govern themselves for the general welfare and common good of their local citizens. Gandhi did not fight for India's independence in order to gain from it himself.

Gandhi put first the interests of his fellow citizens and the nation, whereas many corrupt national leaders seek to serve their own interests first. This is also true at lower levels where for instance, judges and police officers solicit and accept bribes so as to subvert justice of which they are supposed to be the impartial enforcers and custodians!

As for Julius Nyerere, he became the first President of his nation, Tanzania. He refused to accept a huge salary, a huge mansion and an expensive Presidential limousine whereas his country remained poor. Instead, he lived simply like his people and tried to teach them to live together happily in collective villages where they would receive clean water, electricity, and educational and medical services more readily. He called this African "socialist" experiment "Ujaama" (Unity).

Unfortunately, this "Ujaama" experiment failed because of human selfishness and evil. For instance, the people felt that they did not have to work hard on the newly introduced cooperative farms in "Ujaama" villages and just passed time idly instead of doing creative farming on these collective farms.

As you might have already correctly guessed, the results of collective farms were disastrous. There was not enough food grown, and subsequently, there was inadequate food to feed the people in the new collective villages. As a result, Nyerere was painfully forced to abandon this socio-economic experiment and "philosophical idealism." He was a naive victim of human evil; namely, selfishness, greed, envy, and malice. He later discovered that people were most eager to work for individual profit rather than a communal one.

Subsequently, he tried to utilize individual profit drive in order to generate enough food for the people both in the village and urban areas, but tried to control and curb excessive greed for indivual gain at the expense of other people and the nation. As a result, he taxed more of the businesses and the rich in order to provide needed essential human services in rural areas and to uplift the poor. Consequently, though Tanzania still remains one of the poorest and least developed nations in Africa, it has one of the best literacy rates in the whole of Africa.

Furthermore, Tanzania has also been one of the most stable and peaceful nations in the whole of modern Africa. For instance, whereas the neighboring state of Uganda has experienced several civil wars, several coups, political repression and mass murders under Idi Amin and five successive presidents, Tanzania, under president Nyerere, has been the peace-maker and guarantor in Uganda ever since it helped to drive out Idi

Amin in the name of human rights, dignity, morality, and peace.

It is remarkable, therefore, that whereas the other national leaders just watched in amazement while Idi Amin grossly abused human rights in Uganda, leading to the mass deaths of educated Ugandans, conservatively estimated at about half a million people, spread over the eight years "of his reign of terror," President Nyerere got so disgusted and morally indignant that he decided to act positively in order to get rid of Idi Amin and thus put an end to gross evil and mass murder committed just across the border.

Nyerere acted in unconditional love for the neighbor. He did not have much money for the task, nor did he have anything to gain personally by intervening in the tragic Ugandan affairs. It was because of his moral sensitivity, courage, and goodness that he undertook this noble moral task for the redemption of Uganda. This is also the practical moral thinking and practical action that has deeply grounded his support for African freedom fighters and liberation movements in Southern Africa.

Consequently, Nyerere is a very stauch supporter of Bishop Tutu's moral call to the West to stop supporting the evils of racism and apartheid in South Africa out of selfishness, moral indifference, and greed for minerals, wealth, cheap labor (slave labor), and profitable investments.

The moral call is to put human rights and welfare before the cheap acquisition of wealth and profit at the expense of other human beings' degradation, exploitation, oppression, and even extermination. Clearly, this ill-gotten wealth is a disgrace and an offense to both humanity and God.

Unfortunately, this is the kind of evil which absolute capitalism is capable of inducing in most human beings who find it difficult to say "no" to the temptation of easy money and quick wealth. Indeed, there are just a few people who get wealthy by doing good deeds. It seems that the drug-dealers, pimps and thieves often get rich before honest businessmen and women can balance their books! Subsequently, in some poorer urban communities, there is a great temptation to steal, embezzle, cheat, sell drugs and sex, and armed robberies, in order to get rich quickly and effortlessly.

However, the society that allows its members to indulge in such evils and immorality soon destroys itself, for evil is conducive to violence and death, whereas the society's well being and survival requires harmonious socio-economic networks and healthy social relations grounded in mutual love and trust.

Therefore, the human being's welfare, future existence and total survival cannot be assured by modern advances in science, medicine, and technology alone. As we have already seen, the major human problem is the human being himself or herself.

In other words, the present global major problem is the human being's own moral problem which has grown into a global crisis by the virtue of the human being's improved nuclear technology and the great capacity for destroying himself or herself, together with most of the planet Earth, along with life and everything on it. Tragically, that would be the end of all known biological forms of life since in our galaxy it is only to be found on planet Earth, and nowhere else, in this wide, but primarily lifeless cosmos.

Nuclear Weapons as a Moral Evil and a Global Menace

Some people have naively said that nuclear weapons are necessary for world peace since they are good deterrents of war. But we have also heard of national leaders like Ronald Reagan talking of a limited strategic nuclear war which can be won. This leaves most of us wondering how suicidal human beings can be to even take a risk to fight a war in which there will be no winner since both sides and all the inhabitants of the globe will be annihilated in the course of the combatants mutual nuclear exchange and suicidal cosmic destruction.

Since human beings regularly commit suicide, this will be another human mass suicide, but unlike all the previous ones, it will be total and will engulf everything, both living and nonliving. It will be the final page in the tragic human history, with its infinite scope of freedom, greed, selfishness, bigotry, sin and irresponsiblity that made the human being an evil creature; just too evil to live with itself and others, and in the process of killing off others found that it had also destroyed itself in the process! The evil deadly trap meant for the enemy had caught and killed the enemy and the careless trap owner.

In other words, the moral failure of the human being had led to the destructive hatred and intolerance for the others and both had tragically died in the war of mutual extermination. Since it will be only God reading the gruesome end of such a tragic human story, it is also possible that in his/her divine loving, forgiving, redemptive grace, he/she can create yet another human life with a different set of moral agenda so as to avoid a similar history with its tragic end. God will also be terribly disappointed with us human beings for we will have destroyed not just ourselves, but also the world which he/she loves and still seeks through Jesus as the Christ to save from sin, evil inclination, and self-destruction.

Therefore, with human nuclear suicidal self-destuction, along with the rest of God's creation, will certainly also be a great blow to God's work of creation, sustenance, and redemption. Subsequently, the human being, being here as God's representative and steward, will have achieved the ultimate rebellion against God by seizing total control of one's life and that of God's creation and in evil defiance against God's moral law; namely, to love both God and the neighbor. As a result, God is as concerned about human moral sin and evil and its destructive results of selfishness, egocentricity, bigotry, intolerance,

pride, envy, hatred, malice, murder, war, and suicide.
Because of God's ultimate concern about human moral
evil, God has lovingly provided his/her moral guiding
principles in nature and through both prophets and the
saints. Ultimately, God has given his/her love to
humanity through Jesus Christ and there is no higher
moral principle than that divine commandment given
through Jesus to love God and our neighbor unconditionally like we love ourselves. If we obey this divine
moral law or commandment of love, we will live in peace
and happiness with all our fellow global citizens; but
if we disobey, instead we will live in hatred, infinite
fear, insecurity, suspicion, strife, conflict, war,
death, and destruction. What a costly price to pay for
evil and disobedience against God's Moral Law.

To many modern orthodox Christian theologians, such
as Paul Tillich and Karl Rahner, this state of disobedience, hatred, fear, despair, war, and death is identified with hell. And if hell includes real fire, the
nuclear holocaust will be the literal hellfire, kindled
on earth by us through our own sins and to consume us
all in punishment for corporate sins of disobedience
and indifference against God's law of unconditional
human mutual love. Therefore, even if the loving and
redemptive creator God did not want us to perish or go
to hell, nevertheless, because of our great sins, moral
evil, and indifference, we would inevitably invent hell
fire and destruction for those we hate and correlatively, ourselves.

It is, indeed, a strange thing that human moral evil
and sadism lead to human suffering and death in order
to enjoy the short, transient, "evil, sadistic pleasure" of seeing one's enemies suffer and cringe with
pain or die a slow, painful death. What kind of moral
creature is the human being then, that can take pleasure in such cruelty, other peoples' suffering, pain and
death?

Unfortunately, there is abundant evidence that even
many governments do condone and encourage the torture
of political opponents, detainees, and prisoners. All

one needs is to read the annual reports of Amnesty International in order to find out the ugly details and statistics dealing with immoral state political repression, the abuse of human rights, the cruel and inhumane torture of opponents or those with enough conscience to protest against this political, unethical, and repressive totalitarian rule, political murders, and quiet "disappearances" of innocent citizens who are not actively supportive of the government or party in power.

The Problem of the Omnipotent, Loving Good God and the Presence of Evil in the World

The universal awareness of insecurity arising out of human wickednesss and moral evil, has led many to question the goodness of God, given God as the loving, omnipotent Creator, Preserver and Redeemer of the world. Many great theologians and philosophers have, for a long time, battled with this question of evil in the world. Some have sided with Plato that God cannot be both pure goodness and also omnipotent since God's creation does manifest an evil presence and a variety of both physical and moral imperfections which negate both God's goodness and perfection in the world and also the idea that God is both good and omnipotent.

However, others have tried to solve this apparent contradiction of the presence of evil in God's good world by putting both the problem and the blame on the human being as God's free moral agent in the world that has misused his or her unique position and freedom to do evil in the world, and therefore, misrepresenting in the world both God and God's essential goodness and perfection. This shift of the problem of evil in the world from God to the human being is valid in as much as the human being is the concrete, intelligent, free, moral, and effective or consequential representative of God in creation with the supernaturally endowed powers to think, judge, make moral choices, and implement them in the world in God's name and on his or her behalf.

To this end, this moral theory also requires that the human being is to be accepted not just as God's image but also as a true child of God and, as such, a Co-Creator with God, the eternal or heavenly Father and Mother of the human being. And just as human parents are not tried and convicted for the crimes and evils perpetrated by their own children, similarly, God should not be tried or convicted for the evils and crimes committed by the free moral and responsible human beings that he or she has created because the human moral defects are not due to God's defective creation of the human being, but directly due to the human being's moral agency as an intelligent, thinking, moral, responsible, living, free, judging, and independent special creature created for a special purpose and mission in the world.

Therefore, God made no mistakes, nor did he or she do evil to create a free moral human being to take care of his or her creation on his or her behalf. However, the human being made a terrible moral mistake to choose to serve his or her own material self-interest rather than that of the creator of the world. Subsequently, human moral evil and the world's major problems are directly rooted in this human moral evil or greed and self interest. The other evils are mere offshoots, and expressions of this basic human moral problem of egocentricism and the exclusion of others unless they enhance the clearly preconceived self-interest and personal gain.

Subsequently, this solution is more Christian and orthodox than that proposed by Whitehead, namely, that God is neither omnipotent nor perfect since he or she never controls the creative process, but rather, persuades it to actualize itself according to the highest possiblities for the best outcome, which is itself not fully known by God until it has actually occured! That is also the denial that God is not omniscient. And with this denial of God's omnipotence and omniscience, Whitehead thought that he had creatively solved the problem involved in the religious and philosophical of the presence of evil in the world in the presence of a good, omnipotent God who is also the omniscient.

The absurdity of this Whiteheadian solution of evil lies in the affirmation that God is not the knowing powerful Creator, but rather, the weak and ignorant architect working from the limitations of time, space and knowledge, just like fine human "creators." Whereas such a finite, ignorant, weak God may provide a plausible intellectual explanation for physical evil in the world, such as malformed creatures, imperfections, earthquakes, and some diseases, it is a very weak one when it comes to human moral evil. This is the case since the blame is left on God by failing to provide a suitable or an irresistible moral persuasion to choose the good and do it, rather than choosing evil.

Moreover, religiously, Whitehead's weak, imperfect and finite God is very unattractive, because he or she is neither the purposive, loving, mighty, and cosmic Creator nor is he or she powerful enough to redeem the human being from evil both moral and physical that ever plagues the finite humanity.

Nevertheless, for finite human minds in quest for the infinite through the mediation of the finite intellectual means, Whitehead, provides some satisfactory answers by "creating" the infinite Creator God in the "human finite image" so as to to render the infinite God apprehendable and understandable to finite minds. This human temptation to view God in human terms or anthropomorphism, has been the perennial source of idols and idolatry both intellectual and religious.

Human Moral Conscience
and Religion

The human being is also by unique nature a religious creature. Therefore, to be an authentic human being, one has also to be religious. This religiosity may be either affirmed by going to religious activities, such as worship, fellowship, meditation, or prayer, or may be denied by becoming anti-religious, atheistic, and agnostic.

Nevertheless, in both cases, whether in the denial or affirmation of religion, there is a fundamental affirmation of the underlying essential religious element that is a basic constitutive component of the human being, which is being consciously questioned, in the same way a child may grow up to question whether the people that claim to be his/her mother and father are in essence his/her own real biological parents because of the human unique mental qualities of thinking and doubting.

Likewise, it is also just because to be human is also to be correlatively and coextinsively religious, that accounts for the fact that all known human beings, are all known also to have been found to have an established religion of one kind or another, and that even communism itself which was meant to be the very rejection of religion, has itself ironically assumed the previously denounced traditional role of religion!

This universal, religious phenomenon cannot, therefore, be a mere moral or social accident or just a universal coincidence. On the contrary, what is self-evident here, is the irrefutable evidence to support the claim that religion is an intrinsic essential feature of finite human beings found on planet Earth, and that it is an essential manifestation of any being or creature that possesses human qualities.

Consequently, religion and religious sentiments in any recognizable form, constitute the main essential

unique feature of a human being which no other animal
is known or observed to possess. Not even the most
intelligent primates have been seen to practice some
form of rudimentary religion, whereas in other respects, they seem to have some fundamentally forms of
human institutions, such as social organization with a
single leader, social hierarchy, punishment systems,
and feeding and mating rules. However, these same animals appear to be completely devoid of religion since
it requires an intellectual and spiritual capacity for
self-transcendence and the awareness of the Divine
Mystery that is variously referred to as Creator, Deity
and God.

For most religious people, this Cosmic Creative Power
and Mystery known simply as God, has been extremely
revered and personalized as a benevolent, loving, and
caring heavenly parent known to many as Father and to
others as Redeemer and Lord. It is this native and
redemptive mystery that is both feared and loved, as
the Almighty God, Creator, Preserver and Redeemer of
the world of which the human being is the central
created symbol and cosmic representative to God. And as
such, whatever happens to the human beings also happens
to the world of which he or she is the spiritual and
intellectual embodiment and symbol. Likewise, whatever
the human being does, similarly, has a cosmic significance for both God and the world.

Subsequently, since the human being is both divine
and creative, heavenly and earthly, spirit and matter,
human and animal, and divine representative on earth,
the human being is also the world's or the cosmic
created representative and priestly mediator of God.
This is because of the essential need of mutual,
meaningful representation between God and the created
world. The essential dual nature of the human being
endows the human being with supernatural capacity to
communicate with God as readily as he or she communi-
cates with the rest of nature.

As a result, the human being is by nature the cosmic
divine priest, the mediator between God and creation of

which the human being is a key constitutive component.
Subsequently, the human beings, as Cosmic Priests, come
to God in prayer to intercede for the atonement and
forgiveness of the sins of the world committed by
sinful, disobedient, egocentric, immoral human beings,
to pray for more seasonable weather in times of drought
or too much rain, storms, thunder, hurricanes, and
floods. The human being also brings back God's message
of warning, absolution for those repenting of their
sins, love, hope, patience and benediction or blessings.

Thus, the human being, though morally imperfect, is
nevertheless the chosen, divine vessel for God's concrete representation and activity in the world. This
is, indeed, a great responsibility, for unless the
human acts, God does not act either, since the human
being is the divine concrete or physical divine representative in the world through whom God operates to
effect his or her divine creative and redemptive primordial purpose in the world.

This makes sense, since God, being non-physical, can
only work through an intelligent, moral, free agent to
do his or her work in the physical world, where action
on matter requires another matter form to act physically to move it in concrete time and space.

Subsequently, we do not usually see things moving by
themselves from place to place by God's spiritual command. Instead, what we usually see are men and women
doing things in God's name, such as healing, senseless
killings of human beings in war, punishment, murders
and elective abortions. This is because obedient and
moral human eyes, ears, hands, and feet are also the
eyes ears, hands and feet of the divine and as such,
the divine instruments for God's own work in the world.
This is exactly the Pauline meaning when he declared
that Christians are a new creation and God's ambassadors of reconciliation and peace in the world (II Cor.
5:17-20):

Therefore, if anyone is in Christ, he is a new

creation; the old has passed away; behold, the new
has come. All this is from God, who, through
Christ, reconciled us to himself and gave us the
ministry of himself, not counting their trespasses
against them, and entrusting to us the message
(Gospel) of reconciliation. So we are ambassadors
for Christ, God making his appeal through us.
Therefore, we beseech you on behalf of Christ, be
reconciled to God.

Therefore, it is clear and obvious that God works
through human beings in order to effect his or her
divine purpose and carry out his or her work in the
world. Therefore, without us as his or her intelligent
and moral agents, God would be limited and even powerless in what he/she can do on this temporal earth and
in the way it is now. But this fact does not necessarily mean that God is limited or powerless to save us and
the world.
All it affirms is that human beings are intelligent,
creative, and moral representatives of the invisible,
infinite, eternal, and immaterial God in the visible,
finite, temporal, material, and physical or concrete
world. Indeed, it was because of and for the sake of
this special divine purpose that God created a special
creature in the form of the human being at the very
apex of creation and evolution.
Therefore, in the present world, God is still actively creating some new things, fulfilling and redeeming
the old ones, but in the moral and free matters involving moral intelligence, knowledge, judgement, cal-
culations and the like. The primary instrument of God's
activity and intervention is the human being. For
instance, when we pray for the homeless to find food,
clothing, and warm shelter, we never intend or expect
God to answer them in a "supernatural manner" by seeing
them drop from the sky or just pop up from nowhere!
Even the most naive religious person knows that for
this kind of prayer, the divine answer has to be sought
here on earth through the work of other godly, loving,

humanitarian, and generous human beings.

However, this does not mean nor imply that we have to draw the naive, atheistic conclusion that since prayer to God is answered in many cases through the work of other human beings, that human beings are either God or Gods! This was the kind of mistaken atheistic conclusions reached by great philosophers like Feuerbach and Marx and great social scientists like Durkheim and Freud.

These and some other scholars have reached the absurd conclusion that God is just the glorified, idealized, magnified, and deified human moral self-abstraction and self-profection in the sky or heaven, and subsequently, worshipped as God. So that in reality, it is God that has been essentially created by "Man in his own (male) image," and not the reverse.

Subsequently, according to these scholars, the worship of God by human beings, becomes also a mere human activity of self-deification, self-immortalization, self-glorification and ultimately, human worship becomes mere collective self-idealization and self-worship.

Whereas this atheistic explanation of God may sound morally correct, and therefore, plausible, it fails to account for creation itself and the orderly cosmos which cannot be a result of a mere accident or a result of a mere cosmic blind creative forces. Even then, as soon as one admits the existence of an eternal force being involved in the origination of the Cosmos, one is no longer an atheist but a theist!

This can be said affirmatively, to be necessarily the case since by God, most philosphers and theologians mean the existence and pre sence of this external force that is responsible for the origination or creation of this universe. The mode origination or creation can be logically and scientifically comapatible with the theory of biological evolution without negating the fact that God is the ultimate source and creator of the universe.

Consequently, the fundamentalist, naive Christian

controversial insistence that for God to be the Creator
and Redeemer, one has to take the biblical book of
Genesis as an accurate, literal, and historical record
of how the universe originated is scientifically and
historically absurd and is spiritually or religiously
dangerous. This is necessarily the case, because this
kind of religious controversy is rooted in deliberate
religious bigotry and ignorance in the name of God who
is also affirmed to be omniscient, yet the ground of
anti-intellectualism, anti-science, new knowledge, "positive" progress, and the social change that comes
along with it.

For instance, a literal belief in the book of Genesis
would also require a prescientific cosmology in which
the universe is constituted by one big dome-like structure which is rooted in the sea beyond the horizon for
support. And below the dome or sky/heaven, is the flat
earth which is thought of as the center of the universe, being the dwelling place of the humankind, with
God watching above humanity from the advantageous
height of heaven in the sky.

Furthermore, God and his/her heavenly dwelling place
are thought to be positioned high, just above the
cosmic water which is also thought to be located above
in the sky, from which God fetches some to pour down
below, to water the world in the form of rain to water
earth and provide drink for both humankind and the wild
life. The dead are also supposed to go below the earth
into "Sheol" or "Hell" to live a shadowy, meaningless
life.

Subsequently, Noah's flood could only take place in
such a small flat, limited world, since we are told
that it covered the entire world and that all life got
destroyed except that which was preserved in the Ark.
If the entire known world did flood, it must have been
a local, geographically defined flat world in the Middle East which excluded much of the present world which
was only discovered in the fifteenth and sixteenth
centuries by the Portuguese and Spanish sea-goers and
wealth-seekers in Africa, India, and the Americas.

These unknown distant lands were not part of Noah's

world which is said to have been destroyed by floods
due to too much rain. Therefore, they could not have
been covered by Noah's flood, since it is said to have
covered, the world as they knew it, subsequently, ex-
cluding these other distant lands, since they were
unknown, then! Moreover, Noah could not have seen the
flood covering these foreign distant lands from the
security of his watchtower or window in his small Ark
(boat)!

Moreover, it is inconceivable that all the world's
animals and their food and water could have in any way
fitted into Noah's Ark or boat which was a mere 140
feet in length, 75 feet in width and 45 feet in height.
In this kind of limited space, there is not even enough
space for one elephant and all the necessary hay and
water for it to last even a week, since on the average,
an adult average weight elephant consumes more than
five tons of vegetation in only one day!

However, we are very surprisingly, told that a pair
of each kind of unclean animals and seven pairs of
clean ones were preserved in the Ark for more than
forty days since food for these animals would also
continue to be required long after the flood until
there was sufficient new life forms on the land to
support these animals! Even then the carnivorous animals would have required more game on the boat to hunt,
while on the boat and afterwards!

Thus, a literal interpretation or literal belief in
the story of Noah and the cosmic flood is intellectually and spiritually tragic, for it fails to see the
great universal moral value in it as a parable of human
universal sin and moral evil for which the whole world
deserves the divine just sentence of death but through
the righteousness of a few individuals, here and there
like islands in the flood or sea of destructive evil
and corruption, the divine sentence is commuted and
those who heed the warning of the righteous gain divine
salvation.

Therefore, for anyone, especially an educated or
thinking adult, to understand or interpret the Genesis

prophetic moral warning as most effectively communicated in a parabolic moral story of Noah's flood literally, is like taking literally the fairy tale of Snow White and the Seven Dwarfs or Jesus's parable of the Good Samaritan.

Subsequently, going to look for the remains of Noah's Ark, is as absurd as going to look for the forest where Snow White met the Seven Dwarfs or to look for the specific road and the inn in which the Good Samaritan took the neglected victim of armed robbery for shelter and tender treatment or to look for the descendants of the Good Samaritan in order to reward them for the good that their ancestors did.

In the same way, we cannot go to look for Noah's Ark or Boat, his historical descendants, nor can we also go back in the Middle East or Africa to look for the parabolic, primordial, "heavenly" Garden of Eden where the primordial human being or Adam was created. Nevertheless, according to the theory of evolution, the Garden of Eden is to be found in the East African, beautiful Savanna with its abundant wild life and good climate where the original human being emerged and originated.

To this revelation, some of us cry out in "Thanks be to God." But others disbelieve not just because of prejudice that nothing good or of value can come from Africa except natural raw materials, but because the idea that God could have chosen to create the human being by the way of evolution is simply objectionable. For instance, during a conversation on evolution, I was told by a concerned religious friend that "you came from God, you did not come from a monkey!" This is to misunderstand that even monkeys themselves just like us were also created by God!

Subsequently, whether human beings have been created by God, indirectly, through the amazing gradual, slow process of biological evolution from some extinct, non-human lower creatures, such as primates or by God's more direct act of creation is through a mere verbal command or molding clay and breathing life into it, to create living human beings, as the biblical accounts of Creation would suggest if understood literally as history, what is a fact is, that we are now here as intelligent creatures. As such, what really matters then, is that we are now here on this unique planet Earth, and that we are endowed with supernatural powers which distinguish us and set us apart from the rest of creation of which we are part.

Therefore, what is important and counts are our special qualities that make us human and how we use them to actualize fully our divinely endowed full potential as authentic human beings in order to live a more meaningful, humane fellowship with other human beings, God, and the rest of God's creation on which he or she shares a symbolic relationship of mutual interdependence and coexistence.

This mutual coexistence of the human being also illustrates the very essential importance of the presence of the intelligent, spiritual and moral human being in material, non-moral, and non-thinking creation. We have already seen how this special nature and God-given human supernatural qualities force the human being into becoming "the divine Cosmic Priest and Mediator" representing creation and the world to God and God's word, love, holiness, care, and justice to the world. The biblical story of Noah's obedience and righteousness that saved the world from destruction in punishment for human evil clearly illustrates this very symbolic and priestly relationship between the human being and nature of the world.

For instance, Noah's prophetic moral story states that the global human moral evil was so bad that it polluted all God's creation making the world guilty before God, and therefore, deserving of divine judgement and retaliatory punishment:

When the Lord saw how wicked everyone on earth was and how evil their thoughts were all the time, he was sorry that he had ever made them and put them on the earth. He was so filled with regret that he

said, "I will wipe out these people I have created,
and also the animals and the birds, because I am
sorry that I made any of them." But the Lord was
pleased with Noah.

According to the story, Noah's own moral uprightness is
commended by God, and as a result, God tries to save
Noah and his own family on Noah's own moral merit. But
for the rest, God promises destruction or capital punishment for their moral evil and rebellion against his
or her Moral Law:

This is the story of Noah. He had three sons; Shem,
Ham, and Japheth. Noah had no faults and was the
only good man of his time. He lived in fellowship
with God, but everyone else was evil in God's
sight, and violence had spread everywhere. God
looked at the world and saw that it was evil, for
the people were living evil lives:

God said to Noah, "I have decided to put an end to
all humankind. I will destroy them completely,
because the world is full of their violent deeds.
Build a boat for yourself out of good timber; make
rooms in it and cover it with tar inside and out.
Make it 450 feet long, 75 feet wide, and 45 feet
high... I am going to send a flood on earth to
destroy every living being. Everything on earth
will die but I will make a covenant with you. Go
into the boat, with your wife, your sons, and their
wives. Take into the boat with you a male and
female of every kind of animal and every kind of
bird. In order to keep them alive, take all kinds
of food for you and for them. Noah did everything
that God commanded. (Gen. 6:5-22)

It is obvious that what God is interested in is to
punish the world because of human moral evil and sin;
to punish it, yet without destroying it. Subsequently,
Noah is the personification and symbol of individual

human ethical purity and righteousness that becomes the divine instrumentality of a "life-boat"; of a divine saving grace and concrete divine salvation in the surrounding sea of human moral evil, injustice, corruption, sin, and death.

However, for those who seek the literal meaning of Noah's story as history do harm by destroying the ethical value, moral meaning, and teaching of this story or parable since it would be simply dismissed as mere fable since the boat mentioned above is not even large enough to house one blue whale, and all its required food for forty days.

Moreover, there is no way Noah would have gone to all parts of the globe to gather all the species of animals, insects, micro-organisms, and plant varieties in order to obey the divine command to preserve a pair of each creature. And if he could provide the space required to house all of these creatures and the required supply, it would have been greater than the size of Palestine itself.

The Divine Deification
of the Human Being

In essence, the Christian orthodox doctrine of the Incarnation as taught in Catholic, Anglican, and Eastern Orthodox church dogmatic theologies, God became a human being in Jesus as the Christ so that the human being might symbolically also become God by virtue of this divine Incarnation. It is positively affirmed that the Incarnation became permanently and irrevocably united with humanity in the person of Jesus Christ who is truly both God and human in permanent dual natures, co-existing harmoniously in the one person of Jesus Christ.

This Incarnational theology, though radical sounding, actually seems to be in line with the natural dual nature of the human being which is already described above as both divine and human, image of God and crea- ture, and breath of God and dust. The Incarnational theology, also well founded in the New Testament, most especially in the Gospel of John, which identifies Jesus Christ with the eternal Logos (Word) of God who was God's very medium or principle of creation. John writes:

Before the world was created, the Word already existed; he was with God, and he was the same as God. From the very beginning the Word was with God. Through him God made all things; not one thing was made without him. The Word was the source of life, and this life brought light to mankind. The light shines in the darkness, and darkness has never put it out.

God sent his messenger, a man named John, who came to tell people about the light, so that all should hear the message and believe. He himself was not the light that comes into the world and shines on all mankind.

John goes on to decribe this divine and creative pre-existent Logos or Word of God in the following divine redemptive terms:

The Word was in the world, and though God made the world through him, yet the world did not recognize him. He came to his own people; they did not receive him. Some, however, did receive him and believed in him; so he gave them the right to become God's children. They did not become God's children by natural means; that is, by being born as children of a human father; God Himself was their Father.
The Word became a human being, and full of grace and truth, lived among us. We saw his glory, the glory which he received as the Father's only Son. (John 1:1-14)

According to this biblical passage and teaching, Jesus as the Christ and the eternal creative Word (Logos) of God did not just become only a human being; he also gave supernatural power to all those who believed in him to become like himself; that is, to become God's own children. In short, the believers in Christ have been given the power to become God. As children of God, the children have to be like their own Father both in essence and being. However, it is still difficult for most of us, to accept the fact that in Christ, we have become like God our heavenly Parent, for this sounds like some kind of terrible blasphemy.
Ironically, this is the very kind of blasphemy of which Jesus himself was accused of and ultimately put to death for. But as we know, he was innocent of this charge of blasphemy, because what he taught about himself and human nature was the truth. And since the world could not accept the truth that he taught, the religious leaders sought to get rid of him together with his followers. As a result, religion itself cannot have the unchallenged claim to the divine truth or revelation since it rejected the ultimate revelation of

God and the divine truth in the person, life, and teaching of Jesus as the Christ.

This is still the main source of confusion, disobedience and evil in the world. The world still reflects God revealed-truth through the prophets, Jesus Christ, the prayer life of the saints, and the godly sermons of each age and generation. This disobedience constitutes spiritual, moral, political, and socio-economic darkness and chaos in the world which has led many to complete despair and skepticism to whether God is in actual control of the world, and if so, whether this God is holy, benevolent, and loving since the world seems to be engulfed in chaos and destructive evil of which the human evil is the most deadly. Thus, the world is still in need of God's redemptive activity, regardless of the previous entry of God's Messiah to save the world.

However, whereas evil and darkness seem to abound and to threaten the very existence of all human and non-human life on this fragile planet, we should always remember that as long as we who are Christian or peace loving and are obedient to God as God's ambassadors of love and peace in this deeply troubled world, there will always be the guiding divine light just like a light-house of God's eternal and universal light of salvation and peace amidst the great storms of cosmic evil, turbulence, hatred, war, despair, and destruction. This is the eternal light of the redemptive God which has always shined in the cosmic darkness to drive away the primodial darkness of meaninglessness, nothingness, chaos and lawlessness.

Subsequently, in the book of Genesis we read that before God created anything, there was darkness and chaos, and that God's creative word brought light into this primordial darkness and order into the prevailing chaos. Consequently, if the book of Genesis is correct in its affirmation, then, it also follows that without God's continuing activities of both creation and redemption, the world and the entire cosmos would vanish and return back into the primordial darkness and chaos

or "nothingness," from which God had originally both
created and redeemed them.

Fortunately, the Christian doctrine affirms that by
the act of the Incarnation, God has not only "come
down" into the concrete world in the form of the human
being, but has also become irrevocably unified with
humanity itself by becoming a human being in Jesus
Christ, and as such, has also in the act become inseparably bound not just with humanity, but with the
created concrete world or Cosmos itself of which the
human being is an integral part.

Therefore, the dissolution of the cosmos itself would
also to some extent lead to the dissolution of God,
since God has become inseparably bound with his/her
creation through the Incarnation process. The Incarnation means not just mere human deification but also
divine light, peace, and salvation into the world.

It is not surprising, therefore, to find that Christmas is a holiday which is observed almost universally,
regardless of creed and political ideology. For instance, the modern and goodwilled Soviet leader Mik-
hail Gorbachev's New Years' greeting and message reveals that even the non-Christian communist nations
know and value this season as a time to reflect about
the true meaning of humanity and mutual peaceful coexistence. Gorbachev's message was reported by the New
Year's day issues of major newspapers and one of them,
the Tennessean, reported it as follows:

Gorbachev told his countrymen that they must work
much harder in 1987 to overcome economic stagna-
tion.

He spoke of the overriding need for Americans and
Soviets to learn how to "live in peace on this tiny
and very fragile planet."

Gorbachev addressed the Soviet nation for eighty
one and a half minutes on television on New Year's
Eve shortly before midnight..... Gorbachev told the
Soviet people that the world and people of the
world became increasingly aware in 1986 of the

menace of war. "Never before has the earth, our home, been subjected to such a danger," he said. "We are sincerely extending a hand of friendship and cooperation to all who favor immediate negotiations on the complete ending of nuclear tests, who favor immediate reduction and full destruction of nuclear weapons."
Gorbachev wished peace and prosperity to the American people..... and said the realities of the nuclear age mean the superpowers must learn to live together. (Tennessean front page news).

From this message, one can hardly suspect that it is a message from a Soviet Communist superpower leader. Indeed, it hardly sounds different from that of the Pope both on Christmas Day and New Year's Day when the pontiff called global prayers of peace, and prayed for world peace and called for the two superpowers to cease their suicidal nuclear arms race and to destroy these deadly weapons in the name of God and world peace. (In fact, it was largely due to Gorbachev's initiative and response to this global call for reduction in nuclear weapons, that finally led to the December 1987 Summit in Washington, DC and the historical Intermediate Nuclear Freeze (INF) treaty, which is a good guesture towards meaningful global peace.)
For Christians, Christmastide is the special time to reflect on the angelic message of cosmic peace of God the Father; "Glory to God in the highest, Peace on Earth and Goodwill towards all men and women" (Lk. 2:8-14). Indeed, Gorbachev's essential message of peace and exhortation sound very Christian. For instance, it is not far from the Pope's call for world peace; it is very complimentary to prayers for peace on earth and goodwill, such as found in the bidding prayer for Christmas which was read in many Episcopal/Anglican Churches on Christmas Day:

Dear people of God; in this Christmas Season, let it be our duty and delight to hear once more

the message of the angels, calling us to go to
Bethlehem and see the son of God lying in a manger.
Let us hear and heed in Holy Scripture the
story of God's loving purpose from the time of our
rebellion against him until the glorious redemption
brought to us by his holy child Jesus, and let us
make this place glad with our carols of praise.

But first, let us pray for the needs of his
whole world, for peace and justice on the earth,
for the unity and mission of the Church for which
Jesus Christ died, and especially for his Church in
our country and city.

And because he particularly loves them, let
us remember in his name the poor and the helpless,
the cold, the hungry and the oppressed, the sick
and those who mourn, the lonely and the unloved,
the aged and little children, as well as all those
who do not know and love the Lord Jesus Christ.

Finally, let us remember before God, his pure
and lovely Mother, and that whole multitude which
no one can number, whose hope was in the Word made
flesh, and with whom, in Jesus, we are made one for
evermore.

And now let us say together the prayer for
the human family:

"O God, you made us in your own image and
redeemed us through Jesus your Son; look with compassion on the whole human family; take away the
arrogance and hatred which infect our tears; break
down the walls that separate us in bonds of love;
and work through our struggle and confusion to
accomplish your purposes on earth; that, in your
good time, all nations and races may serve you in
harmony around your heavenly throne; through Jesus
Christ our Lord. Amen."

This Christmas bidding prayer is very insightful in
that it views the world not in terms of a global community but in closer kinship and relationship of the
"human family." If those reading or hearing this prayer

were serious to some extent about what they were praying for, then there is still hope that God will indeed redeem us and the whole world through Jesus Christ and the humble efforts of his obedient disciples, even if they may be actually fewer in numbers than the large statistical numbers of Christians in the world of whom only a few are obedient and completely dedicated to God and Jesus Christ's work in the world. But this should never discourage us since we have been warned by Jesus himself that the road to destruction is wider, more popular and overcrowded, whereas the road to God and eternal life is narrower, less popular and less travelled.

Nevertheless, because of the love, selfless sacrificial service, dedication, faithfulness, and obedience of the few saints in the form of humble godly men and women in the world, the world will be saved. God will redeem and save the world from evil and self-destruction by the virtue and work of these few saints who are ever interceding before God's throne of grace for the world's salvation from all evil and suicidal course to self-destruction in a nuclear holocaust, disastrously detonated by the evil and hellish consuming fires of greed, bigotry, and hatred. But because God has "come down" into our world of humanity and its human affairs, God will also find a way to avert and save us from evil and self-destructive egocentricism and hatred.

However, since we also have become like God, in ourselves, by the virtue of the Incarnation, therefore, we have also been given divine supernatural powers to act definitively, in the world, and to intervene in human and global affairs on God's behalf.

Therefore, we have the divine mandate to act in the world in God's name to stop the evil of nuclear weapons, war, genocide, global suicide, and self-destruction. As God's own children, we have the power to accomplish all this for the praise and glory of God, and also in practical obedience to God's commandment of love; to love God and our neighbor in the same way we love ourselves. And since most of us love a good life,

we must also become aware that this is also the primary
wish and priority of everyone else, and subsequently
work together, with all men and women in the world of
good will, in order to accomplish this priority goal,
regardless of creed, race, color, or socio-economic
status.

This is necessarily the case because peace and happiness represent the highest common good sought after by
every living thing; particularly, human beings because
of their higher intelligence and subsequent deliberate
search for the most meaningful, satisfying, and happy
form of living both individually and collectively, in a
harmonious human community in loving fellowship with
each other and with God.

Chapter Two

THE HUMAN COMMUNITY AS THE ARENA

OF GOD'S ACTIVITY

The human community is also the divine arena of the
human being's own creation, socialization or humanization, sin, and salvation. In other words, the individual is the direct creation of the community and each
community creates its own members according to God's
will and command to reproduce and multiply, and also
creates the individual not only in God's image, but
also in its own image.

Consequently, each human being bears the stamps of
both God and the local community in which the individual happens to be delivered into this world. As the
delivery system, the community is here as God's medium
through which human beings are delivered into the world
and cared for until they exit the world to return to
their Ultimate Origin, which is only to be found in the
eternal God who is "the Alpha and the Omega" or the
beginning and the end of the human process.

Humanity cannot exist in a cultural vacuum, for by
nature, human beings are social and incomplete at birth
in terms of human values, culture, and language which
are not innate in human nature nor present or acquired
immediately after birth. Subsequently, the socialization process by which children acquire these human
qualities, can therefore, be correctly described as the
humanization process.

However, whereas this is to affirm that human beings

"are made" or "processed," this does not constitute a denial to humanity to the unborn and those not yet fully socialized. This position holds that human beings, the way we know them in this world, are a direct result of their own parental and socio-cultural heritage. Parental heritage constitutes human biological heritage whereas the social heritage constitutes the cultural heritage or the humanization qualities that sometimes we refer to simply as civilization.

This human dual heritage is expressed most clearly in African philosophy which teaches that "because we are, therefore, I am; and since I am, therefore, we are." This is another way to affirm that both the individual and the community are mutually interdependent on each other, although for any given particular individual, the community is prior and a prerequisite condition for one's creation and humanization as a complete human being.

As a result, if a human child is abandoned at birth or brought up by non-human creatures, that child will never grow up into a human being despite of its human biological heritage and physical features. Similarly, when human beings bring up a non-human child, such as a chimpanzee or a monkey, it will not grow up into a human being! This is because of the dual heritage requirement, namely, cultural and biological in order to complete the creation process of a given creature in raising the human being.

Subsequently, any defect in either one of these dual heritages will also cause the creature to be defective in development or growth. For instance, if there is a biological defect in heredity regarding physical or mental condition, the child will either die or be born with these defects. Similarly, at the cultural level, an evil-filled society also has an evil-filled culture which they pass on to the young and thus taunt them with it. Some examples of evil inherited from an evil culture include color and racial prejudice, bigotry, hatred, war-mongering, and unwholesome sex norms.

Consequently, it can be said that an evil culture

will also produce evil people and that since culture is also a human creation, evil people create an evil culture. Therefore, the culturally inherited human evil is also in turn passed on down to the off-spring in the form of culture, education, and even religion. Fortunately, God's redemptive work in Jesus Christ seeks to challenge the individual and institutional evil in order to redeem both the individuals and their evil or fallen structures riddled by evil and sin.

God works at those two levels because an individual is lost without the community, and therefore, both the community and the individual must be redeemed and saved, for one of these two elements cannot exist by itself without the existence of the other, for both the individual and the commnity are inseparable, since each one presupposes the existence of the other for its own existence. An analogous relationship here, is like that of a good university where both good students and good professors presuppose the mutual existence of each other.

Family and Community

The nuclear family is the basic organic unit component of any given community, whether local or global. Whereas an individual's existence is of great importance, it is like that of an atom unrelated to others whose great importance lies in the relationship capacity and possibility to join with others to form larger clusters, such as molecules. The family is the molecule equivalent in human relationships.

In the family unit, different individuals of different sexes who are not closely related by blood kinship voluntarily enter a legal and religious marriage bond based on mutual love, friendship, and desire to live together as husband and wife, and to bring up their offspring together in the sanctity and loving protection of their home.

The Bible makes it quite clear that in the beginning

God created humankind, both male and female, in his own image (Gen. 1:27) and blessed them; and commanded them to multiply and fill the earth with other human beings through their offspring. From this passage one can, therefore, conclude that homosexual relationships are excluded from the marriage bond for both belong to the same gender and cannot bear children.

It is also true that acccording to the second account of creation, marriage is said primarily to be for the sake of companionship, love, and suitable help (Gen. 2:17). In order to fulfill this need, God did not create another man, but rather, provided an attractive woman (Eve) to Adam. We also read that God blessed them and their sexual union whose chief function was reproduction. And both of them were naked and free with each other until the barrier of sin and the consequent human evil made them uncomfortable with each other.

It was then that the barrier expressed itself in shame, hiding from each other and God. Adam found his egocentricism expressed in male-chauvenism and the oppression of evil. Human evil had truly begun with this primordial couple and it is not surprising, therefore, that their own children, Cain and Abel, became so evil themselves, became envious of each other, and subsequently hated each other until Cain killed Abel his brother! This is the first murder recorded and it takes place within the primordial human family! This was prophetic of what other human families were to be like; namely, evil and self-destructive, mainly due to sins of selfishness, egocentricism, pride, envy, and hatred.

Nevertheless, the family is also the beloved primary place one calls home and feels at home. It is the place of unconditional mutual love, acceptance, and security. One may have many good friends but these do not replace the real need for having close family members, such as mother, father, and brothers and sisters. Friendship will last as long as both of you work at the relationship, whereas being a family member, in a given community, is an essentially given "prior" right, and a necessary prerequisite or prior condition for any meaningful human relationship.

Subsequently, we have no choice of where and when we are born. In other words, we cannot choose to be born in a certain family, ethnic group, nation, or race. Similarly, since we cannot choose our own parents, we have no control over our biological or physical heritage, such as color, height, and intelligence.

Therefore, we have to accept ourselves, parents, and other family members, and the given condition of our being members of a human family. We have to love ourselves as we are and to love others as they are. If we impose conditions on ourselves or others to be met first before we can extend our love to them, then most likely, we will never love anyone since our standards may be too high and unrealistic. In any case, if God had also imposed such prerequisites before we could merit his/her love, then we would never have gained it, since we sin perpetually.

Likewise, we are to extend our love to all without condition, beginning with members of our family, neighbors and members of our local community. Our main goal should be a view to see all human beings as being part of one global family of which God is the parent, and therefore, be able to love and forgive them unconditionally, just as we do with our immediate family members and close relatives. Indeed, in Christ, our big Brother and Redeemer, we all have become closely related as brothers and sisters, since all the other barriers of race, color, nationality, economic status, and ideology have all been transcended by all those who are obedient to God.

The human family is a very important primary human institution, not just because it is the foundation of all human communities, societies and nations, but also because it is the primary divine provision and ideal means for creating new human beings into the world and providing for them through the loving tender care of mother, father, and other family members. And as we have already seen above, according to the Bible, God created the first couple and entrusted it with the divine responsibility of reproducing themselves to fill the world.

The world is now full, and therefore, we have done a very good job of multiplying! Indeed, we have now to pray that we do not overfill the world and destroy it by depleting it of all its essential natural resources needed to support an overcrowded planet. Therefore, birth or population control by proper child spacing is now an urgent necessity in order to ensure the continued well being and good care of all human beings, both born and not yet born.

Nevertheless, in zeal for population control, human beings should never become selfish, and inhumane enough to advocate abortion as either a form of birth control or solving the problem of sexual promiscuity and unplanned pregnancies. Indeed, there is no such thing as "unplanned" or "unwanted pregnancies" because the primary function of sexual activity is reproduction.

Subsequently, each time normal human beings engage in this procreative activity, they should expect to see a beginning of another human life in the form of conception! But because of human evil, sin and perversion, human beings have largely separated sexual activity from its primary function as procreation, within the society and legally approved bond of marriage.

As a result, sex has become another human commodity, to sell and buy, or some casual relationship and activity engaged in primarily for its sake as a source of pleasure, a means to pass leisure time, and an outlet for bodily heightened sexual drives and mere satisfaction; for "animal needs" still present in the "lower animal nature" of the human being. It is the encouragement of this lower animal nature of the human being that has tended to bring both the lofty and the mighty down to the ground at the humbling level of the common prostitute or other despicable and immoral person.

It is also at this animal level that the mighty and the humble have been equalized in sin. Indeed, the Bible is clear that even great kings like David and the wise Solomon ceased to be either holy or wise when it came to sexual sins. King David fell for the naked attractiveness of Bathsheba which he spied on from the height of his balcony and killed her husband in order to marry her, whereas King Solomon amassed about a thousand women for wives! In addition, Samson's tragic story also tells us how sexual sin can lead even a holy man to sin and mortal death.

However, today's threat to the family does not lie in polygamy or casual sex and effective abortion, but rather in increasingly great numbers of women who are defiantly choosing to have children out-of-wedlock, and subsequently, proceed to raise their children as single mothers. For instance, by 1986, it was estimated that of all the Black children being raised in this country (USA), about sixty percent of them were being raised by single parents! And this trend was on the increase and not the decline.

Certainly, this is a tragic example of the destruction of the traditional family and these children, along with the rest of society, which has to pay a heavy price for this unfortunate state of affairs, because most of these Black single parents are also poor and on public welfare. The society will, therefore, have to pay for the sins of its members, and will continue to pay until a suitable solution has been found to rehabilitate the Black and other troubled families.

Another sexual moral problem has been that of homosexuality and its controversy. The Bible explicitly condemns the practice of homosexuality along with despicable acts of beastiality. The punishment prescribed for both sexual aberrations or sins was death (Lev. 20:12; 15-16). We also have the example of Sodom and Gommorrah where homosexuality was severely punished by God through fire and destruction.

Consequently, some Christians may be authentically prophetic when they claim that God is, probably, again warning us through the current affliction of deadly AIDS (Acquired Immune Deficiency Syndrome), which was originally a disease associated with homosexuality and

sexual immorality, that we need to mend or change our
sexual moral ways and return to the traditional norms
of chastity, monogamy, and faithfulness to the marriage
vows.

It is a well known fact that adultery has been rampant, leading to many kinds of venereal diseases, quar-
rels, and divorces; now it may, in addition, lead to
death. Subsequently, because of AIDS, many people are
becoming less sexually adventurous and more careful
with the kinds of persons they choose to go to bed with
or to marry. This is good in itself and should be
encouraged by all those people who love life and all
those who seek the well being of the human family. It
is a good time now to extol the virtues of chastity and
abstinence from sexual relations as both a moral good
and a wise health-care practice.

In this return to the traditional ethics of sexuality, happiness has to be explained as constituted by
successful mastery of the body by our disciplined minds
and the will to live a morally clean life which extols
the virtues of the spirit and not the hedonistic sensory transient pleasures of the body, especially in food,
drink, and sex. Even animals do these things in moderation as required by the body to survive or to reproduce. Subsequently, there are no other animals apart
from us that engage in both eating and sex as merely a
form of pleasure and self or mutual entertainment.

As a result, this is also why only the human beings
are capable of misusing both these natural drives for
food and mating. Consequently, society had developed
norms and laws to guide wholesome behaviors in respect
to food, drink and sex in order to protect the individual and the community from the harm due to the misuse
these God-given gifts might cause. For instance, too
much alcohol is not just a danger to the drunkard, but
to the whole community. Similarly, the harlot and the
pimp are a disgrace; a moral, spiritual, and medical
menace to the local community in which they merchandise
their moral evil and venereal diseases.

Moral laws and cultural sex norms have been developed

in such a way so as to protect all human life, especially in the family home. For instance, incest taboos
and laws have been developed so as to ensure the full
protection of the females in their homes.

If these taboos had not been there, life for the
young females would be difficult and insecure even in
their very own families, since there would be competition between brothers and fathers for them. In short,
without the incest taboos and laws, the human family
would have been impossible because of this incest practice and elimination of any male rivals from the home.
Biologically, family inbreeding would have also led to
the extinction of some families due to some deadly
hereditary diseases.

In order to protect the security, well being, and
sanctity of the family, the Mosaic Law did not only
prohibit adultery, incest, homosexuality, and beastiality; in broad terms, but it also went into specific,
detailed prohibitions and penalties for violations. For
instance, in the Mosaic Law book of Leviticus, we find
the following specific prescribed behavior and sexual
relations, and the prescribed punishments for their
violations:

The Lord gave the following regulations: Anyone who
curses his father or mother shall be put to death;
he is responsible for his own death.

If a man commits adultery with the wife of a
fellow Israelite, both he and the woman shall be
put to death.

A man who has intercourse with one of his father's wives disgraces his father, and both he and
the woman shall be put to death. They are responsible for their own death. If a man has intercourse
with his daughter-in-law, they shall both be put to
death. They have committed incest and they are
responsible for their own death.

If a man has sexual relations with another man, they have done a disgusting thing and both shall be put to death. They are responsible for their own death. If a man marries a woman and her mother, all three shall be burned to death because of the disgraceful thing they have done; such a thing must not be permitted among you.

If a man has sexual relations with an animal, he and the animal shall be put to death. If a woman tries to have sexual relations with an animal, she and the animal shall be put to death.... If a man marries his sister or half-sister they shall be publically disgraced and driven out of the community.... If a man has intercourse with his aunt, both of them must suffer the consequences of incest.... You shall be holy and belong to me; I am holy...... (Lev. 20:9-26)

This sex moral code and prohibitions were not only required to ensure holiness and sexual morality, but also to ensure the survival and the general social and physical well-being of the family since it is the very foundation of the human community and society in general. Subsequently, a healthy family life is the necessary prerequisite for any healthy community or society.

Therefore, this sex moral code which proscribes all forms of incest, was necessary not just to ensure the physical survival and well-being of the human family, but also the survival and well-being of the whole human community which is built on it. Consequently, human community or any society which allows or encourages its family members to practice incest will sooner or later pay the heavy price for this immorality in terms of family disintegration, and ultimately, the very disintegration and dissolution of the evil and immoral community or society itself.

As a result, all societies and communities in one way or another have instituted the sex moral code which proscribes both incest and adultery. The definition and

scope of both incest and adultery may vary from culture
to culture and society to society, but the prohibitions
and taboos are universal, regardless of creed, culture,
race, political ideology, and level of development.

Therefore, it is also not surprising that most cultural, ethnic, and racial prejudices and discrimina-
tions are sexually based and motivated. For instance,
until recently, many racist laws in South Africa had a
clear underlying overtone and agenda of prohibiting
sexual relations and marriages between the people of
different races, particularly, between Whites and
Blacks. In India, the Caste System had also made culturally and religiously illegal for marriages to take
place across different castes.

It is also a fact that in the USA, though the Black
people are no longer slaves, they are still largely
despised and illegally discriminated against on the
account of their color, and that many Whites still look
at interracial dating and marriages with great disdain!

Furthermore, it also seems to many observers and
scholars such as Sigmund Freud, that much of human
behavior and culture can be directly traceable to human
sexuality, which is supposed to explain most of our
conscious and unconscious behaviors, values, religions,
wishes, dreams, and the like.

However, it does not require a trained psychologist
to tell us that much of the human socio-economic values
and conflict in most communities are sexually based.
For instance, in the USA, all one needs is to look at
Hollywood and its sex ideals and symbols as portrayed
in all kinds of entertainment, such as films, comedies,
advertisements, music, and dance. Even new cars are
advertised just in the same way like the sunny tourist
beaches of Africa or Hawaii, by seductive, semi-nude,
sexy girls.

This is almost true of all the public entertainment
and television shows. It seems that the secret ingredi-
ent or recipe to entertainment's success is plenty of
explicit casual sex and senseless violence! If this is
a true observation, then Freud is certainly correct in

saying that sexuality is the unknown yet disturbing foundation of most human values, cultures, religions, and activities. For instance, much of the human conflicts such as envy, hatred, malice, crime; and violence, such as murder or wars, seem to stem from sex and its frustrated outlets or expressions.

Consequently, if any human society or community is ever to survive, it must inevitably find a constructive moral way to deal with human sexuality. The traditional solution has been to proscribe both incest and adultery. But in today's society, especially in the USA, there are increasing reports of child sexual abuse by parents and close relatives in the family home setting. Rapes and cases of adultery and broken homes due to incest, adultery, and divorce, are on the increase, thus endangering the very stable, secure existence and survival of the human family, which is the very foundation on which the rest of the other human institutions are based.

Therefore, unless there is an urgent slowing down and even a reversal of this destructive trend in the human family, the human traditional, secure family will be destroyed and along with it will be all the other traditional societal institutions, such as religion, church, marriage, sexual moral codes, the economy, property rights, procreation, and child-care responsibilities. Without the viable necessary family structure, there would have to emerge a new socio-economic and political order if human beings have to continue to exist and to reproduce their kind without an institution comparable to our present family.

Maybe some kinds of procedures, such as state owned and controlled factories for mass production of test-tube babies with predetermined gender and genetically engineered and improved physical characteristics, according to need, will have to be instituted to replace the shattered traditonal family structure and marriage institution! And in place of the traditional family house, there will be collective dormitories organized according to age, gender, occupation, and interests.

Nevertheless, allowing all those who want to live a traditional family life to continue to do so but at their own expense, without any help from the atheistic state which will consider this traditional family practice outdated and undesirable, or as survival of the "superstitious past era."

However, the concept of God and religion and sexual morality would be preserved forever in this scorned group as testimony of God's love and saving grace in the disobedient evil human state of affairs in the world. This kind of group would indeed constitute a kind of Noah's Ark of divine salvation, amidst the sea of human moral evil and scientific godlessness, waiting for divine anger and destruction.

Fortunately, the above disaster will not occur as long as the world will still obey God's commandments: to fear God, to honor the parents, not to commit adultery, not to kill, not to steal, nor bear false witness, and not to covet our neighbor's spouse or goods; the family will survive the shocks of the current wave of the sins of incest, adultery, rapes, infanticide, and murders, for these are still being committed by a few morally depraved and inhumane men and women who deserve our pity since most of them are also mentally sick and in need of treatment and moral rehabilitation.

With the survival of the human family we also have the survival of the community, nation, and ultimately, the survival of all the global human community in the same degree or measure, for all these human institutions are correlatively and co-extensively interrelated. This is true, regardless of creed, color, nationality, race, ethnic group, or economic status. That is to say that whatever happens to the family in Africa, USA, and China will not affect just those countries, but will also affect those regions and ultimately, the whole world.

Demographic factors such as number of births, deaths, marriages, and divorces will not just affect population growth factors, but will also affect socio-economic factors, politics, and power structures at the local level and also at the national and international levels. For instance, a nation with many strong healthy families will also have many strong healthy productive citizens.

This being the case, it will therefore, become a rigorous world of power since healthy, well educated, disciplined and happy citizens are also more productive in other sectors of life, such as agriculture, science, and technology. Unfortunately, these kinds of well socialized, healthy, strong, satisfied, and happy citizens can only be a product of healthy, strong, noble, disciplined, and happy homes.

Therefore, good, strong, noble, and self-desciplined communities and nations can only be the result of good, strong, noble and well disciplined families and homes as their necessary correlative foundation and grounding. This is because without this essential correct foundation, nothing positive can hardly occur, either in the national or the international scene because only good natured, good willed, and caring men and women work to make good things happen to other people both at home and abroad or both nationally and internationally. For only those from good human families know what a good human community is truly like and seek whole heartedly, to extend their warm family's caring and unconditional, loving spirit to the national and international levels.

Nevertheless, to this end, all these people of good will have to gain the cooperation of others, especially the mean, the greedy, the ethnocentric, the bigoted, the racist, and the exploiters in order to bring unity, human dignity, human rights, and peace to all human beings as God's one big global family. This universal divine family is to be viewed colorfully with all the different skin colors, shades, varying body sizes and looks, combining to form a great beautiful mosaic of one humankind with each color, shape, and size beautifully complimenting the other to form both contrast and harmony in humankind and the human community.

Both humankind and the community would be extremely dull and boring without this contrast of color, size, and gender. Can you imagine what it would be like if all people were the same, including color, size, shape, and all other physical features just like perfect copies or identical twins? It would be extremely difficult for any human being to become an individual, unique and different; for deviation would be due to a defect and imperfection rather than human individualization and self-affirmation as such.

The Human Community

The human community is a necessary extension of the family and its essential activities. In other words, the family is the microcosm of the community; the community is achieved by elevation of families to a higher and more formatted collective level beginning with the local level, such as village, district, tribe, or ethnic group and moving further to a more abstract level, such as nation and the international community or the global family.

The further away the family circle moves outward, the more it is likely to encounter other families who are different in color, physical features, and culture. And with this natural diversity and pluralism, there is always great room for mutual miscommunication and as such, great room for mutual misunderstanding and conflict.

Unfortunately, instead of identifying and correcting the main problem which is usually to be found in poor cross cultural communications, the problem is most often misdiagnosed in terms of race, color, cultural differences, or religious differences. The results have been devastating bigotry, ethnocentrism, and xenophobia.

Consequently, it is to be observed in cultural imperialism and xenophobia from the dominant Western traditional Christian ethos. Subsequently, the West has in the past tended either to capture and enslave or colonize the other people who were deemed as inferior, primarily on the basis of color, race, creed and level of technological development.

As a result of this color prejudice and xenophobia, the darker races, especially the African, have in the past suffered great degradations of slavery and colonialism which have left these people socio-economically, spiritually, and politically traumatized and most severely injured and permanently scarred.

By ungodly and inhumane acts of racism and economic greed, one race of people came very close to the acts of global genocide in order to dominate, control, and exploit the non-White races. To this end, and in order to clear or ease their own Christian conscience, the White imperialists and exploiters declared the non-White races less than human.

Darwin's biological theory of evolution was deliberately extended to human races and their institutions and it was felt that the Whites were the privileged human race at the top of the evolutionary ladder, whereas the darker races in Africa and elsewhere were still at the bottom of the evolutionary ladder, together with their socio-economic institutions.

Therefore, the Africans could be enslaved, colonized, exploited, degraded, and exterminated by whites without a great sense of remorse. This is helpful in explaining the great horrors and inhumane brutality of the African slave trade, colonization wars, and present trends in South Africa today, where the Whites still adhere to this anachronistic doctrine of "Social Darwinism" in order to repress the African people on grounds of racism, and White supremacy; namely, that the White race is superior, and is the elect, and most fitted, by the Creator-God, to rule the inherently inferior African people whose proper divinely given destiny is supposed to be that of obedient subjects and workers, for the material benefit of their White masters!

Tragically, it was also the basis of the superiority

and purity of this White race that Hitler exterminated
about six million Jews during World War II. The world
was not outraged then, and if we are not careful, this
kind of holocaust can reoccur. Since the Jews have
sworn that "never again," the Palestinians may instead
become the victims of the holocaust if they insist on
the extermination of the Jews and the Jewish state of
modern Israel.

On the other hand, the Whites can wipe out masses of
Blacks as a last resort in defense of their present
privileged, economic, political, and racial position.
Nevertheless, the USA, with its racial, intransigent,
and heavily armed groups, such as the Ku Klux Klan
(KKK), White Supremacists, and Neo-Nazis, whose reason
for being is to rid the country of Blacks, Catholics,
Communists, and Jews may actually succeed in carrying
out their objectives, and thus, committing great mass
murders the world has ever seen.

Therefore, one can only hope and pray that God and
our constructive efforts may prevent such a tragic
occurence, and the place to begin is education, most
especially, teaching these kinds of people that their
objects of total annihilation in the name of God are
also the very objects of God's love; namely, that these
are true fellow human beings, created by God in his/her
own image, just like them. Thus creating the sense of a
common humanity which we all share and, as such, to
kill any human being is murder, regardless of race,
color, creed, or ideology. This is because there cannot
be global understanding, clear communication, cooperation, and peace unless we first learn to accept each
other as true human beings who need to learn to work
together as colleagues and correlatively, learn to
live together in mutual cooperation, interdependence,
harmony, and peace.

Therefore, the human community, like any other community, presupposes commonality. It presupposes that the
members of that community have a major self-consciousness as being of one species or sub-species with a
common goal, a common origin, a common destiny, a

common socio-economic organizational structure or government, a common language, and a common good for which to mobilize and work together in order to achieve.

As such, a human community cannot be a mere collection of human beings in a given location. Such a collection of a mass of people in one place even if they all speak one language and have come for one purpose, such as to watch a popular football team's game or for a protest and riot; this kind of human group is not a community. It is merely a crowd and nothing more.

The notion of a community is not just the notion of human beings in a group, gang, team, or congregation. The notion of community includes a dynamic, ongoing, human group living in an ordered and structured form of living network of human relationships and both obligations, formal and informal.

Consequently, a viable human community must be structured, with norms and regulations which guide, govern, and regulate the informal and formal behavior and relationships of the members of the given community with clearly known sanctions enforced for the breach of etiquette and rules.

As such, every viable human community must be an ethical community with clear, moral guidelines regulating human behavior and socio-economic interaction of its members. Ancient Israel with its God-given covenant and law through Moses is a good example of this kind of well regulated community.

However, the legitimate rights of each member of the community have to be recognized and safeguarded. For instance, each individual person's rights to essential privacy, family, education, work, freedom of expression or speech, freedom of movement and travel, freedom of association, and freedom of religion have to be respected and observed even when they may bring pluralism, diversity, and conflict into the community.

Subsequently, there is always great tension in human community because of this diversity of its members and their varied interests which necessarily conflict with the communities' tendency to seek conformity, and therefore, seek to program its members through cultural socialization, education, and indoctrination, to act according to the dogmatic teachings, guidelines, and rules of the community.

This tends to happen more readily in Communist and Islamic countries where the society does not expect or tolerate much ideological, behavioral, social or religious dissent. In the Soviet Union, dissenters are treated as mental cases, whereas in Iran it is an extreme current example of Shi'ite Islamic fundamentalism and its determination to crash any deviance or opposition through intidation, coercion and public mass executions for all forms of religious and social dissent.

It is mainly due to this religious bigotry, fundamentalism, and intolerance that is responsible for much evil, poverty, destructive war, deaths, human suffering, and misery in the Middle East, Northern Ireland, and many parts of Africa. Authoritarian governments and dictators, such as Hitler and Idi Amin never tolerated any opposition or dissent. Those who opposed these dictators did not last long and it was in such an evil manner that some self-serving, ambitious, evil men have deified themselves, swept away all the established rules governing human relations and behavior to impose their own and reign in terror and bloodshed.

These are the kinds of evil men and leaders that have been responsible for much of the global human moral evil, degradation, suffering, pain, war, and death. World history bears great testimony to this sad and humbling human evil and moral tragedy. Indeed, history seems to be made by evil men and women such that the evil acts these people do receive more comprehensive coverage in the mass media and history text-books, whereas what the good human beings do seems to receive less publicity both in the mass media and history books unless it is very outstanding, such as the Camp David Agreement, the Pope's call for a day of prayer for global peace, and a truce between President Aquino's

government and the communist dissident resistance guer-
rilla movement in the Phillippines. Otherwise, the mass
media tends to regard good actions as noble but not
sensational enough to sell to their listening or reading mass audiences.

However, one is almost led to ask whether it is not
actually true that good news does not sell well just
because human beings are more inclined to do evil. And
that if they cannot persuade themselves to do evil,
that they will, instead, want to read about those who
have done it! Is it not also possible that most of us
are privately or unconsciously sadistic enough to take
pleasure in reading about other people's misfortunes,
pain and tragedies? Isn't this kind of need to unite,
and even see other people suffer pain or cry out in
pain that leads most people to go to rough boxing,
football, and wrestling contests?

If there is some truth that many of us use these
rough games for psychological self-treatment and subli-
mation as many psychaiatrists think, then it could also
be said to be true for the human need to read or see
more of massive tragic events in the news media and
history books than good events which challenge them to
a better performance or a higher moral standard of living.

In this respect, then, one should expect morally
depraved human beings to read more or see more of their
own kind succeed or do what even others think of as
gross, in order to entertain and motivate themselves to
greater aggression and the commission of greater evil.
Such is the case with the people who read pornographic
material or those who go to see sexually explicit and
obscene movies. Thus, evil feeds on evil to motivate
even greater evil.

As a result, the American young indiscriminate television viewers who have been for long subjected to both
sex and violence, and subsequently, live with violence,
and practice loose casual sex themselves, as if these
vices were normal and the acceptable social ways of
life in today's society. And this being the unfortunate

case, the American society is today paying heavily for the unchecked public vice and sins committed in the name of show business and uncensored public entertainment.

These evil and immoral merchants of free casual sex between "consenting adults," homosexuality, abortion on demand, divorce on demand, sex and liquor for pleasure and leisure, "might makes right," and violence being the way to get one's way and vindication have destroyed the moral fabric of our society by corrupting the youth into living an immoral life of casual sex and drugs for both leisure and pleasure.

Consequently, the public has also been brainwashed and programmed by a variety of entertaining war films into believing that war is fun if you are the winner, and as such, some see no problem with President Reagan's Strategic Defense Initiative (SDI), popularly known as "Star Wars" like the popular cosmic and space war film after which the program was modeled!

It is very telling about us when the programs for children in the form of cartoons seem to be more than 70% concerned with aggression, violence, and war. When these children, programmed to love war games, firearms, and violence become fully grown adults and scientists, these animated cartoon warfares and toys can actually be turned into real modern forms of war machines, instead of mere toys and cartoons, since with modern technology, it is almost possible to say that whatever the mind can conceive logically and clearly, technology can be utilized to turn it into reality!

Therefore, we have to be extremely cautious about what ideas we entertain as funny, ideal, good, and bad. We have also to be concerned with what our children see, hear, learn, feel, and think. The television programs our children see may affect them the rest of their lives both directly and indirectly and therefore, it should be our chief concern to preview and approve them, whenever possible.

Since generally the mass media has no good moral values to impart to our children, we must support

public educational television channels and insist on
good, sound, and morally upbuilding educational programs. This may prove controversial in a pluralistic
society, such as ours but there are always universal
ethical values we all can agree on, such as those based
on the Ten Commandments.

On the other hand, we can always introduce our own
ethical and educational programs to view in place of
the morally objectionable ones from the commercial
public media. This boycott and appropriate legislation
can help to clean up some programs aired during the
times when children are at home and awake, and therefore, most likely to view them despite the rating or
request for parental guidance where minor children are
concerned.

Society has a moral obligation to help parents bring
up the young well and instill in them the right social
and religious norms and values. But the American television entertainment producers seem to have forgotten
their own moral values along with those of their own
traditional society.

Subsequently, they have become the evil, rich, op-
portunist, greedy, and capitalist merchants of war and
nuclear war machines, and have also become the horrible, onmipresent pimps of casual sex and pervasion.
Therefore, unchecked, indiscriminate television and
movie-going can soon be the greatest moral degradation,
and source of societal self-destruction and suicide in
this country, if ill-advised nuclear warfare does not
do it first.

However, despite the gloomy picture of the human
community painted above, this is still nonetheless the
very human community in which God's unconditional love
and redemptive grace have become permanently embodied
by the virtue of the Incarnation. In other words, this
sinful human community that appears desperately evil
and wicked is the same community which God loves so
much and seeks to redeem in Jesus Christ from the evil
grips and bondage of overwhelming evil and sin. And
because there is evil and sin, we know that there is

also God's love and saving grace present for all those who are tired of evil and its hellish consequences and need salvation from it.

In the Incarnation, God has become a concrete and temporal, holy human being in this temporal human community, so as to provide a concretely, holy, living, human example of what it really means to be truly an authentic human in this temporal world. And also what it means to be ethically and morally upright while living in the midst of evil, sin, pain, suffering and death without being corrupted by evil or being influenced and corrupted by peer pressure and friends who may be party to evil-doing.

In addition, Jesus' own temptations show us how to resist the great temptations of sin even when there are great promises and real possibilities for instant wealth, fame and political power. These were the same temptations faced and conquered by Jesus. Instead of becoming a wealthy mighty king, he preferred to live a simple life of poverty, while serving God among the society's marginal, neglected poor and outcasts.

Instead of the supernatural show of irresistible force or coercion of sinners to repentance and divine holiness, he chose to invite and persuade them into the kingdom and holiness of God. He respected human rights and dignity and, as such, he never tried either to coerce or hoodwink sinners into repentance. Rather, he taught them what was right and wrong and then invited them to make an introspection, self-examination, evaluation, and decision for God and his kingdom "of global, unconditional love of neighbor and peace."

In other words, Jesus Christ's main mission on earth was to teach, preach, and persuade men and women in the name of the loving heavenly Father, God the Creator, to live a simple, holy, loving, and joyful life in the universal, unconditional "Fellowship of Love." And to this heavenly end, Jesus promised that God would send his/her Holy Spirit to aid men and women to enter the fullness of life in the blissful joy of the heavenly ecstasy of God's spirit of love and true happiness that can only come from God and being fully unconditionally accepted and loved.

Hence, all Christian teaching and all God's commandments being correctly summed in: LOVE YOUR NEIGHBOR WITHOUT ANY CONDITIONS! Consequently, unconditional love for the neighbor, and the neighbor being every human being, is the only true test of any true and redemptive religion, regardless of what it calls itself.

Subsequently, if Judaism, Christianity, Islam, Hinduism, Buddhism, or even Communism fulfills this divine commandment of unconditional love for fellow human beings, including the enemy, then that religion and that person who practices this love has already qualified for divine salvation and he/she is on her way to heaven!

Indeed, such individuals have included diverse men like Jesus, Mahatma Gandhi and Martin Luther King who were great exponents of the universal brotherhoods and sisterhoods of human beings, since all of them were created by the one Almighty loving God to become his or her children to live together in unity, harmony, and to love each other as God's children and members of the same divine global family irrespective of creed, color, race, and nationality.

Consequently, all these three denounced bigotry, hatred, racism, violence, and war. Jesus, Gandhi, and King had a very clear common understanding that all human beings are essentially one, interrelated, and interdependent children of one heavenly loving Creator and Parent that we call God and that the other differences that divided humankind into castes, classes, tribes, nations, colors, and races were secondary and superficial. These secondary qualities were for the sake of contrast and beauty within the one and indivisible global human family.

Jesus Christ, like his faithful disciples, such as Gandhi and King, was acutely aware that in order for there to be peace in the world, human beings had first to learn to live together in harmony and that in order for different human beings to live together in harmony, they had first to learn to accept and love one another as human beings without any conditions attached.

However, in order for this unconditional love to occur, there had to be the necessary teaching and transformation of men and women; Black and White people, Red and Yellow people, Jew and Gentile; and Christian and non-Christian, to view each other as full human beings. They have to accept each other, unconditionally, as God's people, sharing one and the same common humanity with one common supernatural origin and destiny in the one loving Creator and God, the Ultimate Father and Mother of us all as human beings and his/her own beloved children or daughters and sons, and as such, true brothers and sisters.

In short, this awareness, confession, and positive affirmation of a common humanity, is the only sure foundation on which unconditional acceptance and love can be extended by any given family, tribe, community, nation, color, race, or group of people to another group of people which may look or be perceived to be different either on the basis of gender, culture, educational background, creed, ideology, color, race, language, nationality, or merely on the basis of socio-economic class.

However, this requirement for human beings to ignore and transcend the natural apparent barriers and boundaries of gender, creed, color, race, and nationality, in order to embrace other people in love and to regard them as our equals, especially if we think that we are the special chosen people of God, and therefore, better or superior people, then, this acceptance of others as full human beings and our own equals before God, must essentially occur either as a result or as a direct act of divine supernatural transformation of our natural human nature. This is necessarily the case because our natural human nature tends to glorify apparent differences and to elevate them into divinely ordained barriers and boundaries of humanity, love, socialization, and interaction.

This is why Hitler could exterminate six million Jews without a sense of guilt for the mass murder, and this is also why in South Africa Black people continue to die in great numbers, whereas most of the Western world keeps quiet or even supports the White Minority racist regime. This realization that both Black and White share a common humanity and destiny has not yet taken place and that is why many Whites still view the innocent killing of a Black person as not a horrible murder.

Subsequently, Blacks in South Africa and abroad, especially in the USA, have in the past endured the indignity of being called less than human, discrimination, exploitation, and physical and sexual abuse with almost no protection from the law and the predominantly White law enforcers, who most often were overt racists than the rest of the White population.

This kind of history led Martin Luther King to speak out against intrinsic color prejucide, racism, and oppression, and to mobilize all the humane, peace loving, and godly people to resist the intrinsic global evil forces of dehumanization, forced racist segregation, poverty, injustice, and oppression.

King called for the acceptance of people of different colors, races, and creeds as equal and true human beings, being truly the very children of God. He also called his nation to account before God for its declaration of human rights and constitution which state that "all men are created equal by God" and have inalienable rights given to them and guaranteed by God. King went on prophetically to declare that no one is free until all human beings everywhere are free and that injustice anywhere is a threat to justice, everywhere.

Subsequently, and this being the case, for King's true justice would not come until all human beings, everywhere, on this globe have learned to accept other human beings unconditionally and to judge them not on the basis of their color but on the content of their moral character. Consequently, his non-violent protest mass movement in the USA was modeled after that of Gandhi in his successful non-violent mass protest and fight for Indian independence from the British colonial power.

He was prepared to fight injustice and racism, but to do so only through love and non-violence. However, non-violence succeeded in both India and the USA because the political leaders in power had a sensitive moral conscience which could be pricked, pained, and even agonized.

Subsequently, Gandhi's philosophy of non-violence and peaceful resistance strategy failed miserably, in South Africa when he tried them there. They have recently failed again, when the oppressed, peace loving Black people tried them in their peaceful mass resistance and protest against the evil repression of apartheid and racism. Instead, thousands of them got killed! Therefore, this creates room for violence to be met with violence, not because all the people want violence but because non-violence has failed to solve a violent problem.

Unfortunately, violence is neither a good tool nor a moral means by which lasting peace, love, trust, and fellowship can be achieved, for violence breeds counter-violence and enemity; and liberation wars leave behind them a dehumanizaing trail of bloodshed and destruction morally, spiritually, politically, and economically harmful to those liberated, the liberators, and those they defeated.

This being the case, then all forms of violence, both provoked and unprovoked, at home and abroad, national and international, political and economic, verbal and physical, traditional and nuclear, big and small, limited and global, and natural and supernatural are all evil and not to be condoned by any God loving, humane, and peace loving persons, groups, organizations, and nations.

This is even more so for those people and nations, such as the USA, which regards itself as the Christian nation, and whose motto is: "IN GOD WE TRUST." If this

is God in whom we trust, then our universal divine
mandate is that of loving our neighbors as ourselves
and non-violence, rather than being the self-elected
nuclear armed cosmic or international policeman and law
enforcer or international nuclear and military terror-
ist in the name of God, technological superiority, and
military might.

Ironically, the explicit teaching of Jesus Christ on
love and war contradicts this naive "Christian militarism." On this controversial subject, Jesus is reported to have taught as follows:

But I tell you who hear me: Love your enemies, do
good to those who hate you, bless those who curse
you, and pray for those who mistreat you. If anyone
hits you on the cheek, let him hit the other one
too; if someone takes your coat, let him have your
shirt as well. Give to everyone who asks you for
something, and when someone takes what is yours, do
not ask for it back. Do for others just what you
want them to do for you. (Luke 6:21-27)

And concerning the unconditional acceptance and love
for all one's fellow human beings, Jesus went on to
teach and command his hearers as follows:

If you love only the people who love you, why
should you receive a blessing? Even sinners love
those who love them. And if you do good only to
those who do good to you, why should you receive a
blessing? Even sinners do that! And if you lend
only to those from who you hope to get it back, why
should you receive a blessing? Even sinners lend
to sinners to get back the same amount!

No. Love your enemies and do good to them; lend
and expect nothing back. You will then have great
reward, and you will be sons of the most high God.
For he is good to the ungrateful and the wicked. Be
merciful, just as your Father is merciful. (Luke
6:32-36)

Consequently, Jesus went further to command the hearers not to judge others but rather to forgive and be generous since it is by our own very measure of giving to others that we too will receive:

Do not judge others and God will not judge you; do not condemn others, and God will not condemn you; forgive others, and God will forgive you. Indeed, you will receive a full measure, a generous helping, poured into your hands all that you can hold. The measure you use for others is the one that God will use for you. (Luke 6:37-38)

This is the heart and essence of God's message in the creation, Incarnation in Jesus Christ, redemption, and God's Kingdom. God created the world out of unconditional love and redeemed it in Jesus Christ out of his eternal unconditional love. If human beings had to merit God's salvation, out of holiness rather than sin and despair, then they would not need nor require this divine or supernatural salvation for they would have already earned and achieved it by their own moral efforts and self-discipline.

Nevertheless, due to the actual confused state of human affairs and egocentric nature of human beings, this personal holiness and salvation from overwhelming evil and sin are most difficult and almost impossible since it is like saying that an exhausted, semi-conscious, drowning, helpless person is able to save himself or herself from the grip of a swift current. Such a person does not only need a "thrown life-line," but also another loving and cable person who can jump into the water to save the helpless, and the drowning in the cosmic sea of evil and needing loving, able saviors to come and save them from the slumber of sin and eternal death.

It was both ironic and prophetic that most prophets and moral teachers of inclusive global love for the neighbor without conditions, in order to achieve the global unity of humankind, harmony, violence, and war, themselves became the very object of human skepticism, hatred, rejection, and violent death which they had uncompromisingly denounced as evil and dehumanizing.

Jesus was rejected by the religious leaders and condemned to die a cruel and dehumanizing death on the painful criminal's cross whereas both Gandhi and King were felled by the assassin's bullets. The sad and tragic violent end for the advocates and teachers of love, forgiveness, and non-violence in an evil, hating, and violent world.

However, in death, these individuals have reached, touched, and blessed the lives of far more people than they ever did during their earthly ministries. As a result, evil and the death of Jesus on the cross had been defeated and the cross transformed by God into the very object of triumph and victory of justice, holiness, and truth over injustice, sin, and falsehood.

Consequently, the subsequent resurrection of Jesus by God to eternal life, is the ultimate triumph of life over death, light over darkness, good over evil, holiness over sin, love over hatred, non-violence over violence, and forgiveness over retaliation. By the resurrection, God and unconditional love had the last definitive shot and irrevocable triumph over the devil (or evil), hate, violence, and death.

Similarly, Gandhi and King's violent death had been negated and transformed by God into the very definitive and culmination of these individual's non-violent holy crusade against evil, hate, injustice, violence, and senseless death into a head-on conflict and collision with the powers of evil in which the devil (evil), feeling threatened, resorted to the cowardly last trick of ambush and assassination!

However, both Gandhi's philosophy and King's great dream of a just, humane, and integrated society have lived on even more strongly than ever before, since with the death of these holy crusaders for unconditional inclusive love and global peace, their crusade has now become elevated from the local scene to the global scene.

As a result, both men have achieved the highest
honors the local, national, and international community
could ever bestow on great holy men, compelling peace-
makers, advocates of unconditional human love, and
martyrs of peace dying a violent death in witness and
testimony that courageous love for life and humanity
overcomes the evil of the violence and fear of death
because in order to live a full life committed to the
crusade against evil, oppression, injustice and violence, one has to love one's cause and humanity enough
to be willing to challenge these evil powers and even
die courageously in this quest so that one's innocent
death might become an atoning sacrifice to prevent such
evil, violent death.

To this end, martyrdom can be considered to be a
greater good that does away with some kinds of human
evil and violence if the perpetrators are, indeed,
moral human agents endowed with reason and a moral
conscience to be aroused, agitated, and moved into
positive action as a result of repentance and transformation. Otherwise, invitation of martyrdom in
circumstances where there is a total lack of moral
conscience to affect, is not only foolish, but also a
form of ill-advised senseless suicide! Analogously, it
would be both foolish and suicidal for a Christian to
kneel and pray when faced by a ferocious wild beast,
instead of fleeing to safety.

Therefore, non-violence is not the naive, passive
philosophy of not resisting evil and just turning the
other cheek. Conversely, it is a morally compelling,
dynamic, and powerful way of saying "no more" to evil,
whether in individuals or structures, withdrawing one's
moral, physical, spiritual, economic, and political
support from this evil individual, structure, or organization with the full willingness to face all the
consequences, such as going to jail, losing a job, or
even getting beaten, injured, or killed.

In other words, you have to be willing to stand firm
and even die in this moral crusade for the sake of love
or the neighbor, personal moral integrity, and just for

all human beings. It was to this very end and realization that Jesus himself invited all those who would
become his followers to carry their crosses of suffering and possible crucifixion:

"If anyone wants to follow me," he told them, "he
must forget himself, carry his cross and follow me.
For whoever wants to save his own life, will lose
it; but whoever loses his life for me and the
gospel's sake, will save it. Does a person gain
anything if he gains the world but loses his own
soul? Of course not! There is nothing he can give
to regain his life. If a person is ashamed of me
and my teaching in this godless and wicked generation, then the Son of Man will also be ashamed of
him when he comes in glory of God his Father with
the holy angels." (Mark 8:31-38)

Therefore, it is through our obedient response to
this divine invitation for us to pick up and carry our
crosses and follow Christ in his committed crusade
against evil, sin, hate, bigotry, prejudice, injustice,
oppression, violence, intolerance, war, and death that
God will transform this human evil community, bent to
do evil and violence, into the holy "Fellowship of
Love" or the redeemed community of the people of God.
In short, God can only work concretely through us in
order to transform evil in the world into good, and
discord and armed conflicts into harmony and peace. And
the longer we delay, is correlatively also the longer
the world will wait and languish in evil, prejudice,
hatred, division, violence, and self-destruction. This
is necessarily the case because we are his effective
ambassadors in the world charged with the full responsiblity for the moral, spiritual, socio-economic, and
political reconstruction and rehabitation of both humanity, the human community, and the rest of God's
creation of which we are the divine stewards and moral
custodians.
In other words, God is actively working in this world

of evil and we as human beings created in his/her
divine image, the intelligent moral agents capable of
judging and doing what is good, ethical, and right in
the spirit of love, are the very divine agents and
instrumentality of God's redemptive activity by which
God seeks to redeem and transform this world from a
"Fellowship of evil" engulfed in hatred, division, and
violence into a "Fellowship of Love," committed to God
and the divine work in the world, seeking to bring
about the fullness of obedience, holiness, generosity,
unconditional love, and acceptance of all God's created
people as his/her children and equal members of the
same universal divine and human family.

This is very close to what St. Paul meant when he
wrote his letter of advice to the confused, prejudiced,
and divided Galatian Christians. He warned them that in
Christ:

> there is no difference between Jews and Gentiles,
> between slaves and freemen, or between men and
> women; you are all one in union with Christ Jesus.
> (Gal. 3:28)

Since Christ is preexistent and all creation and all
human beings were made by God through him as the creative Word of God (Gen. 1 and John 1:1-18), the eternal
divine light that enlightens every human being into the
moral and intellectual awareness of what is good and
what is bad, what is right and what is wrong, and what
is holy and what is sinful, in which all religions are
universally grounded and in which ethical values are
rooted, then what St. Paul has written to the Church in
Galatia can be correlatively extended to include all
God's people everywhere, regardless of creed, who obey
God's definitive commandment of unconditional love for
the neighbor.

Consequently, all human beings are essentially one in
Christ, since ultimately, it is in and through Christ
that they all came into being, have their redemption,
and regain their reunion and fellowship with God which

had been previously, either partially or totally lost through rebellion against God's will and moral law, and subsequently, through sin and evil deeds.

Fortunately, sin and evil were negated by Jesus Christ's coming into the world; his innocent death on the cross at the hands of evil doers, and his subsequent triumphant resurrection in divine glory to create a new social order. And therefore, creating a new and transformed world whose priorities and agenda have also been correlatively transformed and changed from those of economic greed, territorialism, violence, aggression, and war, to that of global, economic, mutual, equatable sharing, acceptance, in fellowship, and interdependent; equality, freedom and peace.

Then, God's Kingdom would truly have been established here on earth in its full beauty, glory, love, heavenly bliss, and peace! And our daily prayers to God for his/her kingdom to be established on earth and his/her will to be done on earth as in heaven will have been fully answered and fulfilled in reward to our prayers, faith, hopes and concrete efforts.

The Socialization and Humanization
of the Young

Human beings are more than just complex thinking biological organisms or creatures. Human beings are not
only born but also made. Human beings are constituted
by both their own biological heritage and equally so by
their social or cultural heritage. And both of these
two heritages are equally required in the making of
authentic human beings and the human community.

As such, mere human biological heritage does not
result in a human being, nor does the cultural heritage
by itself result in a human being, unless there is a
person to inherit it. The process by which the young
inherit their respective cultures is known as socialization.

It is also by this same process of human socialization that the new young members of the humankind and
society are humanized and "tamed" into civilized, informed, technical, authentic, moral, responsible, humane, intelligent, and linguistic beings or people. In
this respect, the socialization process of the young is
like the social river or link providing continuity and
link between the past, the present and the future
generations.

This vital human process of socializing and human-
izing the new young members of society and the global
human race takes place primarily in the home in which
the young are born, adopted within the social interactive context of the family, the community, and the
larger society.

In other words, whereas biologically the individual
inherits directly from the parents the accumulated
genetic material from past generations; socially, the
individual also inherits culture and civilization from
past generations through the family's and society's
culture and civilization. The individual achieves this
both informally and unconsciouslly, and also formally

through education which is an organized formal method by which the responsible knowlegeable adults transmit culture, values and civilization to the the young in order to socialize and humanize them. Nevertheless, this process is slow, gradual, free, and selective, whereas the biological one is a given, and therefore, swiftly appropriated within a short time following conception or the fertilization of the egg.

However, unlike human biological heritage which is determined and fixed since this heritage consists in a precise genetic programming code whose results and effects can now be scientifically and correctly predicted and analysed in advance, and even radically changed by medical and biogenetic intervention results that are socially, physically or medically undesirable.

However, socialization as humanization is such a gradual and slow social, cultural, and educational process, that whereas it is most important during childhood years when the child acquires basic human values, language, skills, self-identity, and gender roles, this process continues during adolescence and later maturing years.

As a result, in some cases, socialization continues until death, if it is properly understood to include learning new values and information that require social change and adjustment in one's ways of life and social interactions so as to fit in a new role better or just to live a more adult, mature, social, humane, and satisfying life. Since we say that learning should never end until one's death, similarly, it is also conceivable that as long as this learning process does continue, also after the learner's social behavior, if this leads to more humanization, then it has also led to continuing socialization.

This is more so in our own time when modern, increased, scientific knowledge and new breakthroughs have led to great successions of technological revolutions which have profoundly affected human society with the result of rapid social changes requiring innovations and renovations of job and life skills required

to live in a modern technological society which is
always rapidly changing and rendering the new obsolete
as soon as it is off the manufacturing assembly!

Nonetheless, this rapid change, requiring all human
beings to keep pace with its learning, changing, and
making necessary constant cultural, social, and personal adjustments; to keep up with the pressure and cur-
rents of socio-economic changes. And do so without
being left behind or breaking down under the great
pressures from constant changes and threats of inade-
quacies intrinsic in learning new job skills quickly in
order to retain or protect the job one already has.

In this kind of situation where old experiences are
soon outdated, and as such, worthless, one has to keep
on being socially adjusted throughout life, since old
experiences will be inadequate to prepare the individual for new experiences which require new knowledge,
new skills, and therefore, new experiences and new
social adjustments.

However, this does not mean that we should ignore the
traditional methods of socialization. For it is the
well socialized, fully integrated, and well educated
person that can best and most successfully fit into the
mainstream of modern society with its constantly changing requirements for new information and new skills.

Therefore, the most well educated will also make the
most personal adjustments quickly, efficiently, and
easily. This being the case, the human society, both
local and global, is best served when its members are
well socialized, "tamed," civilized, humanized, highly
motivated, educated, and skilled.

This being the case, then, the human community is
also conversely misserved and harmed by poorly socialized members who happen to be also uneducated, savage,
ignorant, unskilled, poor, unmotivated, lazy, xenophobic, and racist. These individuals also happen to be
criminals since they lack the essential noble values
and virtues to keep them from the life of vice and
crime, such as stealing, burglary, fraud, prostitution,
drugs, rapes, vandalism, child abuse, violence, hate,

blackmail, and murder.

Unfortunately, these poorly socialized individuals grow up to have families of their own and perpetuate the kind of undesirable socialization process which creates evil human beings due to incomplete and poor methods of socialization, or to poor and evil role models inherent in the bad, poor, criminal, and uneducated families.

Since socialization is also a process which primarily occurs within the family context, the family being the microcosm of society and global community; therefore, bad or evil homes and families can only produce bad and evil children since these children get exposed to the daily evils of their own parents, and learning to accept and imitate them both consciously and unconsciously as a moral way of life. Values are also taught and learned in the home, both explicitly by words and implicitly by deeds, whether intended or unintended, public or private. For instance, a family in which parents steal either for survival or fun, children also learn to steal, either by being directly taught or used by their own parents to steal.

This teaching can take many forms, such as being taught how to do it without being caught or by being asked to stand and keep watch while the parents do the actual stealing, being asked to lie, or to conceal or sell stolen goods. In this example it is like Charles Dicken's The Artiful Dodger; he could have been taught how to pickpocket by his own parents instead of a street hardened gang of criminals with their "Mafia Boss" type for their chief, teacher, employer, and guardian. In other words, the behavior of the young is a mirror for adult behavior and the values of the local community.

Psychologists such as Freud, Skinner, Erickson, Piaget, and others have clearly shown us how both family and child rearing practices are so important for the society in terms of what kind of adult human beings these children later become as a result of their family background and socialization methods and processes.

Socialization is in some major sense a form of social and cultural patterning and programming. This being the case, human beings tend to remain faithful to their own cultural heritage and social programming which often determines and governs most, if not all spontaneous human social behavior, gender roles, and relationships to both friends and strangers or foes alike.

Subsequently, human beings who have been conditioned and programmed by their own crooked or evil families to hate and do evil will most likely succeed in doing just that, namely hating and doing evil. Human beings reap what they sow both in their gardens and in their hearts and minds. In the same way one sows rice and reaps rice, and not beans or wheat, similarly, those who sow evil, malice, hatred, and violence will, likewise, reap the same; namely, evil, malice, hatred, and violence. The bonus or interest in this case may come in the form of murder or war.

Is it surprising, then, for us to find in the inner urban communities of the USA a very high rate of poverty, crime, child abuse, divorce, unwedded mothers, teenage pregnancies, school drop-outs, drug problems, prostitution, illiteracy, lack of skills, unemployment, and con artists? These kinds of people have been fenced in and isolated into some subcultures of poorly educated, unskilled, poor, and unemployable masses of dehumanized, directionless, and hopeless men and women with very limited options for self-improvement and employment. Subsequently, because of despair, boredom, and spitefulness, these people have resorted to sex, drugs, and crime for leisure and pleasure.

In some cases, it has been observed that crime was intentionally committed in order to survive or attract public attention to the unattractive plight of poverty, neglect, and public indifference. In this and every other respect, the society will pay a heavy price for allowing some of its members to suffer from such socio-economic evil, discrimination, neglect, and injustice.

Consequently, unless society or the government intervenes to redress and reverse these evil and destructive trends within these poverty and crime-ravaged urban communities, future generations may hold us accountable if the evils and violence from these communities get out of hand and destroy the surrounding middle class neighborhoods and communities in revenge for being neglected and abandoned in their hellish life in the housing projects or ghettos.

Putting more schools in the housing projects is not the answer to the problems raised above because there are enough schools for most students to go in or near the inner city communities. But these problem students do not attend school regularly, do their homework assignments, or obey school rules. And finally, they drop out of the school system altogether and subsequently take to the life of crime on the street in deadly gangs, selling drugs or stealing from the other poor members in the projects.

Pickpocketing, mugging, and robbing armed youth gangs have terrorized many inner city neighborhoods themselves; hence, the inner city communities themselves are reaping what they have sown. They have taught their own young to rape, rob, steal, and defraud, but because the middle class income communities are removed and better protected by vigilant police patrols, the young thugs have, subsequently, turned to robbery, rape, fraud, and stealing from their own neighbors and kindred, from whom they are cannot be kept away.

The current socialization of someone in most of the American inner city community is definitely mostly dehumanizing, and an evil programming process of learning the art of crime in order to survive in an environment heavily steeped in evils, such as poverty, crime, violence, and premature deaths. This may be achieved by telling lies, stealing, learning how to fight, carrying weapons, joining gangs, prostitution, and the like. These may be directly learned from parents, surviving relatives, siblings, or peers.

Tragically, in this kind of community, the young tend to get their role models from imitation, aspiration, and identity from parents, pimps, successful harlots, drug pushers, and gang leaders. This is unfortunately the case, and if the inner city communities have to be changed and morally rehabilitated, the children must be given better successful moral role models, but within reach if they stayed at school long enough.

Unfortunately, drug dealers have little education, yet have much more spending money than the local teacher, policeman, carpenter, and electrician, and therefore, it is very difficult for appropriate, positive role models to be provided in this kind of evil environment until the drug dealers and pimps have been eliminated from public view. For these smooth talking, evil culprits have fewer moral competitors in this respect because of their evil, easy way of life and quick wealth.

In the middle class families, generally, the young tend to get positive socialization and humanization. Rewards for good or approved behavior and punishent for the very undesirable ones tends to be the method followed by many parents in this group. Good language, property rights, communication skills, decency, loyalty, time consciousness, and job skills for success in future employment are emphasized.

Subsequently, these young people get good education and preferred professional or job training. As a result, they also are the ones who get good employment, earn good money, and perpetuate their own middle class values and standards of living. These in turn socialize and marry from their own class and raise their own children in the same middle class and work ethic or values in which they were themselves raised.

The greatest taboo in this middle class community being, "Thou Shall not Steal," whereas in the lower income group in the inner city, it seems to be the silently accepted norm since most of these people seem to engage in it and also to become its deadly victims themselves.

It is also true that on the whole, the middle class families also do a better job of teaching their children religious and moral values. As a result, they also tend to go to church and Sunday school more regularly than the people in the projects whose usual excuse is the lack of transportation though the young tend to be straightforward and say they have no need for going to church.

In addition, it is also the middle class people that give money to support not only the church work, but also the charitable organizions that do work to change or improve the plight of the disadvantaged and the poor in the world, including the local project or inner city food or child care programs and feeding the homeless or the poor people of the Appalachian region.

Therefore, these people, particularly, the members of the upper and middle classes, ought to be both commended and encouraged to be less prejudiced, and therefore, in unconditional love, be able to do more for the poor masses both at home and abroad in the global community. They ought to do this as a divine duty, incumbent upon them as morally responsible, accountable, reliable, intelligent, and faithful stewards of God's creation of which we are the divine, privileged custodians, including natural resources, wealth, the poor, the weak, and the developing peoples of the world.

Subsequently, modern technology is not for giving us power, wealth, and dominion over the poor and the undeveloped nations of the world, but rather technology gives us the means by which we can benevolently and freely develop more wealth cheaply to share both at home and abroad, and to develop the undeveloped nations so that they too come into the international economic fellowship, mutual exchange, trade, interdependence, and ultimately, come into the fullness of a good, safe, and happy life of which we all aspire and pray for.

However, in order to achieve this noble goal, we must socialize; program our citizens in the global unity of humanity and the need for mutual interdependence, fellowship, cooperation, economic exchange, and unconditional aid and develop the undeveloped so as to make them viable friends and allies in search of one common good and one common destiny and fulfillment of each other's natural needs and incompleteness in the spirit of mutual unconditional love, generosity, togetherness, sharing, fellowship, accountability, unity, goodness, virtue, justice, duty, and moral obligation.

This becomes a moral obligation because we are all God's children, moral agents in the world, intelligent, social, and political beings, humane, peace loving, and obedient servants or stewards of God who view each human being as our brother or sister and lovingly seek to be each other's keeper without any conditions attached except the joy of sacrificial giving and service one gets back for reward.

This kind of ethical teaching and globalization of the socio-economic responsibility can easily be incorporated in the education and socialization process of the children born and reared in the middle class because in the developed western societies, the middle class is the largest and the most powerful class. It has great numbers of well educated people in it.

Consequently, it also has a great socio-economic impact on the world because its values tend to be cosmopolitan and global. For instance, most material consumer goods are manufactured to meet the demands and high standards of living of this class. And since the middle class has the money and the socio-economic needs and values of this class, thus shaping the world's economy structure and priorities.

Similarly, this middle class shapes the dominant social and political trends and values of their local communities, nation, and ultimately, the global community itself which is increasingly becoming homogeneous in ideas, lifestyles, and standards of living. The middle class is politically powerful because of the great number, good education, and wealth of this group.

Since members of this class are also, on the whole, very well educated, better informed of global current events, politically and economically dominant, and therefore, powerful both at home and abroad, they can most easily work as not the mere economic masters of the universe, but as its moral conscience, moral creators, shapers, catalyst peacemakers, and advocates of international close cooperation, harmony, peace, and unity.

Consequently, men and women of good will who are also members of the upper or middle class of goodwill are better moral agents for international peace, cooperation, and unity because they also have an international economic interest to protect and be promoted abroad.

For instance, wars in the Middle East, Africa, and Latin America international terrorism effects more middle class average Americans than the American's lower class and the poor masses. This is because the poor have no money invested in stocks on Wall Street to be threatened by international wars and sabotage of economic targets such as crude oil shipliners or oil fields and refineries in the Middle East, whereas the rich middle class Americans may have some kind of stocks and investments in such sensitive petroleum oil markets.

Furthermore, international terrorism affects the middle class far more than the lower class because it is the middle class that has the economic resources and luxury to go on tours abroad just for the mere delight of seeing the regions of the other parts of the world, its people, culture, foods, landscapes, vegetation, and wild life.

However, whereas tourism and leisure is the pleasure of the rich, the poor are homebound, and they are locally and daily terrorized by poverty, crime, and disease, and as such, have no interest in foreign affairs or politics unless these have a direct bearing on their local problems of poverty, crime, injustice, and how to either remove them or survive better.

In fact, the local poor are usually opposed to national programs for foreign aid, mainly because they reason that, that is the money which should have been better used locally, to aid the poor in order to uplift them from the dehumanizing horrors of poverty, rather than being donated and sent abroad.

However, what the poor usually fail to see, is that

there is always enough money and resources available in
the nation, but the nation's priorities are different
and do not usually include them and their betterment or
increased welfare. For instance, the money spent on
just one nuclear carrier and all its military hardware,
accessories, and personnel could help a great number of
poor Americans overcome their dehumanizing poverty and
improve their own plight as human beings.

This is just a simple example of how we have been
conditioned and programmed by prejudiced, bigoted,
ethnocentric, hateful and xenophobic war-mongers to
think and believe that in order to protect ourselves,
we have to build more expensive and more deadly nuclear
weapons and stockpile them at all costs. Unfortunately,
these dangerous nuclear weapons are very often also
built not merely at great costs, but sadly also at the
very expense of the poor citizens who happen to have
nothing to protect except to be protected from us and
our uncaring indifference, insensitivity, unloving and
unforgiving prejudiced attitudes.

For instance, many politians very often view the
local poor people, especially, those in the inner city,
as a nuisance, and as a socio-economic and polical
liability, rather than an asset. This attitude is,
usually, due to the fact that these poor people while
voting, pay no taxes because they have no money or
taxable property, while they look to the government to
provide them with timely welfare monthly payments,
foodstamps, medicaid and other welfare services, such
as free or low income housing.

However, as we have already clearly seen, ignoring
the poor, in order to build nuclear armaments, only
invites socio-economic problems at home, and aggression
abroad. Furthermore, there is an increased temptation
to use these deadly weapons, in order to solve a perceived conflict or threat, which would have been otherwise, a simple problem.

Therefore, and contrary to, the arms invite war and
naive philosophy of arms race and no one is any more
secure because of the deadly nuclear arms that the

mutual antagonistic super powers now possess. On the contrary, we all feel like global hostages of the military nuclear arsenals of the two competing super powers contending for unchallenged global military supremacy.

It is in this unfortunate manner that the two super powers have both become evil international nuclear terrorists, holding as hostage the whole of humanity, creation, and the planet itself, whereas her citizens languish and die neglected in poverty due to malnutrition and preventable disease, which were never prevented nor adequately treated, because they could not afford to pay for it, having no money and no adequate medical insurance coverage due to being both unskilled and unemployed.

Therefore, in order to positively change the community and the world from petty jealousies, prejudice, bigotry, hatred, violence, and war, and transform these into mutual global acceptance, unconditional love, nonviolence, cooperation, harmony, and peace, we must start this positive procedes at the family level. This may be achieved namely by socializing the young, especially those of the middle class to accept these global, socio-economic values as the standard universal norm for all, fully harmonized, civilized, education, humane, considerate, and responsible human beings. Thus seeking to proscribe parochialism, prejudice, ethnocentricism and bigotry, crime, violence, arms, and war-mongering.

It is conceivable that by this approach of rearing and educating the young to accept global values, mutual cooperation, peace, and interdependence, and lasting global unity, harmony and peace may be realized in the world. Global cooperation and peace are important and that without them, this planet and its currently warfaring, divided inhabitants may actually destroy themselves in their mutual hatred, blindness, folly, and misculturation. And only unconditional and universal acceptance and love for the neighbor can avert and prevent this catastrophe and disaster. But since children learn better by listening, seeing, and imitating good examples and playing out their own roles both mentally, playfully, verbally, and later physically, we need to teach them the values of good, harmonious, neighborly, peaceful, social interaction and living by both word and example.

The parents and teachers must reinforce each other's teaching and peaceful living both at home and in the formal school environment. If there is violence and hatred at home or at school, it will negate the verbally or the theoretically learned values of the unconditional acceptance, love, cooperation, and peaceful coexistence.

Nevertheless, all human beings are by nature finite and imperfect; coorelatively, all human institutions, knowledge, education, relations, ethics, and values are also imperfect and will remain as such until the unforeseeable future when human beings will probably become more humane, loving, and less greedy, less selfish, less self-centered, and less imperialistic, therefore, becoming more perfect.

All human institutions and creations bear the stamp of creativity, aesthetics, limitations, sins, and imperfections of their human creators. This is the way it is and has, therefore, to be accepted, as such, because all human creators with God, and responsible for these institutions, since they are the individual's or collective concrete expressions of their, otherwise, an abstract humanity.

Subsequently, we cannot sit and wait until human beings are perfect and morally upright in order to begin a global crusade for international closer cooperation in fields, such as economic development and exchange, education, scientific research, technology, medicine, audiovisual and performing arts, communication, agriculture, trade, tourism, and fights against war, crime, injustice, imperialism, terrorism, deforestation, environmental pollution, poverty, hunger, malnutrition, disease, and premature death.

To this end, there must be a closer knowledge, under-

standing, and acceptance of each other as real people
and nations. And to facilitate this process, there must
be an initial mutual trust and goodwill to enable the
rest to follow. In this initial quest for mutual knowledge and understanding, international studies are abso-
lutely essential.

These international studies should, ideally, include
world history, world cultures, world geography, world
religions, international trade and international organizations (such as United Nations and North Atlantic
Treaty Organization) and their structures, international languages, problems of developing nations, the distribution of natural resources, global population
growth, and other major global and demographic factors
which require global human cooperation and socio-economic planning in order to continue to survive as human
species despite the rapidly increasing populations,
whereas there is a corresponding dwindling of natural
resources and food.

The study of international studies and listening to or
reading current world news, undoubtedly, foster the
needed understanding and feeling of global unity, the
oneness of the human race, the interdependence of nations and the universal common human quest for peace,
longevity, happiness, justice, acceptance, technological knowledge, accountability, sharing, and prosperity.

Therefore, positive international studies will reduce
prejudice, ignorance, bigotry, and indifference and
subsequently pave the way for gradual moral international understanding, dialogue, cooperation, tolerance, peaceful coexistence, and global peace.

The global peace can only come and last when human
beings realize their common humanity and common good
being, constituted by living together in unconditional
acceptance and love of each other as fellow human
beings whose happiness consists in the happiness of all
human beings. And therefore, the ultimate shocking
realization as King warned us that no human being is
free until all human beings are free, and that injus-

tice anywhere was a threat to peace, everywhere, in the world.

This is certainly true in today's world where wars in the Middle East cause global hardship when oil prices go up or when oil is used as a weapon against those who fail to support the Arab cause. And as we have already seen, this is all true of wars and terrorism in oher parts of the world. It is also true that the past World Wars also started as limited local violence and small wars and gradually, escalated into major destructive global wars.

Consequently, injustice and violence are just like tiny flames of fire that set whole buildings ablaze, causing great losses and property destruction. Conversely, teaching the young to be nonviolent, and to love peace and their fellow human beings without conditions, is setting a small fire that will gradually set the world ablaze with the spiritual and intellectual enlightment and realization that violence, aggression, injustice, discrimination, and poverty are wrongs which need to be universally negated. And to be, subsequently, replaced with unity, love, fellowship, justice, sharing, cooperation and both internal or personal, and social or global peace.

Chapter Three

THE PROBLEM OF PREJUDICED HUMAN LANGUAGE

AND THE CONTROVERSY

OF THE INCLUSIVE RELIGIOUS LANGUAGE

The human being can be said to have truly become human and the very unique creature representative of God when he or she spoke, and communicated in a complex spoken language with its essential complex time consciousness as signified by verb tense conjugation. Subsequently, to be God-like, and human being created in God's image means to be linguistic!

However, since the human being is also a "fallen" creature and a sinner, the human being's language is also equally fallen and correlatively sinful in its various expressions, such as sexism, racism, cursing, obscenity and profanity. The human language can only be as good and perfect as the people that create and use it.

Therefore, the problem of theological language is the problem of language in general, and this being the case, then the controversy of the The National Council of Churches of Christ in USA (NCCC) inclusive lectionary, which was first released in October 1983, is therefore, a controversy over the traditional English language, in terms of its structure, vocabulary and general usage.

However, in this chapter I will, primarily, deal with the general function of language. To this end I try to

outline its relationship to culture, cognition, thinking, epistemological process, metaphysics, religion,
and human communications in general. The controversy of
the inclusive lectionary will be dealt within this
wider context, since religion and its language have
their function in this wider societal context, and not
in an isolation or a vacuum!

The Essential Nature
of Language

The great importance of language both verbal and nonverbal, and both written and spoken, can hardly be
overemphasized since it is the main characteristic
which differentiates us from the rest of the animal
kingdom, of which we are the only ones that speak,
write and leave behind a documented record or a carefully formulated and professionally guarded oral record religiously handed down from one generation to
another to inform each new generation of the great
inventions, achievements, special blessings to inherit
and rejoice in, as well as noting past mistakes and
calamities to be avoided.
   This is the way in which history, religion, culture
and civilization have been handed down to us in the
human community. But there is nothing like this going
on in the rest of the animal kingdom, since there is no
evidence to support either any form of higher thinking, speech, language or the accumulation of collective experience in a form of history or civilization.
   However, this is not to deny that animals do, indeed,
learn new things, nevertheless, this is to deny that
animals have a language by which this learned knowledge
can be handed on, down to the next generation, apart
from habit or conditioning. In other words, this line
of reasoning has been adopted in order to define the
human being as a linguistic creature. Therefore, for
the purpose of this chapter, language will not be

viewed just simply as the tool of human communication, but as the very instrumentality or vehicle of humanization itself for these thinking creatures, usually referred to in some scholarly anthropological literature as the "homo sapiens."

Subsequently, any creature which speaks or utilizes some form of well developed system of communication, will be accorded the status of a human being, and will be treated as a human being regardless of the color and physical looks of the creature, since speech is to be viewed as definitive of what a human being is. This approach deliberately leaves it open for inclusion of some forms of the extra terrestrial beings, such as "E.T." in the category of human beings!

The Divine Nature
of Language

We are not very sure when and how language came into being, but we can speculate that it is as old as the human race itself. Indeed, some primitive societies associate language with the very divine origin of humanity itself. For instance, the ancient Hebrews understood their God, "Yahweh" to be a God whose essence was to speak. For instance, in the book of Genesis we are told that God created the cosmos by his own words! So we read in Genesis chapter one, "And God said, 'let there be light'; and there was light.... 'Let the earth bring forth living creatures.... Let us make human beings in our image, after our likeness.... male and female he created them, in his own image." (Translation is my own.)

According to the Bible, God is the primordial or quintessential linguistic Being. God just speaks, and things happen! It is in this sense that the Prophets spoke of God's word being a very potent power which accomplishes all that it has been addressed to by God, thus never ever failing in its mission so as to return empty:

so shall my word be that goes forth from my mouth;
it shall not return to me empty,
but it shall accomplish that which I purpose,
and prosper in the thing for which I sent it.
(Isa. 55:11)

We are also familiar with the warning messages of the
angels and the Prophets with their claim to authority
in the well known formula: "Thus says, the Lord." This
prophetic cry of "Hear you people .... for thus says
the Lord," carries the implicit meaning that God is the
quintessential Speaker of the Word/Message and subsequently, the human being is the essential Hearer of
this divine Word/Message.

This is probably the main explanation underlying the
fact that all human beings have a religious inclination
and need, for it is in religious worship that most
ordinary human beings Hear God speaking to them, more
directly, whereas some few lucky ones tend to hear God
speaking in all situations, and indeed, in all places,
including earthly historical events, people, and ordinary cosmic processes. For these kind of people the
silent Word/Message of God can be found imprinted on
everything in the created universe, for everything
bears the divine seal of God as its creator, and therefore, in one way or another bearing and telling the
divine story of the creative cosmic Mystery and wonder
which we usually associate with God as the Creator.

Furthermore, we read in the prologue of the Gospel
According to Saint John: " In the beginning was the
Word, and the Word was with God, and the Word was God."
The Greek word here translated as "the Word," is the
"Logos" which is a philosophical term with a very
complex metaphysical explanation and complicated theo-
logical implicit doctrine.

For instance, the term "Logos" used in the Gospel has
the implications for God being not just linguistic, but
also rational, creative and male! As you can probably
see already, language is not neutral in terms of content, metaphysics and therefore, meaning. As we shall

see in more detail later, very often language has meaning, metaphysics and the local world-view already built into it either implicitly or explicitly.

In the final analysis, what is being said here is that God is the quintessential linguist, and indeed multi-linguist since he/she has to know and speak all the human languages for they all belong to the people whom he/she has created in his/her own image which we have already seen to be constitutive of both masculine and feminine characteristics as evidenced by the creation of both male and female human beings in God's image, and likeness. It would therefore, seem logical to assert that in this respect, language is both human and divine. It is a divine gift from God, like the very intellect and thought or cognitive processes themselves.

Subsequently, it would also follow, that to participate in either a linguistic or thinking process is to participate not only in a natural human activity, but also to participate in a divine or supernatural act in that language and mind or intellect are more than just natural, since they are divine qualities, and ultimately, flow to us from God as unmerited gifts to us, as his/her special creatures in the world, charged with the resposibility of being the created custodians or stewards of this created universe.

As a result, we can always, measure, judge, classify, identify, accept or reject people on the basis of their own language, for apart from human deeds, there is no good way to judge a person, except by their own words or language.

Therefore, bad language is supposed to express evil nature, and good language, to express noble intentions, and good nature. In other words, a person is his/her language! That is one of the reasons why most of our professional education is oriented to the manufucturing, and acquisition of prestigious professional language/jargon of highly specialized vocabulary.

However, my saying that language is a divine gift to humanity does not mean that human languge as it is now, or was in the past was ever created by God in terms of vocabulary, grammar, structure or intonation.

Therefore, what is given to us by God is the capacity for language, in the same way God has given us the capacity for thought in terms of the intellect and intuition, all made possible by the superior brain capacity of which we have been freely endowed by the humble divine creative activities operative in cosmic history, quietly and usually in very non-glamorous incognito manner.

The Imperfection of
Human Language

Since the actual human language is not a direct creation of God, but rather a direct creation of the human being who is imperfect, then we should also expect to find the human language itself imperfect, and ever undergoing review, modification in its evolution and slow change just like the human being its creative spirit.

Furthermore, since language is of a human creation, it can be affirmed that no human language is ever good enough to be called, divine, and that any human language is subsequently, a fit vehicle for divine revelation, holy scripture, liturgy and religious worship!

This statement is also by nature a denial and a refutation of some old-fashioned, religious fundamentalist views found in Islam and among some poorly educated Christians that claim that God speaks only either in Arabic or in King James Bible version of English! But as most of us know, God does not have a special language to communicate with us in, nor does he/she have any preference for Latin or English when it comes to liturgical worship.

Therefore, each human language is a fitting language for the worship of God, and no language has the advantage over any other when it comes to God, for God loves his/her people unconditionally, as they are, for all of

them are collectively his/her own beloved children even
when they are all sinful, and imperfect along with
their languages which they have created in their own
sinful and imperfect reflection or image. It would have
been very strange indeed, had the imperfect human
being, with his/her limited intellect, succeeded in
creating a perfect language, for it is impossible for
an imperfect creator to create something more perfect
than himself/herself.

The analytical philosophers of language such as Benjamin Lee Whorf, C.G.E. Moore, Betrand Russell and
Ludwig Wittgenstein have very clearly pointed out in
their scholarly, but controversial works how this imperfection of the human language has been responsible
for the major problems in metaphysics, epistemological
or cognitive process, and the inadequacy of theological
language, and the erroneous philosophical and theological constructs or doctrines this gives false basis to.

THE FUNCTION OF THE HUMAN LANGUAGE

Language performs several essential human functions and tasks which are necessary and vital to human life and the nature, and quality of human existence as we know it today. Some of these functions and tasks performed by language are directly related to the subject under discussion, and therefore, will be briefly discussed within this context.

Language as a Medium of Humanization and Socialization

Language is a very necessary tool for human beings in their incessant quest for a better form of existence in which leisure, pleasure and happiness are maximized. This is one of the reasons why there is no human society that has ever been found lacking in this most essential human tool, which is in itself an abstract essential constitutive element of the human being. This is another way to say what has been said before that the nature of the human being is essentially linguistic.

However, language being human and also being a tool for the humanization of the new born, it has to keep up with the societal changes in which the new born are socialized into civilized members of the society. If language fails to do what society wants to do, then it is either discarded gradually in favour of a new one or it is modified with the addition of new words, professional vocabulary/jargon, slang and new idioms. Examples of discarded antiquated languages include Koine Greek, Latin, and King James English!

Languages are not static because they are as alive as the people who use them. But if for one reason or another, any given language should become static, then that language will die and be replaced by a more dynamic one.

Subsequently, we see new vocabulary, and new language usage come about as a result of the felt need to think better, and communicate better. For example, we have new "high-tech" words such as "modem," "bug and debug," and "logon," which have been invented to describe interaction, problems, and software for computer communications hardware or gadget.

This is an example of how professional language has become so specialized so that different branches of knowledge can hardly be utilized by others just because of too much formidable technical jargon employed in that particular discipline by some misguided experts who seem to think that the more professional vocabulary is employed in ones speech or written work, the more scholarly and prestigious it will come across!

However, what is often forgotten in this situation, is that language is basically a medium for communication, and that good communication takes place when the language, symbols, signs, gestures, sounds or codes used are familiar and known by both the originator of the message, such as the speaker, sender, writer, preacher, communicator and his/her intended recipients or the audience.

In short, communication only takes place if the communicator and the audience speak the same language, irrespective of whether this language is verbal or nonverbal. This includes the Indian smoke signals, the Chinese picture language, modern sign language, computer language, mathematics as well as the African "talking drums."

Language as the Chief Medium
for Human Communication

Since the human being is by nature a social being, therefore, the major function of language is essentially that of communication and socialization. Both of these functions are aimed at the creation of good interpersonal networks of social relationships.

It is in this manner that language truly becomes a medium of humanization, since our own humanity, identity and selfworth are gained from our society, and from our social networks of relationships. We see ourselves through the linguistic mirror of our society. We see ourselves as wise, kind, beautiful, great or vice versa, if we have been constantly told by those around us that we are that! Similarly, we too, often see other people in the familiar linguistic mental images of "good" or "bad."

Unfortunately, these linguistic terms are so relative and fluid that we rarely agree on what they mean! This is one of the great problems of language, since words derive their specific meaning from the particular context in which they have been used. Subsequently, words alone are in themselves less meaningful and even completely meaningless, if they are without the original context in which they were used.

For instance, the word "space" will mean one thing to a house-wife in a small kitchen, and mean another thing to a psychologist, and yet mean another thing to a physicist or a philosopher! This is what was probably meant when Mcluhan the great communications' expert made the famous statement that "the medium is the message."

This also means that not only are the words very important and meaningful, but even more so is the very structure of the sentence, and ultimately, the structure of language itself which is itself a reflection of the mind, culture, philosophy, religion and technology of those people who created the language and those who

continue to use it to express themselves, to themselves
in thought, to express themselves to God in prayer and
liturgical worship; and probably, most importantly for
most people, to express ourselves to our fellow human
beings in interpersonal relationships, such as in
speech, love songs, poetry, proverbs and writing.

Language as a Lethal Weapon

Whereas language is what makes us all human and therefore, inherently good in itself, it has also the con-
verse inherent power to exclude, isolate, insult and
dehumanize when it is used by morally depraved or
malicious evil people with the intention of inflicting
social or psychological harm on other people. Name
calling, mud slinging, slander, malicious misquotation,
insults, character assassination, profanity, dirty
jokes, evil gossip, cursing, telling lies and falsehood
belong to this category.

However, in these and other human problems, our counter weapon is the teaching of good language to the
young so that they grow up with respect for language,
and other people with whom they come in linguistic
contact.

Since in the Church, it has been the usage of exclusive male dominated language in terms of nouns and
pronouns, for both God and humanity, some sensitive
female Church members have felt personally excluded,
from the Church, its Scriptures, and its liturgical
worship whose language is heavily influenced by this
male dominated, patriarchical language. This is the
language that refers to God as "Father," "Lord," "His,"
"King," "God's Kingdom," and refers to Jesus as "Son of
God," "Son of Man," "a man," "Prince of peace and Lord
of Lords," "Lord," "Master," and "His Kingdom."

These are some of the theological words and the
theological thinking underlying them that feminist
theologians seek to exorcise from the Bible, liturgical
books, such as prayer books and hymnals, as well as

from all forms of public religious discourse in the form of sermons, lectures and Sunday School instruction both for the young and the adults. This is the main spirit and great motivation behind the positive venture of the highly controversial NCCC Inclusive Lectionary.

This venture presupposes the vital importance of language in not only creating human beings in the process of humanization of the young ones into the various linguistic communities into which they are born and eventually initiated into full membership as they become fully socialized and accepted adults, but also as thinking members of the community who will use language for the purpose of cognition, and thought.

This being the presupposition, then, language becomes the perceived weapon with which the linguistically excluded, oppressed and dehumanized members of the human female gender defend themselves from such abuses, and correct the sexist situation which has given rise to this offense.

Again, the underlying assumption is that linguistic semantics do affect human thinking, philosophy, world-view, religion, and ultimately, human existence in general. Subsequently, it follows that the NCCC's attempt to change religious language, is also an attempt to change not just language, but also to change humanity itself in the above respects which are themselves influenced and shaped by language.

Therefore, language is a double edged sword which can be used as both a weapon for self-defence, as well as a lethal offensive weapon with which one can silence opponents or dissect them and their valuable work into worthless junk to be thrown away on to the trash dump of history!

Furthermore, since our society tends to identify us, judge and evaluate us by our language, then our language is more than a tool or handy weapon. Our language is us in self-abstraction, and self-expression or self-communication to other "selves," to God, and to the world around us.

In short, we are our own language. This is necessarily the case since it the greatest medium for self-expression and self-communication to others.

It is not surprising, therefore, that the ancient people identified and named tribes, and races by their spoken language! For instance, you were French if you spoke French, and you were English if you spoke English! But this categorization does not apply today because we have to speak other languages other than those of our own parents.

Therefore, some of us can speak both French and English whereas we are neither French nor English! This phenomenon of language and identity is probably more pronounced in Africa where there are well over 1,000 distinct languages, and corresponding ethnic societies derogatorily referred to by imperialists and colonialists as "tribes."

THE PROBLEM OF THEOLOGICAL LANGUAGE

Whereas language is most often imperfect, vague and equivocal, and inadequate for some specialized disciplines of study, theological language presents us with the best example of such a problematic phenomenon. The main problem facing religion and philosophy is that of limitation of the human language due to its imperfection, semantics and inadequacy.

Human language is finite, yet its object, content and subject claim to be divine, and as such, infinite in nature. It is therefore, a great problem for the finite ever to have a full grasp of the infinite, and fully express it without distortion.

It is, indeed, a contradiction for us to claim that God is an infinite Mystery, and yet insist that we can have the right theological understanding of such a cosmic Mystery, and to insist that we can be sure of our doctrinal formulation about this incomprehensible Creative Mystery, we call God. Yet, most Churches claim absolute doctrinal truth, and subsequentlty, any questioning of their theological language, and doctrinal formulations is viewed grimly as a question of unbelief, ecclesial insubordination and rebellion.

This being the case, in most religious establishments, theology, religious language and the liturgy have not been given the creative expression they need. Consequently, religious dogma and creedal statements of faith have come to dominate our religious lives, and those who do not comply are either censured or they just leave the religious establishments alone to live either in quiet indifference or loud skepticism.

However, a few people have always stayed behind to try and reform the religious language, theology and the liturgy, from within. The translation of the scriptures, the Protestant Reformation, the Evangelical Revivals, and now the NCCC Inclusive Lectionary are just a few examples of this courageous group.

The Nature of Religious Language

Since the object and content of religious or theological language is abstract, infinite and incomprehensible, human finite language is inadequate and unable to embody and express this divine cosmic creative Mystery.

Nevetherless, we will disagree with Wittgenstein who suggested that Language mirrors reality, and that what cannot be grasped, and expressed in language should be consigned to silence and the realm of non-existence, for this is to confuse languistics with metaphysics, to confuse logical coherence with empirical reality, and ultimately, to confuse language with ontological reality.

Language does not necessarily mirror reality, it just mirrors our mind, culture, philosophy and technology. Language is nothing more than a conventional system of codes and symbols of any given group, culture, society, discipline, school, profession and the like.

Consequently, language is simply a conventional meaningful system of symbols, codes, names and tenses for the sole purpose of naming objects, communicating, storing and retrieving information for either processing or transfering from one person to another or from one computer terminal to another.

However, language in itself, has to do with positive or empirical truth and the correctness of the information itself of which it is the medium and means of codification and decoding. Therefore, language in itself is simply a means of thinking and data gathering, processing, storage, retrieval and transfer, in as much as it is the primary and essential medium of encoding and decoding of any messages, regardless of whether these messages are verbal, electronic, written, physical, pictorial, visual or symbolic.

In this respect, religious language is, therefore, no exception. Religious language does not in any way contain the reality it describes or claims to stand for.

In order for us to speak humanly, yet meaningfuly about the supernatural God who is the main object of religion, worship and theology, we have to realize that human language is finite and relative, and as such, we should remain open to the question of relativity in our own religious beliefs, liturgical language, scriptural translations, theological knowledge, and doctrinal formulations including our creeds and dogma.

Unfortunately, this has not always been the case, and as a result, most people have come to equate theological language with the Absolute Truth! This serious error of confusing language with reality, has led religion to serious doctrinal errors, anthropormophism, and idolatry! For instance, many people have failed to appreciate the nature of mythlogical, parabolic, symbolic, poetic, figurative and metaphorical religious language found in the Bible, and have interpreted it literally and historically, and therefore, falling into this deadly trap of confusing language with ontological reality.

For example, some people believe that God is a supernatural Great Man. Some more naive ones, even think of God to be some kind of superman or Cosmic King, mainly because the scriptures refer to God in male terms, such as "our Father who art in heaven," "King, and Lord," "the Father of our Lord Jesus Christ." But all these are simply human metaphors, analogies, figures, imageries for the infinitely transcendent, abstract and incomprehensible, Creative, cosmic, holy Mystery we call God.

Therefore, if we take literally these human metaphors, analogies and figures, or treat them as sacred symbols, we will be guilty of idolatry, for we have been forbidden to make images and any other representations of God! Subsequently, maleness does not represent God any more than "femaleness!" In any case God did create both male and female in his/her own image, so no single gender could be adequate to represent God, even if this representation was acceptable.

However, we should never give in to the suggestion of

great theologians like Rudolf Bultmann, that since the religious and theological language has become more of a hindrance than an aid in the understanding of the faith, it should, therefore, be demythologized, in order to make the hidden religious meanings become plain and clear to all.

The problem here is that myth itself is religious content since it has religious meaning which cannot exist apart from the myth itself in which it is enshrouded and embodied. In other words, religious myth is itself the medium and the very message itself. Here, a good analogy is, probably, that of the relationship between the human body and the mind. In this respect, demythologization would be like killing a person in order to analyze his/her mind! Myth, parable, symbolism and mystery constitute the heart of religion and subsequently, its language, beliefs, scriptures, and liturgy.

For instance, can you visualize a Church devoid of its symbolism of the cross, water, bread, wine, light, colors, vestments, music or the Bible? Are sacraments themselves not ecclesial symbols pointing to the sacred which they embody in a religiously meaningful manner? Are they not part of the Christian central myth and mystery which cannot be demythologized without destroying the Christian message itself whose center is Mystery, and whose human linguistic religious embodiment is myth itself?

The fact that every human race has its myths about the ultimate origins, meaning and destiny or creation, particularly that of human beings themselves is a case in point. In this respect, Christianity is not unique, and its language is not unique either, although Christianiy tends to be more exclusive than the other universal religions.

In addition, Christianity like Judaism and Islam were all three born in the same region, around Palestine and the surrounding Arabian desert. This region did not only give birth to these religions, but it also gave rise to all the major canonical religious books or the scriptures of these religions.

Since the people of this region were patriarchal, their understanding of God, and the scpritures they wrote down were subsequently influenced, and expressed in their own languages which were male-dominated in its gender nouns, pronouns, metaphors, and imagery. This was of course acceptable to these patriarchal cultures in which women were generally supposed to be of inferior gender, and therefore, to be subordinated to men who were considered to be of a higher and better gender.

However, in our society, today, the sexes claim equality before God, the law, employment, and also before the Church. Therefore, women and racial minorities now demand change in Church official language so as to be equally included in Scripture readings, hymns and the liturgy as God's people equally chosen, and redeemed, just like their White male counterparts. After all, it is mostly the women who come to Church in large numbers.

Therefore, when women come to worship, they should not to be insulted by male-chauvinist Ministers or by being referred to in male terms, such as "men" or the generic "man," and the male pronouns, "he" and "his" which go with male-dominated religious language both in sermons and liturgical worship.

It is this evil and religious linguistic abuse and exclusion of women from the scriptural readings and the liturgy that the NCCC Inclusive Language Lectionary was meant to redress. However, it is expected that some people both men and women will oppose the proposed inclusive language, for it poses a great challenge and threat to the security of the old religious language they knew so well, and probably, had to identify with God, and ontological reality.

Therefore, for these kinds of people, changing the familiar religious languange for either the Scripture or the liturgy, is tantamount to the destruction of their religion, God, and religious security which had been built on these idols!

These people lack the necessary faith to believe in

the reliability, salvific power of the Incomprehensible God of mystery, who has chosen to reveal himself/herself in the human imperfection, and the cosmic historical process by the virtue of the Incarnation. In this respect, the fear of change is faithlessness in God's ordained cosmic evolutionary creative activity, which is ever actively engaged in renewing creation, as new things are created, including the human language itself.

Commendation for the NCCC Lectionary's Inclusive Language

Since human language itself is a creation of evolving and changing human beings, it cannot be perfect enough to become divine, immutable or static since the human being, along with the rest of God's creation, is still undergoing this evolutionary process, change and transformation.

Therefore, all the human institutions must keep undergoing a corresponding change, at the same pace with the human being's change, if these institutions are to remain essential, meaningful, and helpful to the versatile human being in his/her endless search for knowledge, meaning, fulfillment and happiness.

Consequently, therefore, if any of the human institutions resists change, and remains behind in development, it will subsequently, get discarded as a meaningless historical relic to be thrown away on the trash heap of fossilized history. Religions, philosophies, theologies and languages are no exception to this principle.

Therefore, any genuine religious attempts at self-examination, self-reformation, and redirection in faith, prayer, study and guidance of God's redemptive Spirit of Truth, revelation, creativity, and divine renewal, should be encouraged by all those who love God, and whose faith in God is strong and mature enough to believe that our Creator God is still creating new things today, and that this Redemptive Creator God, is also the God of Change, residing right at the heart of turbulence so as to call creative order right in the midst of chaos. Our God is the God of Babel as well the God of Pentecost!

In the new redemptive, and unitive spirit of Pentecost, let us therefore, welcome the efforts of those trying to make sure that God's holy Word will be heard in their own language! This is the message of the divine Incarnation, it is the meaning of Pentecost, and it is also the meaning and motivation of all scriptural translations, including the new NCCC Inclusive Language Lectionary.

The lectionary is not perfect in its translation, and new references, and metaphors for God, but it represents a noble venture of making the Christian faith relevant, and meaningful to female members of the Church, who constitute the bulk of our Church membership. This lectionary translation, is therefore, a very timely prophetic, religious and social venture in faith, and witness to the continued presence of the Holy Spirit Jesus promised to guide the Church into further truths.

Therefore, the main issue before us now and in the time ahead, is whether we will hear this divine truth, and obey or kill God's prophets, just like God's rebellious people have often done in the past! Jesus and his redemptive Gospel truth are only ever true and relevant in every era and culture, only if they are expressed and heard in the contemporary language and culture of the people of that society and that era.

Our society and era is that of social equality and nuclear space age. Subsequently, we need new contemporary social, philosophical, scientific, and theological language and metaphor, in order to be able to communicate more meaningfully the eternal timeless truths to the people of our era. To this end, King James Bible religious language, Patristic theological formulations, the language of the Nicene and the Apostles creeds are worthless and meaningless blind guides!

Therefore, we must keep up the search for new and better social, racial, philosophical, scientific and religious language expressions, metaphor, imagery, analogies and theological formulations. However, as the Methodist Hymnal Revision Committee has clearly demonstrated, this important religious, human finite venture, has to be undertaken in both humility and prayer for God's guidance, but also with the clear understanding that not all the people, will be either satisfied or pleased, with new inclusive theological language and metaphors or analogies for the invisible and infinite, mysterious God.

FOR FURTHER READING ON THIS SUBJECT:
A SELECTED REFERENCE

Black, Max. Language and Philosophy: Studies in Method. New York: Cornell University Press, 1949.

Gross, Barry R. Analytic Philosophy: An Historical Introduction. New York: Pegasus, 1970.

Hoijer, Harry, ed. Language and Culture. Chicago: The University of Chicago Press, 1955.

McFague, Sallie. Speaking in Parables: A Study in Metaphor and Theology. Philadelphia: Fortress Press, 1975.

The NCCC Inclusive Lectionary, Years: A, B & C.

Whorf, Benjamin Lee. Language, Thought and Reality. Cambridge: MIT Press, 1966.

Chapter Four

THE AMBASSADORS

OF GOD

Since all human beings have been made in the image of
God, then all human beings are also charged by God with
the divine mission of becoming his/her true representatives and ambassadors in creation, the world, and the
whole cosmos, both known and still yet to be discovered.

This divine mission, charge, and calling of human
beings to become God's ambassadors of messages of unconditional love, acceptance, forgiveness, cooperation,
sharing, and peace in the world is for everyone. This
divine message and charge is for every man, woman, and
child, regardless of any conditions, such as gender,
color, race, creed, nationality, education, historical
background, socio-economic class or status, level of
technological development, age, or era.

All Human Beings Created and Called
to Become God's
Ambassadors in the World

This universal, divine calling to human beings to serve
as his or her ambassadors of love and peace in the
world is a reality in every place and in every generation, for it is an eternal and universal divine free
calling, that is ever eternally extended, to every

human being, everywhere.

This is necessarily the case because being God's concrete representative in creation is the quintessence of what it means to be an authentic human being in the world created "in the image of God." Consequently, to be like God or to be created in the image of God is not only to be linguistic, intelligent, creative, and moral beings and creatures in the world, but it also means to be holy, loving, caring, and peace-loving, just like God the heavenly Father and Mother.

The divine charge to the human being to become the concrete, divine ambassador, master, and the divine steward in creation is tied in with creation. As a result, in the book of Genesis we read the following:

> Then God said, "And now we will make human beings; they will be like us and resemble us. They will have power over the fish, the birds, and all the animals, domestic and wild, large and small." So God created human beings, making them to be like himself. He created them male and female, and blessed them, and said, "Have many children, so that your descendants will live over the earth and bring it under their control. I am putting you in charge...." (Gen. I:26-28)

According to this passage, the human being resembles God not by accident, but by divine will and act in creation. The human being's special divine privilege is having a divine nature together with an earthly concrete "animal" body so that the human being can become the unique being endowed with both natural and supernatural qualities; both divine and animal in nature, both spiritual and material physical qualities; both humane and beastly; both holy and sinful; both mortal and immortal; both heavenly and earthly; and both loving and hateful.

The dual nature of the human being has torn him/her in both good and evil, and both God and devil. But it was originally given to the human being by God so that he/she could truly become the effective divine instrumentality or ambassador of God in the world, being able to represent the abstract God to the world in more concrete terms, such as intelligence, creativity, organization, construction, repair, reproduction, intervention, and control.

This is what the book of Genesis means when it says that God put the human beings in charge and control of creation. This is also implied in Genesis, chapter two, when we are told that God put Adam in the garden and asked him to cultivate it and take care of it.

It is important that we note that the charge given to the human beings by God was that of representing him or her, taking tender and loving care of creation as a divine steward, whereas conversely representing creation to God as its capable, intelligent, linguistic, mobile, creative, and moral representation in both prayer and thanksgiving. Here, the emphasis is correctly placed on taking care of creation as being God's faithful ambassador and steward in creation and the world.

Unfortunately, the human being has egocentrically placed more emphasis on dominion and mastery control, instead of stewardship. As expected, results have been the godless human usurpation of God's power and control in the world. The consequences for this sin have included thoughtless suicidal deforestation and the misuse of the environment, mishandled industrial and nuclear waste pollution, and increasing destruction.

This is the tragic story of the environment based on previous Judeo-Christian teachings which demythologized and secularized the universe and its fragile, ecological balance system which had been previously carefully protected and guarded by religious myths and taboos which Christianity thoughtlessly and carelessly condemned as mere evil, pagan superstition. Subsequently, now we have to pay the costly price for this sin in terms of soil erosion, desertification droughts, hunger, starvation, death, pollution, disease, death and environmental destruction.

Consequently, global human interdependence, cooperation, and peace cannot itself come or last long unless
the current critical problems of ecology and the environment are immediately addressed and current destructive trends slowed down and/or negated. For human
beings themselves, whether at war or at peace, cannot
continue to exist unless there is a healthy environment
to make their existence possible and to continue to
support them.

Subsequently, the global peace which is greatly
sought after cannot just be merely, peace between human
beings, nation and nations, and the secular and the
sacred; and not just the mere absence of hostility,
strife, conflict, aggression, violence, and war, but
should also include peace, love, and harmony with the
rest of nature or creation as God's vineyard and flower
garden of which we are the faithful chosen stewards and
custodians.

Indeed, just as Adam is symbolically created and
placed in the garden or world by God with the specific
charge and command to cultivate and take good care of
it, so are we today. For each person is that Adam in
himself or herself since this primordial divine charge
and purpose for humanity has not been changed.

Consequently, the plight and destiny of the human
being is also bound up with God's creation. It was
because of this mutual unity and interdependence that
Genesis records the disobedience and sin of Adam and
Eve, his wife, as having affected the rest of God's
physical creation by causing enemity between human
beings and creation such as snakes and the subsequent
growth of thorns and thistles.

In addition, we are also told that because of human
sins, God destroyed not only human beings in punishment, but the whole of creation with the exception of
what was saved and preserved by God in Noah's redemptive Ark of physical survival and divine supernatural salvation.

In this religious parabolic story of Noah, we see
most clearly what it means to be a faithful ambassador

of God in this sinful world. The parable or story makes
it quite clear that whereas the people and the world
were engulfed in the pleasures of sin and apparent
total rebellion against God's moral law and commandments, Noah remained faithful to God, despite the temptations of evil and sin that completely surrounded him.
And as a result of Noah's faithfulness to God and
subsequent righteousness, God was able to punish the
wickedness of human sin, yet saving a remnant to re-
plenish the earth.

In addition, some prophets like Isaiah, also foretold
of the future definitive act of God's salvation and
restoration of the earth through the coming of the
Messiah. This future restored new era would constitute
a new divine creation in which there was perfect eternal peace between human beings, nations and creation.
This ultimate eschatological divine restoration of
creation to its essential perfection was pictured and
described in grandiose imageries and metaphors, such
as, God's Kingdom, heaven, paradise, unconditional love
for the neighbor, healing, wholeness, peace, justice,
joy, plentifulness, and the restoration of deserts with
rivers of pure water, whereas lions and calves eat
grass together in peaceful coexistence on the river
banks.

The Prophets of God

Although all human beings are essentially created by
God to become his/her ambassadors in the world, because
of human sin and rebellion against God, God has subsequently, from time to time, chose, equipped, and sent
some special messengers or ambassadors in the world in
the form of prophets, teachers, saints, leaders, re-
deemers, reformers, healers, peace-makers, writers,
preachers, and ministers.

These special divine ambassadors have been sent by
God in each generation to a particular group of people
in a particular place, and their mission and message

from God have always been specific and designed for that particular group of people in order to be communicated most effectively, contextually, relevantly and meaningfully.

To this end, this mission has been usually given to the messengers who not only speak the same language as their audience, but also share the same world-view and a common culture in order to ensure maximum and most meaningful communication of the divine message in appropriate, clear inclusive language, metaphors, signs, and symbols.

It is for this reason that God chooses prophets, teachers, priests, kings, queens, and other leaders from the people of the same language, history, culture, and geographical location. This indicates that God does not condone human acts of cultural, political, or socioeconomic imperialism or colonialism which favor the subjugation and domination of one group by another, on the basis of superior technology, economy, race or military might.

The prophets of Israel are some of the good examples for our discussion here. However, this does not constitute a denial that God did not choose viable prophets elsewhere outside Israel, such as Gautama Siddhartha in India who founded Buddhism, Prophet Muhammad in Saudi Arabia, the founder of Islam, and hundreds of prophets in pre-colonial Africa of whom little has been written down, but whose message still lives on today in the form of African Traditional Religion and religious "cults."

To deny that God had not universally spoken his/her redemptive Word through his/her chosen prophets would be also to deny God's universal work of creativity, sustenance, renewal and redemption or restoration which is clearly wrong, ethnocentric, bigoted, malevolent and evil. This is necessarily the case since this would constitute a sinful attempt to limit God's universal grace and activity by our own selfishness and sin; namely, that in our own bigotry and sadism, we want others to perish unless they are just like us, sharing

153

our common racial and cultural heritage or being in
agreement with us religiously.

This is more so within the fundamentalist Judeo-
Christian and Islamic traditions. For instance, fundamentalist Jews excluded Gentiles from God's supernatural salvation whereas fundamentalist Christians
excluded all non-Christians from the divine salvation,
including both the Jews and the Muslims.

Whereas this is the case with these major world
religions, other religions like Hinduism, Buddhism, and
the African Traditional Religion have tended to be more
flexible and inclusive to the extent that most of them
teach that all true religions are given to their followers by the same One Creator and redemptive God, and
that they all lead their true followers back to the
same and one cosmic God, regardless of what the local
name and attributes might be.

However, Christianity generally rejects this teaching
and sends its missionaries to convert all non-Christians because it is firmly believed by many Christians
that only the baptized and the obedient or the "born
again" people that confess Christ both in word and deed
are the ones to be saved by God.

This Christian position is a mere shift from the old
Jewish teaching which claimed that God's salvation was
only available within the Mosaic Covenant community
alone to the unloving Christian dogma that salvation is
only available within the Jesus Covenant community or
the explicit, social, historical, and concrete Church
alone. In the Mosaic Covenant, circumcision was the
male initiation rite of entry, whereas in the Jesus
Covenant or the Church, baptism is the required initiation entry rite.

In each of these cases, a special divine ambassador
or messenger is supposed to be difinitive in regards to
God's message and representation to the respective
community, era, and group of people. For instance,
Moses was given the Commandments and the charge to
forge the redeemed people of Israel from bondage and
slavery in Egypt into a new theocratic nation, whereas

Jesus as the Christ of God was given the charge to redeem and restore all humankind from the bondage of sin and forge all nations into a new global kingdom of God in the fellowship or mutual unconditional love and forgiveness.

Consequently, if Moses is appropriately designated as a great prophet, Jesus is still a greater prophet. And indeed, as the Christ of God, God himself came down on earth to become permanently one with his people in the Incarnation, and never to be separated from them again.

However, there are other prophets who came before and after the coming of Jesus Christ. Within the Judeo-Christian context, the greatest of these prophets as we have already seen is Moses. But this does not necessarily mean that Moses is greater than other great prophets outside the Bible, such as Buddha or Muhammed.

Nevertheless, in this book we are primarily concerned with the Judeo-Christian prophets, and as such, this is the context in which Moses, Jesus, and the other major prophets of justice and peace, such as King, will be discussed. This is not necessarily to accept the Old Testament, biblical, Jewish, naive, exclusive claim: "Of all the nations on earth, you are [Israel] the only one that I [God] have known and cared for." (Amos 3:12)

Moses as the Greatest Prophet

As a prophet, Moses is one of the most outstanding prophets in the whole world and for all time. Moses was by biological heritage a descendant of Hebrew slaves held in bondage in the Ancient African great kindgdom of Egypt along the fertile Nile River banks and the surrounding desert.

Culturally and religiously, Moses was one of the most well educated and privileged African priest-princes, having been adopted by the Pharaoh's daughter, and subsequently, reared in the African royal court as one of the princes and possible heirs to the Egyptian throne as Pharaoh or King. And we also know that he later married a Cushite (Midinianite) or African (Sudanese) and that his own racially sensitive and prejudiced family members, namely, Miriam his sister and Aaron his brother, criticized him for it and sought to overthrow him until God intervened on his behalf and not only reproved them, but also punished Miriam by striking her with the dreaded disease of leprosy, which disfigured and ate at her face until Moses interceded to God for her healing and restoration to wholeness (cf. Numb. 12:1-13).

This story of prejudice, racism, and punishment of leprosy which Miriam suffered at the hands of God has not gone unnoticed by some religious militant advocates for racial socio-economic harmony, integration and peace, because in the catechism written for and used by Marcus Garvey's Universal Negro Improvement Association, we find a full reference to this story. After the story, the catechism then goes on to ask: "What is the cure for color-prejudice and racism in the world today?" And the resounding catechitical answer given for this question consists of one word: "Leprosy."

However, the main importance of Moses' example, is not to challenge and or even invite us to marry the people of different ethnic groups, color and races in the face of strong opposition from our family members

and friends. But it is a good example for us to follow
in order to affirm the fundamental oneness and unity of
the human race, and subsequently, the pragmatic affirmation of the equality of people and the equality of
different ethnic groups, as the constituent members of
the one divine global family.

This is indeed, an important prophetic affirmation,
and practical peace-making strategic mission in our
world today, which is strongly divided, primarily on
the basis of color, race, creed, and nationality.
Nevertheless, the main importance of Moses does not lie
in his racially mixed marriage. Instead, it lies in his
steadfast obedience and faithfulness as God's special
calling as God's ambassador of peace and God's prophet
deliverance in the world, for the people of God suffering harships and oppression.

For instance, even when Moses had committed murder
and fled from Egypt into the Sinai Pennisula for safety
and refuge, he obeyed God and returned to Egypt when
God encountered him on Mount Sinai in the burning bush
and called him to become his instrument of liberation
of the Hebrew slaves who were suffering greatly in
their bondage under a new Egyptian King who was less
humane and considerate for the Hebrews as both a race
of people and as slaves.

When Moses was born, there were such hardships that
he had to be hidden away by his own mother, but since
we are told Aaron his brother survived such hardships
and later aided Moses in his Messianic mission in
Egypt, it can be concluded that the persecution of the
Hebrew slaves in Egypt was just sporadic and not the
official consistent policy of the Egyptian court.

This helps to explain why Moses had a very difficult
time and some Hebrews wanted to return to Egypt rather
than face the hardships of the wilderness under the
leadership of God and Moses towards the fulfillment of
the promises made to Abraham that God would make his
descendants as many as the sand on the shore and would
also give them a land in which they would become a
special nation through whom and by whom God would bless

all the world's people and its nations (cf. Gen. 12:1-3; Numb. 14:1-4).

The prophetic writer of the book of Numbers, like the other Hebrew prophets before and after them, viewed Moses as the most special prophet among all the prophets, and to this end, they report the following divine affirmation of Moses by God as being this most special human representative of God, God's ambassador and prophet to the Hebrew people and the world:

Moses had married a Cushite [Midianite or Sudanese] woman, and Miriam and Aaron criticized him for it. They said, "Has the Lord spoken only through Moses? Hasn't he also spoken through us? The Lord heard what they said. (Moses was a humble man, more humble than anyone else on earth.)

Suddenly, the Lord said to Moses, Aaron, and Miriam, "I want the three of you to come to the tent of my presence." They went, and the Lord came down in a pillar of clouds, stood at the entrance of the tent, and called unto "Aaron, Miriam." The two stepped forward, and the Lord said, "Now hear what I have to say! When there are prophets among you, I reveal myself to them in visions and speak to them in dreams. It is different when I speak to my servant Moses; I have put him in charge of my people in Israel. I speak to him face-to-face, clearly and not in riddles; he has even seen my form. How dare you speak against my servant Moses?" (Numb. 12:1-8)

Therefore, it is quite self-evident that Moses was regarded as the most special prophet, direct ambassador of God and representative since he saw God face-to-face whom no other human being had ever seen! Subsequently, since his message was also supposed to be obtained directly from God his sender, it is also the most revered and treasured prophetic message in the whole of the Hebrew Bible or the Old Testament, as commonly known among the Christian laity.

Moses was also the priest and mediator of the Sinai covenant between God and the newly liberated and redeemed people of Israel. Therefore, through Moses and his prophetic and priestly leadership role among the Hebrew slaves, God's liberated and redemptive work is effected among them.

As the Hebrew slaves are liberated from the burdens of bondage and suffering in Egypt and through the covenant, they are claimed and cleansed by the Almighty and Redeemer Holy God, to become his/her special holy people, and elect nation of Israel through whom God would cause his/her eternal holy light to shine most fully in the world through the Incarnation of Jesus as the Christ or the Jewish expected God's Messiah that would restore Israel's lost freedom due to sin and oppression, and also restore all nations and creation itself to the primordial divine obedience, righteousness, harmony, and peace (cf. Isa. 9, 11, 35, 42, 52, 53, and 61).

Among the messages given to Moses by God to convey to his people is the Torah or the moral law that was given to regulate all the aspects of the Hebrew life. The Torah covers matters which are both religious and civil in nature. Like the African environment in which Moses was born, reared, educated, lived, and worked, the Torah has no division between the sacred and the secular because in both the African Traditional Religion (whether in the Egyptian Mysteries or the Subsaharan Traditions), and in Judaism, God is the supreme overall Lord of the secular and sacred spheres of human life, and as such, a distinction and diochotomy being both untenable and meaningless.

Some unprejudiced scholars now see clearly the continuity of the Egyptian religion and modification in the Mosaic Law and teaching. This teaching includes similarities in the "creation myths" found in Genesis, cosmological views, periodic destructive floods, God being associated with mountains and fire, monotheism, priesthood, animal sacrifice, circumcision, polygamy, ritual laws, position of women and their supposed impurity during their menstrual periods, children as God's blessings, and probably most important of all, the close similarity between the Ten Commandments and the "negative confessions of Oni" found in the <u>Ancient</u> <u>Egyptian</u> <u>Book</u> <u>of</u> <u>the</u> <u>Dead.</u>

Focusing on similarities is a greater academic virtue than focusing on the differences in the traditions and religions because the former is positive and unitive, whereas the latter is negative, divisive, and most often, destructive. Unfortunately, some scholars selfishly and sadistically thrive on negating and destroying other people and other scholars' works either because they are threatened by them or out of sheer malevolent envy and destructive malice.

Nonetheless, this is the kind of academic environment that has done a lot of good as well as great harm, in the form of blatant prejudice, racism, and subsequent omission and distortions of true facts and correct interpretations, when the truth was clear, but against them, and their prejudiced or racially biased positions, ideas, interpretations, and published works.

As regards this form of evil, most academic disciplines have been seriously implicated from history to theology; from sociology to psychology; and from biology to medicine. For instance, whereas a philosopher of religion like John Hick was discussing in a footnote the primordial, monotheistic origin in Egypt, most especially in the thought of Aken Aton, the thoughts of the divinely enlightened and benevolent ruler of Egypt in the fourteenth century before the coming of Christ (BC) or "Before the Common Era" (BCE), some scientists were actively seeking a rational way to avoid or distort the self-evident historical and anthropological evidence pointing to East Africa as the ultimate origin of all human beings and human civilization (including the origin of White people and the Western civilizations and religions).

However, for some people this kind of truth is too shocking to be accepted and therefore, these kinds of prejudiced people will prefer to ignore the truth, believe falsehoods, and live a life based on a lie because the truth is too much to bear. But true freedom cannot be found in falsehood. And therefore, for all those who love God and humanity, truth is a welcome divine light that sets free all the enlightened and obedient people of God to become truly themselves and humane.

Subsequently, in cases where the truth has been rejected in favor of a life based on a lie, the lie that Black people are not true human beings just like their White masters, has led to the dehumanization, exploitation subjugation, repression, oppression, mistreatment and extermination of the Black people with consequent protest and armed rebellion of the Black people which is going to turn South Africa into a protracted battle zone with the Blacks fighting for liberation, freedom, and independence, whereas the Whites are trying tenaciously to protect their privileged way of life, wealth, power and control, even when they know fully well that these things are unfairly acquired and based on injustice, oppression, and dispossession of the indigenous Black people.

Nevertheless, even for these kinds of ruthless, prejudiced people, Moses is still, nonetheless, a great challenge because the center of the Torah is the decalogue, and the decalogue is the basis of universal civil law systems and human rights. The decalogue is also a key part of the Christian moral law of which both Jesus and St. Paul summed up in unconditional love for both God and the neighbor.

This moral code which God gave to the world through Moses is binding not only the Jews, but all human beings because it is a general moral guide of how human beings should live in good and ethical relationships and peaceful, loving fellowship with both God and each other. This important, divine moral code, which is both universal and timeless, is read daily in most Churches during the Lenten Season. In its outline, the decalogue is found in the book of Exodus 20:1-20 and it runs as follows:

1. I am the Lord your God who brought you out of bondage. Therefore, you shall have no other gods but me.

2. You shall not make for yourselves any images nor shall you bow down before an idol or worship one.

3. You shall not invoke with malice the name of the Lord your God.

4. Remember the Sabbath Day and keep it holy and a day of peaceful rest.

5. Honor your father and mother so that you may live a long life.

6. You shall not commit murder.

7. You shall not commit adultery.

8. You shall not steal.

9. You shall not tell lies.

10. You shall not covet what belongs to others.

It is very obvious that the first four commandments deal with the human relationship with God whereas the rest of the six commandments deal with the social and neighborly ethical and moral relations between human beings themselves. What is also clear is that God is only known and obeyed as God not through an experience of creation of which we are oblivious, but rather through personal liberation or redemption from some threatening evil situation or that of bondage in sin and guilt.

This experience is more meaningful in our perception and thinking about God both as loving heavenly parent, protector, provider, creator, and redeemer. But the faith in all these divine attributes depends primarily on our own experience of some kind of supernatural intervention and salvation or liberation. This was as true for Israel as a nation as it was also true for individuals. The proof for this is to be found in Psalms where individuals express personal faith in God's omnipotence, goodness, love, grace, and eternal salvation based on their own particular past experiences of divine intervention and deliverance from evil and danger (cf. Ps. 25-28, 34-40).

As regards to the commandments dealing with good moral and ethical social and neighborly relationships between human beings, including parents and neighbors, it is clear that these divine commandments have a universal appeal and validity, regardless of era, race, culture, and socio-economic class and technological development. This is because a community which does not respect its own parents and ancestors cannot honor itself nor live in mutual fellowship and peace since the family is the foundation of society and all essential good socialization, kindness, caring, loving, faithfulness, morality, and goodness which are learned here and begin from there.

Similarly, a community which allows unchecked murder, adultery, false witnesses, coveting, and stealing is not a moral and a viable human community in any sense at all. But rather it is an evil crowd of restless and mutual suspicious, ruthless evildoers, sinners, and criminals whose end is self-destruction through mutual, unmitigated, cold-blooded murders. This is what happens where there is no respect for life and other divine moral guiding principles. By doing unrestrained evil and living an evil life, human beings can only achieve one thing; suicidal self-destruction through corrosive, excessive, evil deeds.

Therefore, in order to avoid this tragic end, human

beings must observe the Mosaic kind of divine moral code whether it was given to them by God through Moses or another local prophet before or after Moses, and the human community has to be morally responsible enough to become the moral custodian, and guarantor of morality and freedom, and as a must on God's behalf, sanction, judge, and punish the violators of the moral and civil laws and all other evil-doers.

Moses himself had to enforce the laws he brought from God, and he entrusted and charged the elders, political leaders, judges, and the priests with the responsiblity for teaching the people God's moral law and for enforcing it on God's behalf. This was to ensure the survival of the community, its general well-being, justice, harmony, and peace.

This is as true for all other human communities as it was for the community of Israel. For all human beings are essentially the same, and all have similar needs for law, protection, justice, security, well-being, harmony, and peace.

Consequently, for any community sincerely looking for harmony, justice, and peace, it must observe the basics of God's universal moral as clearly revealed in his servant Moses, and subsequently, his son Jesus Christ, who both affirmed and summed up all these ten commandments into one, namely, "Love God and Love your Neighbor as yourself."

Jesus Christ has this as the definitive commandment and the new moral law for all human beings everywhere to follow in order to live a most happy, satisfying, moral, and spiritual life most fully oriented to both God and all one's fellow human beings here on earth in which God has become most personally and concretely manifested in the person of Jesus as the Christ.

In this respect, Moses was merely a prototype of Jesus Christ of God who, as the cosmic Messiah of God, was to come and enter the world in the fullness of God to liberate and redeem the world and everyone in it from the universal grips of the bondage of sin, evil, and death.

Amos: The Prophet
of Socio-Economic Justice

It is well known how the people of Israel conquered the fertile and rich land of Palestine. This was the very coveted land which was also considered the divinely promised land by the ancient Hebrews who up to now had had no land to call their own.

Subsequently, the Hebrew people constantly referred to this land as the promised land. If this rich land of Palestine or Canaan had been described correctly as the wonderful, primordial Eden or paradise colorful and fertile land of divine promise which was "flowing with milk and honey," before the arrival of the Hebrews from slavery in Egypt, it must have soon ceased to be so attractive because of strife and incessant tribal wars, which have most omenously and viciously persisted up to the present day!

As a result, after a period of an unstable weak system of the Hebrew tribal alliances and the sporadic, emergence of charismatic leadership in the form of God-sent judges or liberators who were both religious and military leaders. These religio-military charismatic leaders were, on the whole well received, since they were considered to have been sent by God to save the people of Israel from their enemies, having been allowed by God to defeat Israel, in punishment because Israel had broken the Mosaic law and God's covenant, which the people of Israel constantly breached, finally, Israel asked God for a king, in order to be like the other strong nations that were afflicting them.

Subsequently, we are told that God reluctantly allowed Samuel to annoint first Saul, then David as kings of Israel, and from then until the sixth century BCE when Judah fell into the hands of the conquering Assyrian armies, Israel existed as a monarchy. And there were many years when Israel was truly very prosperous and a great political power, despite internal divisions into two kingdoms following the death of the great, prosperous, and benevolent King Solomon who was also supposed to be one of the wisest men in Israel and the world, despite the fact that he unwisely married about a thousand wives all at one time, and that he did not train well his sons for succession and wise governing of the people, after he and David, his father, had done all the necessary work to make Israel into a united and great nation under God, one place of central worship; the beautiful and majestic temple newly built by Solomon in Jerusalem.

It was during a period of this great success and prosperity between 760-750 BCE that prophet Amos appeared on the scene claiming that God had chosen and called him from farming and sheep-keeping in Tekoa, and Judah had given him a serious message of warning for Israel. This message consisted primarily of God's warning for the rich and self-righteous kings and priests that God was going to punish the whole nation because of their rebellion against God's moral laws, sins, breaking the covenant, accepting bribes to pervert the legal system, cheating, exploitation, and most of all, injustice to the weak and the poor who were being cheated and sold as slaves by the rich for a mere debt of the price of a pair of sandals.

Consequently, the wealth of the rich had been largely acquired through ungodly and evil means, such as bribery, cheating, robbing, fraud, and selling the debtors and the poor as slaves. This was what moved God to denounce the wicked, rich people who slept in beds of gold and mansions of ivory, whereas the poor masses were getting poorer, neglected, exploited, cheated, and sold as slaves by the wicked, rich people who were subsequently getting even richer at the great expense of the poor masses.

For these kinds of uncaring, evil and oppressive rich people, prophet Amos had the following discomforting message from God:

The Lord says, "The people of Israel have sinned again and again, and for this I will certainly punish them. They sell into slavery honest men who cannot pay their debts, poor men who cannot repay even the price of a pair of sandals. They trample down the weak and the helpless and push the poor out of the way. A man and his father have intercourse with the same slave girl, and so profane my holy name. At every place of worship, men sleep on clothing that they have taken from the poor as security for debts. In the temple of their God, they drink wine which they have taken from those who owe them money. (Amos 2:6-8)

Amos goes on to tell these wicked, rich oppressors and exploiters of the poor that God would punish them with destruction through catastrophes, drought, famine, war, death, and exile into slavery. He also goes on to warn the political civil leaders, priests, kings, and judges against injustice, oppression, corruption, bribery, and pervasion of justice in law courts.

You are doomed, you that twist justice and cheat people out of their rights.... you who hate anyone who challenges injustice and speaks the whole truth in court. You who have oppressed the poor and robbed them of their.... I know how terrible your sins are and how many crimes you have committed. You persecute good men, take bribes, and prevent the poor from getting justice in the courts. And so keeping quiet in such evil times is thought the smart thing to do! Make it your aim to do what is right, not what is evil so that you may live. Then the Lord God Almighty will really be with you, as you claim he is. Hate what is evil, love what is right, and see that justice prevails in law and the courts. (Amos 5:7-15)

In regard to the religious, elaborated rituals and ceremonies of these wicked, rich exploiters, unjust oppressors, corrupt robbers, and defrauders of the poor

through deceit and false measures, God had this message
to declare through his prophet Amos:

The Lord says, "I hate your religious festivals; I
cannot stand them! When you bring me burnt offerings and grain offerings, I will not accept them. I
will not accept the animals you have fattened to
bring me as offerings. Stop your noisy songs; I do
not want to listen to your harps. Instead, let
justice flow like a stream, and righteousness like
a river that never goes dry. (Amos 5:21-24).

Prophet Amos' denouncement and rejection of the empty
religious ceremonies, rituals, festivals, and activities of the wicked people who put on a public hypocritical show, whereas in private, they readily break the
commandments of God, exploit, oppress the weak and the
defenceless, and hate their fellow human beings, is
univerasally relevant and valid today. It should be
reaffirmed universally today because we have too many
religious hypocrites among the ranks both the clergy
and laity.
These are the kinds of people that steal, cheat,
exploit, kill, discriminate, take or give bribes, and
pervert justice in the quest of political or economic
gain, and yet, still claim to be very religious since
they can buy their way into the church or religious
community favor with "big money" in the form of pled-
ges, tithes, special gifts, and support for the community's special programs and projects.
Subsequently, in this manner, the Church and the
religious community itself get bought off with "blood-
stained money," and gifts from known evil people that
should not be accepted by the Church which seeks to
remain godly, holy, and prophetic in the world, and
therefore, seeks to denounce evil, corruption, bribery,
injustice, exploitation, racism, hatred, oppression,
violence and war.
On the contrary, the Church should always be free and
economically independent so as to remain faithful to

168

God and always be able to be the prophetic voice of God by uncompromising in the denouncement of evil at all levels of society. Otherwise, the church and other religious institutions will be held hostage by the money of the wicked rich people, and then silenced in face of discrimination, racism, injustice, violence and murder because of fear of losing the necessary financial support or outright fear of blackmail and public scandal.

Tragically, most churches have been bought and their religious and prophetic voice for the holy, loving, and just God has been badly distorted or completely silenced, leaving behind a mere social organization and Sunday meeting club, instead of God's redemptive church. The main test for this is how well integrated the church is at all its various ranks, and how much time is spent ministering and seeking local and global solutions to end poverty, prejudice, sexism, racism, hatred, injustice, oppression, violence, and war.

Why is this the authentic test for the true Church of Christ? The answer is simple; the ministry of the Lord Jesus and the charge given to the Church was to follow him and continue his ministry. Luke reports the manifesto of Jesus' ministry for which God's Church is called into being to implement in God's Name:

Then Jesus went to Nazareth, where he had been brought up and on the Sabbath he went as usual to the synagogue. He stood up to read the scriptures and was handed a book of the prophet Isaiah. He unscrolled the scroll and found the place where it is written:

"The Spirit of the Lord is upon me, because he has chosen me to bring the good news to the poor.
He has sent me to proclaim liberty to the captives and recovery of sight to the blind,
To set free the oppressed
and announce that the time has come

When the Lord
Will save his people."

Jesus rolled up the scroll, gave it back to the
attendant, and sat down. All the people in the
synagogue had their eyes fixed on him, as he said
to them, "This passage of scripture has come true
today, as you heard it being read."

In short, the ministry of Jesus as the Christ and the
Chief Ambassador of God in the world was primarily
targeted at the poor, the oppressed, the sinful, and
the social outcasts. The good news for them was that
God had heard their cries of pain of injustice, oppression, poverty, neglect, disease, ignorance, and despair
and God had finally come down in flesh so as to minister to them himself.

Subsequently, Jesus healed, taught, fed, forgave, and
saved these people from their problems and evil. And he
gave them the new self-identify, hope, satisfaction,
and happiness. It is this noble ministry to the weak
and the poor that the church is called and entrusted.

Unfortunately, with some exceptions of groups, such
as the Daughters of Charity of which Mother Theresa is
the best known example, most churches are content to
serve the rich and the middle class people and ignore
the poor masses in the housing projects and the Third
World, especially Subsaharan Africa, which has most of
the world's most poor and least developed nations.

Fortunately, just like the prophet Moses refused to
be bought so as to be silent about injustice, there are
still modern leaders and prophets who have refused to
be bribed and bought by evil forces. The best examples
have included Mahatma Gandhi and Mother Theresa in
India, Pope John XXIII, Martin Luther King, Jr. in the
USA, and the retired President James Carter; martyred
Archbishops Romero and-Luwum in El Salvador and Uganda,
respectively, Bishop Festo Kivengere of Uganda; L.
Walensa, the peace maker in Poland, Mwalimu Julius
Nyerere, the retired president of Tanzania, Bishop Tutu

in South Africa, and the daring Terry Waite the new Saint of the Anglican Church of England who like his Lord Jesus Christ, out of exemplary unconditional, redemptive, divine love risked his own life several times in order to save others, from inhumane captivity, torture and cruel death.

These courageous men and women have devoted their lives to the service of both God and humanity as they sought to serve the weak, the needy, the poor, the oppressed, and the captives, and by their global efforts of unconditional love, sacrificial service, and peace-making, they have made a positive mark on the world and made it a better world to live in, though still an imperfect one and still in need of God's saving grace, more prophets, special ambassadors, messiahs, and God's redemption. This will inevitably remain the unfortunate case as long as there evil and sin in the world as opposed to goodness, perfection, justice, unconditional love, harmony and peace.

Jesus as Both the Christ of God
and God

It has already been pointed out that Moses was the prototype of the Cosmic Messiah and universal definitive Moral Law code giver who was predicted by the Hebrew prophets, such as Isaiah, and expected to come into the world during the last days when God would fulfill creation, remove evil and imperfection, restore sinners to holiness and justice. And ultimately, therefore, restore the whole creation, to its primordial goodness, harmony, perfection, and peace.

The prophets described the expected Messiah in both human and divine terms. As a human being, the Messiah of God was expected to be the royal descendant of King David, and therefore, to become a just, wise, benevolent and godly king of the Jewish people, just like King David, and like King David, to restore the unity, prosperity, harmony, godliness, justice, might, and peace to the divided, weak, and impoverished nation of Israel.

Consequently, after 63 BCE when the Roman imperial forces conquered the nation of Israel and occupied Jerusalem, the Messiah was expected to save the nation from this disgrace of foreign colonial occupation by militarily driving the Romans out of Jerusalem and all the Jewish Territories. And as a divine personage of God, the Messiah was expected to restore human beings to wholeness along with the rest of creation.

To this end, the Messiah was expected to heal the sick, restore sight to the blind, and restore the lame so that they could walk and get the full use of all their limbs, forgive sins in order to remove spiritual guilt and death, and therefore, restoring the dead back to the fullness of life. And since it was believed that only God could give life and forgive sins, consequently, by forgiving sins and raising the dead back to life, again Jesus did not only claim to be the expected eschatological messiah, but also claimed to be God himself come down in the human form so as to dwell with human beings, fellowship with them, love them, and communicate with them at their own very human level, in their own language, culture, and local symbols systems.

This complex, dual nature of Jesus as the Christ, as both God and human has been the subject of great debates, controversy, and division in the church. The major problem for most people has been simply the apparent contradiction and illogicality of the problem of affirming that an infinite God could become finite and therefore be born as Jesus was and die on the cross as Jesus did. The Jews found this absurd and subsequently, rejected the expected Jesus as a dangerous religious teacher and a sinful blasphemer.

Furthermore, Jesus had not only failed to become a real political king and liberator as their expected Messiah, but he had instead contradicted their wish and mosaic teaching by introducing a new commandment that required all human beings to love each other and to love all human beings unconditionally, including their own enemies.

In addition, he had rejected all forms of violence, including capital punishment (as in the case of the woman caught committing adultery), just retaliation, or war. In place of retaliation, he had instead commanded the turning of the other cheek and walking the extra mile.

Nevertheless, Jesus did fulfill the essential messianic prophesies where they dealt with peace, justice, and spiritual restoration of the people. The following being an example:

> The people that walked in darkness
> have seen a great light.
> They lived in a land of shadows,
> but now light is shining on them.
> You have given them a great joy, Lord;
> You have made them happy.

A child is born to us!
A son is given to us!
And he will be our ruler.
He will be called "Wonderful Counselor,"
"Mighty God," "Eternal Father,"
"the Prince of Peace."
His royal power will continue to grow;
his kingdom will always be at peace.
he will rule as King David's successor,
basing his power on right and justice,
from now until the end of time.
The Lord Almighty is determined to do
all this.
(Isa. 9:2-7)

This Messianic passage clearly requires God himself
to fulfill it and to rule Israel directly, establishing
an eternal, peaceful reign in justice and righteousness. The Messianic ruler expected cannot, therefore,
be less than God himself, since he is referred to as
"Mighty God," "Eternal Father," and "Prince of Peace."
These cannot be titles for any human being without
incurring the problem of blasphemy or idolatry. But
Jesus, as both God and human in nature, fits this
description extremely well. He was born to us as a
child and yet he also remains fully God.
    In addition, Jesus directly fulfilled the following
Messianic expetations:

The blind will be able to see,
and the deaf will hear.
The lame will leap and dance,
and those who cannot speak will
shout for joy.
Streams of water will flow
through the desert;
the burning sand will become a lake.
(Isa. 35:4-7a)

It is very clear that the expected Messiah was, in essence, God who would be coming to the world to save his people from sin, evil, disease, inperfection, and death; and also to renew and restore the physical creation into newness, freshness, fertility, and perfection, along with and correlative to the renewal and restoration of human beings to the primordial wholeness and perfection.

Subsequently, human beings are healed of diseases and physical defects, whereas the deserts become watered by streams of fresh water and hot sand gives way to a beautiful, cool lake. This kind of transformation, both among human beings and in creation, calls for God's own coming, supernatural intervention, recreation, and salvation.

Accordingly, Christianity strongly affirms that in Jesus Christ, God has come into the world and has also become a human being in order to effect this process of human, supernatural salvation and transformation in the most personal, free, persuasive, and meaningful manner, given the fact that God respects our humanity and personal freedom, and that this being the case, God will not in any way force or coerce us to be saved.

It is within this very context that John writes the following:

> For God loved the World so much that he gave his only Son, so that everyone who believes in him may not perish but have eternal life. For God did not send his son into the world to be its judge, but its savior.

> Whoever believes in the Son is not judged; but whoever does not believe has already been judged... This is how the judgment works: the light has come into the world, but people love darkness rather than the light because their deeds are evil. Anyone who does evil hates the light and will not come to the light because he does not want his evil deed to be shown up. (John 3:16-20)

It is in this manner that Jesus Christ became not only the divine instrument of liberation, restoration, and salvation to all those who believe and follow his teachings of mutual love, forgiveness, and nonviolence, but he also becomes the instrument of divine judgement for those who reject him and his teaching and continue to do the evil deeds of sin, hatred, and violence.

In this respect, Jesus Christ and his message of good news of salvation are the most definitive, eschatological divine instruments in the form of an ambassador, prophet, messiah, teacher, and message from God. Therefore, there cannot be any greater messenger or message from God than what we already have in Jesus as the Christ.

Consequently, being both truly human and truly God, Jesus came into the world personally to save us from the power of evil that holds us firmly in the bondage of evil and mere transitory pleasures experienced in rebellion and the sinful gratification of bodily, insatiable, "animal" or lower, and base sensuous desires.

Jesus Christ himself, as a human being is the perfect example of how to be an authentic human being that God had originally created us to become. Jesus examplifies perfect humanity by virtue of his own perfect life of sinlessness, simplicity, unconditional love for his fellow human beings, full openness and fellowship with God his heavenly Father, willingness to serve the poor and the oppressed, willingness to forgive, suffer innocently without fighting back, and die a dehumanizing painful death on a criminal's cross, in order to redeem and save his enemies, persecutors, and other world's sinners.

Jesus was tempted in every respect just like us, but did not yield to sin; and he was subjected to evil, violence, and physical abuse and pain, yet he did not retaliate. Instead, he forgave his enemies and torturers. Even as Jesus tragically and unjustly died on the painful, cruel cross, he was still able to love and forgive his enemies, and to intercede for his murderers to God, praying aloud, "Father, forgive them, for they do not know what they are doing."

Consequently, Jesus Christ has also become the cosmic eternal Messiah and High Priest who is ever in God his Father's eternal presence interceding on our behalf, being ignorant sinners in need of God's redemptive grace, forgiveness, teaching, judgement, correction, and salvation, along with the rest of creation of which we are inseparably bound.

Therefore, Jesus as the Christ or eternal Word of God (the Logos) is as much the very divine, primordial medium of God's creation as he is also the very same supernatural and God's medium of perfecting, renewing, and redeeming and restoring this creation to its original and primordial goodness, holiness, restoration, and supernatural salvation in the eternal Word of God who is both Creator, Savior and Redeemer.

Some liturgically-oriented churches, such as the Anglican Church, celebrate appropriately the definitive, redemptive role of Jesus Christ as both truly God and truly human in the Eucharistic liturgy. Part of this liturgy (Eucharistic prayer B) goes like this:

We give thanks to you, O God, for the goodness and love which you have made known in creation; in the calling of Israel to be your people; in your Word spoken through the prophets; and above all in the Word made flesh, Jesus your son. For in these last days you sent him to be incarnate from the Virgin Mary, to be the Savior and Redeemer of the World. In him, you have delivered us from evil, and made us worthy to stand before you. In him, you have brought us out of error into truth, out of sin into righteousness, out of death into life.

This prayer is a very good summary of what God has done in Christ as the Word from creation through Israel, the prophets, and finally, the Incarnation and cosmic divine redemption and restoration. The alternative Eucharistic Prayer C is provided in the same Episcopal Prayer Book of 1979 to celebrate the above sounds not just mere celebration of God, but also of beauty, the cosmos, and the eternal Christ as the Word through whom it was both made and redeemed by God. It reads as follows:

CELEBRANT: God of all power, Ruler of the Universe, you are worthy of glory and praise.

PEOPLE: Glory to you, O God, for ever and ever.

CELEBRANT: At your command all things came to be: the vast expanse of interstellar space, galaxies, suns, the planets in their courses and this fragile earth, our island home.

PEOPLE: By your will they were created and have their being.

CELEBRANT: From the primal elements you brought forth the human race, and blessed us with memory, reason, and skill; you made us the rulers of creation. But we turned against you, and betrayed your trust; and we turned against one another.

PEOPLE: Have mercy Lord, for we are sinners in your sight.

CELEBRANT: Again and again, you called us to return. Through the prophets and sages you revealed your righteous Law. And in the fullness of time you sent your only son, born of a woman, to fullfill your Law, to open for us the way of freedom and peace.

PEOPLE: By his blood, he reconciled us. By his wounds, we are healed.

CELEBRANT: And therefore, we praise you, joining with the heavenly chorus, with prophets, apos-

178

tles, and martyrs, and with all those
who, in every generation, looked to you in
hope, to proclaim with them your glory, in
their unending hymn:

ALL: Holy, holy, holy Lord, God of power and
might, heaven and earth are full of your
glory. Hosanna in the highest. Blessed is
he who comes in the name of the Lord.
Hosanna in the highest. AMEN.

When this liturgical celebration is well done, even
those who claim to be devoid of religious emotion might
be moved to shout a spontaneous "Amen!" For it tells
the story in moving terms of the origination of the
cosmos and the human beings in graphically modern scientific terms, yet without losing God's loving, purposive, and redemptive will and freedom.

The role of evil and sin against God through personal
free will is weaved in well in the role of the prophets, sages, and saints, and ultimately, of Jesus
Christ, are positively affirmed within the total ground
context of the vast cosmos, in which we are called to
exist meaningfully in the right, loving, and fulfilling
fellowship with God and each other in a global community of unending goodwill, love, and peace.

For truly "Blessed are the peace-makers, for theirs
is the kingdom of God" (Matt. 5:9), which has already
come into the world with the coming of Jesus as the
Christ of God. And his atoning death and resurrection
which has conquered the tragedy and finality of death,
enabling us to experience new being now, and eternal
life.

Chapter Five

EDUCATION FOR ETHICAL LIVING

AND HAPPINESS

In all human societies, and most especially among the Ancient Egyptians (Kemites), Hebrews, Ancient Greeks, and later, among the Christians and Muslims, formal education was wholistic, and the main goal and objective was to impart the necessary correct knowledge required to live a virtuous life whose intrinsic, noble end was the attainment of happiness.

In other words, education was pursued as the primary means to gain the necessary knowledge of how to live a happy life. And the happy life was perceived to be a divine quality achieved by living virtuously, according to the knowledge of the good, just like God.

Education and Moral Values

Traditionally, education was, by nature, moral and ethical. Socrates, the famous philosopher, made it most plain to his generation and era that the greatest evil which threatened the well being, peace, and happiness of the nation and the world was ignorance. The solution to this problem was found in good education that taught the young as well as adults, the soldiers as well as political leaders, slaves and free people, Greeks and non-Greeks, and the religious and the superstitious (pagans) how to think critically and ethically.

Socrates did not claim to have a new, special knowledge which was not already available. His chief claim
was that he taught people to think more analytically
and critically about what they were previously taught
as the truth and lived by as the right guides to correct moral behavior and happiness. And by so doing, he
said these people learned to discover what was true and
what was false.

However, the Greeks were not alone in this quest for
correct knowledge, virtue, and good moral life and
happiness. Indeed, the Egyptians and the Hebrews had
been engaged in this pursuit for hundreds of years and
had written quite a lot on this subject before the
Greeks themselves had even become civilized or had
organized themselves into viable city states which
enabled the luxury of philosophy, performing arts,
democracy, and the rule of law to flourish.

Furthermore, the ancient major Greek philosophers,
such as Socrates, Plato, and Aristotle were persecuted
for teaching controversial foreign doctrines. And were
forced to flee Greece with the exception of Socrates
who refused to escape, and was subsequently executed
for his controversial religious, ethical and philosophical teachings. Therefore, it makes good sense to
trace these new philosophical teachings from Egypt with
which they were in close political, cultural, and economic contact.

In fact, Aristotle later moved his own academy itself
to Alexandria in Egypt where there was an already
flourishing Egyptian university and a large library
containing Egyptian scientific, philosophical, medical,
and religious books, going back thousands of years in
civilization which had resulted in engineering feats of
the building of the great pyramids and irrigation canals. We know that Aristotle and his students both
utilized and translated some of these Egyptian books,
which were unfortunately ascribed to them as the au-
thors, rather than being credited with mere translation.

This is definitely unacceptable today as not just

mere academic dishonesty, but also as an illegal act of plagiarism. But there were no copyright laws then. Nevertheless, we need to correct this mistake by doing careful research and giving proper credit here to the Egyptians just like the Old Testament scholars are beginning to credit Egypt with a good portion of the material found in the first five books of the Bible known as the Pentateuch or the Books of Moses (Torah).

Until recently, education was always part of the Church, temples and mosques, where the priests were the professing masters of divine knowledge, and scientific and artistic creative skills required for a wholistic and integrated, enlightened, virtuous life of knowledge of God and God's will.

Consequently, thereby living the good life which is the necessary prerequisite for true happiness that all human beings constantly crave, and try to achieve in whatever they do, whether good or inadvertantly evil. That is to assert that nobody does evil knowingly unless there is some form of perceived good to be derived from it even if it may only be finite, limited and short-lived.

This universal human quest for good education and knowledge as the means to the good life and happiness is also the human quest for divine eternal knowledge, virtue, supernatural salvation, and eternal bliss. This is true for Christianity, Judaism, and Islam as it is also true for Hinduism, Buddhism, and the African Traditional Religion. In other words, education, knowledge, and divine salvation have always been correlative and extensive for thousands of years.

The evidence for this traditional, indissoluble, and correlative relationship between education and salvation is the fact that ancient universities were mere extensions of the clerical education, and were also located on Church, Temple and Mosque grounds. These religious places of worship also served as the very halls of learning lectures, ethical sermons, and centers of higher education directly under the expert, "professional" guidance of the clergy (priests and ministers) who were the privileged few "professors" of knowledge.

The clergy had, in most cases, been students of more famous masters in whose esoteric or mystical knowledge they had to be initiated by both ritual and obedient, disciplined study of the divine, revealed mysteries, carefully guided by the testimony, expertise, skill, knowledge, and religious or ethical codes of life and behavior which was a necessary precondition for initiation and subsequent education.

Egypt had such an elaborate system of education which was duplicated in Judaism where the priests were the Rabbis (professors and teachers and masters of knowledge), and in Christianity and Islam, where the clergy and the monks are the traditionally recognized teachers, lawyers, judges, healers, and counselors. In this respect, religious terms, such as "deans," "professors," "masters," and "preceptor" have remained part of modern secular education.

In addition, most universities still begin their academic year with a religious service known as "Convocation Service" and end the academic year with a "Baccalaureate Service." And as we know, all universities, both public and private, are still expected to provide chapels, chaplaincies, and departments of Religion and Philosophy.

President Ronald Reagan and the conservative right wing in USA are asking for public prayer to be constitutionally allowed in public schools. Their argument is that "God was expelled from public schools when public prayer in public schools was outlawed."

Nevertheless, whether these people know it or not, this is a request to return to the traditional university system of pre-Enlightenment Era and to pre-Rationalism which brought the split between Religion and Science, based on the new skepticism which regarded all knowledge as suspect myth unless it could be rationally proven or imperically verified with scientific experiments.

Wholistic and Integrated Education

In this traditional educational system, unlike modern education, what is important is not the mere acquisition of information and skill in order to compete successfully in the job market and get a well paying job with attractive fringe benefits. Instead, what is important is measured in the quality of education and how well it has enabled graduates to live a full, integrated, ethical life in the community, relating well in a civil and cultured manner with their fellow citizens, and playing a major role as moral leaders of the community and also as a good role model for the young.

Therefore, in essence, the traditional, educational system seeks to enable graduates to love both God and their fellow human beings and seek to serve them well. Subsequently, it seeks also to make a positive contribution and thus to make a positive difference in the world. And that is the way it should be for equipping the individual with mere technical information and skills without imparting moral values, accountability, responsibilty to both society and the Almighty God the Creator, is to create a dangerous, immoral, clever, technological monster capable of destroying us, along with the rest of God's creation.

Therefore, scientists and leaders need most of this traditional, wholistic system of education which emphasizes ethical values, the love of humanity, and the love of God; the accountability and human responsibility as God's moral agent and concrete intelligent representative in both creation and the cosmos.

Both leaders and modern scientists meed most of this kind of wholistic and ethical education because they have greater moral and ethical decisions to make constantly, on behalf of humanity, creation, and God. And as such, they need all the humanistic, moral, religious, ethical, political, economic, scientific, and technologically necessary education and information in order to make a sound decision in all these important perspectives.

Whereas teamwork is important in providing the mentioned essential above expertise, it is important that the leaders and those who make key decisions in any society, especially among the super powers, the persons should be well educated and well informed in order to be fully accountable and responsible to both humanity and God, in their important decisions which tend to have both cosmic, concrete ramifications and irrevocable consequences.

It was in this respect that Plato himself, prophetically declared that there will not be any meaningful peace in the world until philosphers become rulers (or kings) and rulers, philosophers. For Plato, philosophy was a systematic inquiry and study that included all branches of knowlege, and this being the case, recommended wholistic systems of education for all those destined to become good leaders and global peacemakers. For ignorance, shortsightedness, naive egocentricity, parochialism, and ethnocentrism are the greatest obstacles and enemies for good leadership, wise governance, and global peace.

The Ancient Egyptian System of Education and Salvation

The primary objective of the Ancient Egyptian system of education was human attainment of the divine secret mysteries or knowledge which was expected to lead to virtue, a moral good life in accordance with the divine decrees, righteousness, justice, love, happiness, growth in personal knowledge, and divine or supernatural illumination, culminating in the union with (Atum Amen Ra), and thus supernatural salvation.

Like the rest of Africa, the Ancient Egyptian education had as its primary objectives human deification and salvation. Subsequently, this Egyptian system of education, like the one Moses introduced to the Hebrews in the form of Judaism, which was itself a modified form of the Egyptian system of the divine mysteries, traditionally combining both education and religion, had no boundaries between secular education and religious or theological education. For such a distinction did not exist in life itself. Life was viewed and perceived as a whole. And as such, unlike the Western modern times, there was no distinction between the sacred and the secular realms.

Consequently, both secular and sacred studies were combined in general or wholistic systems of education known as "The Divine Mysteries," which were kept secret and hidden away from the lay people and all those who were not trained, disciplined, and initiated into the cult and knowledge of these Divine Mysteries by the authorized masters who were also temple priests of God (Atum Amen Ra), the One Supreme God of Egypt and the whole world.

This ancient African God-centered system of Education was designed not only to ensure a virtuous life, but also a skilled life in the world, harmony, peace, and happiness as a blessing from God in reward for virtue and disciplined search for knowledge and the spiritual enlightenment that transformed the knower or the enlightened initiate into the "Son of light."

The educational curriculum consisted of language (both Grammar and Rhetoric), Mathematics, Astronomy, Music, Geography, both Divinity and Philosophy (which were known as "The Mystery of the Secret Word"), Political Science, Law (also known as the "Mystery of Pharaoh"), Communication, and Teaching skills (known as the "Mystery of Teachers"). It is to be noted that it was at the highest level of learning, in the Mystery of Teachers that the secret mystery language and the hieroglyphics were taught.

Since much of what was taught in these African mysteries was secret and only to be taught to the initiates only, the individuals were prohibited from writing down these mysteries and so was the publication of books on these secret teachings.

However, the Temple Chief Priest, could from time to time, commission some of the scholars to study certain subjects and write down their findings in book form. It is also known that long before Moses was born, there were many books and libraries in Egypt which inspired the Hebrew Scriptures and Moral Law through Moses, and later, the Greek philosophy.

Furthermore, we also know that later, some of these libraries were both plundered and burned down by invading foreign armies although the one that later became known as Alexandria following the Egyptian conquest of Alexander the Great in 332 BCE, remained fairly intact and turned into the first great world university which even attracted notable Greek philosophers, such as Aristotle, who moved there with his whole academy and helped to translate some of these Egyptian scientific books into Greek.

In this understanding, the first scientists, mathematicians, and philosophers were not the Greeks as we tend to think, here in the West, but rather the Ancient Egyptians were the true pioneers in these subjects, which were heretofore, unknown and not yet developed in the West which was still, largely "primitive and barbarian, including the Greeks themselves."

Nevertheless, the Greeks should be credited with the more systematic development and writing down of these Ancient Egyptian mysteries which are the understanding foundations of Judaism, Greek philosophy, Christianity and Islam, all of which benefitted and came into being in the richness and fertile vicinity of Egypt. After all, it is self-evident that we can trace all civilizations from the most ancient one which happens to be Egyptian and where the Hebrews were held in bondage and enculturation for about four hundred years before Moses freed them.

However, because of prejudice and racism, the West has preferred to ignore the great Egyptian civilization, just because it was African. Subsequently, the West has sought to begin with the "Ancient Greeks,"

rather than with the great "Ancient Egyptian Civilization."

Similarly, the West has chosen not to begin with the
Hebrews because the Hebrews point us back to Egypt,
their origin, and the origin of their corporate civilization and religion through Moses the Egyptian priest,
prince, and professor, turned into the Hebrew Liberator
or Messiah.

Unfortunately, we have ignored the truth deliberately
and chosen to believe a lie because the truth ruins the
comfort and false sense of superiority and security,
we obtain from our unfounded myths, especially, the
myth of White racial and intellectual supremacy that
the Africans are inferior people who have contributed
nothing to world civilization.

Subsequently, here in the West, we seem to be still
of great prejudice and conviction that nothing good can
come out of Africa except cheap raw materials, minerals
and cheap labor. But if the scientists are right that
this is our common birth place, then each time we
disgrace Africa and its people, we inevitably disgrace
ourselves too.

The Egyptian priests and teachers such as Moses were
trained at the highest level of the mysteries which is
the "Mystery of the Teachers." The teachers had to be
themselves the initiates and masters of this "Order of
Mystery," in order to teach the other Mysteries, which
they had themselves to be initiated in, learn and
master before they could communicate it and teach to
others, largely from memory, without any distortions or
variance with what they had been themselves taught.

Authentic examples of this kind of oral traditional
education, and oral transmission of knowledge, still
exist in non-literacy cultures of Africa where history
and other skills, such as medicine, religion, philosophy, moral codes of conduct, laws, handicrafts and
cooking are all transmitted orally from one expert to
another by means of apprenticeship and from one generation to another.

These Egyptian masters or teachers, having attained

the highest level of knowledge and training in the mysteries and divine knowledge for both spiritual and intellectual enlightment, were regarded as being very close to God through the deification process of divine knowledge, a disciplined virtuous or holy life, and ultimately, through divine illumination that is correlative of correct moral or ethical knowledge of what is true and what is false, of what is right and what is wrong, and of what is important and what is trivial.

This process of human deification to divinity through knowledge and illumination was later appropriated by the Greeks neo-platonic philosophers under the term "theosis" which literally translates as "divinization," "deification" or "Godification."

It is also to be noted that Africa, South of the Sahara, still deifies its heroes today and gives them the rank of "gods" which is beyond the rank of the "ancestors" who are the western equivalent of Saints in the Catholic Church, but below the One Supreme God who is regarded to be above all gods, and all gods are considered to be subject to his/her power, though this power is ever delegated to these subordinate gods, saints, ancestors, priests, and holy people."

For the Egyptians, all those people illuminated and divinized by God through this deification process through initiation, study, knowledge, self-discipline and the mastery of the mysteries, were referred to as "The Sons of Light," and "The Sons of God," since God as "Atum Amen Ra" is symbolized by the very light, never-failing brightness and warmth of the African sun.

The sun was the symbol of God because it also drives away the darkness and insecurity of night to usher in a new day with new hopes of success, better life and happiness. In addition, the sun was considered an appropriated symbol for God because without it, our planet would cease to be in its orbit and life on this earth, as we know it today, would cease to exist. They may not have known how gravity worked, but they knew that the sun as well as the water were appropriate symbols for both God and life on this planet. Subsequently, some African groups still view God through these primordial symbols of light, fire, air, and water (rivers, lakes and oceans).

The Egyptian system of education was not open for everyone. The inquirers had to be instructed in the need and function of divine knowledge. The prerequisite condition was self-renunciation, self-discipline, and purgation. Those passing the test and the hurdles of rigorous self-discipline were then initiated into the Secret Mysteries of God in the Temples by the appropriate ranks of the priests.

As we have already seen, the Egyptian curriculum was designed to make the student whole. Therefore, all students had to learn mathematics not just to be able to count, but to be able to carry out sophisticated engineering projects like building canals, houses, temples, sphinxes, and probably most imposing and lasting of all, the great pyramids to immortalize and eternalize the deceased Pharaohs, and humanity which these Pharaohs both embodied and symbolized, both in life and death.

It was also in this tradition that Plato and Aristotle, his successor, required of their philosophy students to be masters of mathematics, science, language, and logic before they could advance into metaphysics and ethics which were viewed as the epitome and crown of both knowledge or philosophy and life itself since virtue, the good life, and happiness were regarded as the necessary fruits of both knowledge and the correlative divine salvation.

For these ancient Egyptians, the main problem was ignorance and how to know what is good and right, rather than the problem of weakness of the will and the failure to do what one knows to be both right and good. Consequently, this moral and ethical standpoint is found both in Judaism and Greek philosophy which inherited it with little modification from the Egyptian ethical teachings.

It is only in Christianity, particularly in the Pauline letters, that we find a strong emphasis on God's

free, redemptive grace, due to the weakness of the
human will, and subsequently, failure to live a good
and happy life of virtue based on one's knowledge of
the good God's moral law as found in the Ten Commandments as well as in the teachings of Jesus Christ.
This Christian teaching on God's universal redemptive
grace is a needed corrective for both the ancient
Egyptian Mysteries, Judaism, Greek philosophy, and
Islam, on the question of education, knowledge, virtue,
a good life and salvation.

Judaism and Christianity:
Education for Righteousness and Divine Salvation

It has been pointed out already that Moses modified the
Egyptian mystery teachings which he introduced to the
Hebrew as a new religion we now know as Judaism. Atum
Amen Ra, the God identified with fire, water, and the
sun in Egypt was introduced to the Hebrews as Yahweh,
who was known to Moses through "the burning bush" on
Mount Sinai.

Again, the well known system of an elite, professional priesthood which was to be the physical, intellectual, and moral custodians of the Torah reveals a
continuity with Egypt. In Judaism, the Priests and
later the Rabbis were the educators of the community.
They too taught all the subjects and there was no
boundary between the secular and the sacred.

However, Judaism, unlike the Egyptian Mysteries which
were secret, opened education to all males who wanted
to learn the law, whereas it barred women from this
pursuit. But it has also to be noted that for the
patrirchal Hebrews, God was also perceived as being
male, and the covenant contracts had always been made
between God and the Patriarchs in the notable absence
of women, including their wives, and that circumcision,
which was the initiation rite into the covenant and of
which it was also regarded as the symbol, did not
include the females and there was no equal alternative

ceremony to incorporate them into the covenant community and its obligations.

As a result, Judaism, like Islam, almost became male
religions, since they excluded women from the inner
part of the Temple and Mosques, and also barred them
from becoming priests and ministers or studying the law
which in both cases covered civil matters as well as
religious and moral matters.

This is how religion, in the name of God, elevated
and deified the male gender, whereas surbordinating,
subjugating, denigrading and ultimately, dehumanizing
those of the female gender as weak, inferior, and
defiled beings because of menstrual periods. Up to this
day, some churches which strictly follow the Mosaic Law
and the Pauline Epistles in the New Testament, in the
name of God, still bar women from the ordained ministry.

The problems of gender in the Bible can be easily
summed up simply as follows:

1. The Patriarchal Hebrews had a male dominated culture.

2. The Patriarchal Hebrews despised women as weak and
   inferior.

3. The Patriarchal Hebrews viewed God as male and
   good.

4. The Patriarchal Hebrews viewed female and "femaleness" as un-God-like and evil.

Given this kind of background, it is easy to see how
and why Eve is the one who is supposed to have caused
the original disobedience and sin in the world, even
when the commandment was only given to Adam and not
Eve, who was not yet created when God commanded Adam
not to eat from the tree of knowledge of the good and
the bad as well as death (Gen. 2:5-17). This divine
command is significant not because it led to the pri-

mordial human rebellion, disobedience, and sin against God, but because it clearly testifies to the fact that the knowledge of the good and the bad is primarily a supernatural divine quality.

Therefore, to possess this moral knowledge and consciousness is to be viewed as a divine privilege which human beings can only gain and enjoy by divine permission and benevolent divine tutelage for the human being's enlightenment; a good, habitual state of the life of virtue, self-discipline, harmony, peace, and blissful happiness.

In this sense, it is through the human "a priori" divine intrisic attributes of self-transcedental, greater mental capacity for infinite intellectual activity, free thinking, reasoning, value judgement, moral consciousness, good education, and knowledge that which human beings truly become Godlike (or become God).

Subsequently, following Eve and Adam's disobedience and eating of the forbidden fruits of the tree of knowledge and death, God is reported to have said the following:

"Now the man has become like one of us and has knowledge of what is good and what is bad. He must not be allowed to take fruit that gives life, eat it, and live forever." So, the Lord God sent him out of Eden and made him cultivate the soil from which he had been formed.

Therefore, within Judaism, just like the Egyptian Mysteries, it can be said that knowledge is supernatural and divine and its quest is also the quest for salvation, the supernatural and the divine. Subsequently, its possession does not only confer wisdom, but also divinity, salvation, virtue, right judgment, righteousness, goodness, peace and happiness.

Consequently, in these religious and philosophical systems, God can only be God because he/she is the ominiscient source of knowledge, creativity, providence, perfection, and salvation in the world. As a result, the Whiteheadian finite and ignorant God would be utterly rejected as meaningless, since he/she was unable to create, direct, and save at will, and at any time, both in history and eternity.

After Moses and the Sinai Covenant between Yahweh (God) and the people of Israel, the Torah or the Law of Moses began to be the Hebrew focus and center of education. Indeed, God himself is credited with the command to teach this law, especially to the young so that they would grow up in the fear of the Lord and the observance of his moral code as was given to Israel through Moses. On this subject, Moses is reported to have said:

> These are the laws that the Lord your God has commanded me to teach you. Obey them.... As long as you live, you and your descendants are to honor the Lord your God and obey all his laws that I am giving you so that you may live in that land a long time.... The Lord and the Lord alone is our God. Love your God with all your heart, with all your soul, and with all your strength. Never forget these commandments that I am giving you today. Teach them to your children so that they observe them when they grow up. Repeat these commandments when you are at home and when you are away, and when you are resting and when you are working. (Deut. 6:1-7)

And as we have already seen, the priests, scribes, rabbis, and Pharisees later developed privileged, authoritative, and expert teachers, developers and interpreters of the Law (Matt. 23:1-3), and that most of the lay people, known as common people or "sinners" lived a life which was generally obvious to the details, and therefore, the observance of the Law.

Subsequently, by the time of Jesus, the religious "priests," such as the Pharisees avoided contact with the ordinary populace because it was strongly believed that the religiously pure would become contaminated and defiled by physical contact with those who did not know the Law, such as foreigners, and those who did not strictly practice or observe it. If such physical contact took place, the Pharisees had to purify themselves with a ritual of handwashing up to the elbows.

This is the kind of Pharisaic legalism that Jesus denounced and did away with in his own ministry and religious teaching. In deed, it was this very neglected large group of common and ordinary people which the Pharisees shunned as defiled "sinners" that Jesus primarily sought out, taught and ministered to (Luk. 4:16-21).

Explicitly, Jesus also affirmed that it is the sick that require a physician for healing, the lost that need to be found, the blind that need restoration of sight, the lame that need to walk, the ignorant that need teaching, and the sinful that need forgiveness and restoration to wholeness and that it was for this supernatural and divine redemptive work that God in Jesus came into the world (cf. Mk. 1:21-2:12).

Nevertheless, Jesus himself knew the divine quality of knowledge and its redemptive and divinizing value that his ministry was almost entirely devoted to the essential teaching of the ignorant masses in the open fields and on lake shores so as to reach the unreached masses of people. He sought to teach them God's moral law and to impart to them God's redemptive knowledge and message of the good news of the availability of God's free salvation in God's own free loving and saving grace for all human beings who turn to him in faith and need of this supernatural salvation and divine restoration to wholeness, harmony, unconditional love for all people, peace, and happiness.

Therefore, it is in obedience to Jesus Christ's examples and command to his followers to carry out his uncompleted work and to reach out to all human beings on earth and teach them what Jesus taught about God's unconditional, forgiveness, non-violence, peace and salvation that the church today should be the primary instrument of education, particularly religious, moral, and ethical education in the world, if there is to be

any meaningful global harmony and lasting peace.
The fact that Jesus saw education and knowledge as
part of salvation and theosis or divinization of the
active and obedient knower is found in clearly stated
in the following encounter and discussion between Jesus
and the teacher of the Mosaic Law:

A teacher of the Law was there who heard the discussion. He saw that Jesus had given the Sadducees
a good answer, so he came to him with a question:
"Which commandment is the most important of all?"

Jesus replied, "The most important one is this:
Listen, Israel! The Lord our God is the only Lord.
Love the Lord your God with all your heart, with
all your soul, with all your mind, and with all
your strength. The second most important commandment is this: Love your neighbor as you love yourself. There is no other commandment more important
than these two."

The teacher of the Law said to Jesus, "Well done,
teacher! It is true.... It is more important to
obey these two commandments than to offer on the
altar animals and other sacrifices to God."

Jesus noticed how wise his answer was and so told
him, "you are not far from the kingdom of God."

Therefore, it is self-evident from this passage that
according to Jesus, all those who wish to be godly and
to become his redeemed and obedient disciples, and
thus, the children of God and enter God's Kingdom, must
not only love both God and their fellow human beings as
the universal neighbor, but must also study God's law
and God's works in nature so as to prove wise and to
live more meaningfully according to God's Law, goodness, holiness, truth, justice, and unconditional love,
which only occur where there is good and godly education.

It was for this kind of good and wholistic education that churches founded all the ancient universities in Europe and in America. Good universities like Cambridge, Oxford, Harvard, Yale, Princeton, Duke, Vanderbilt, Wheaton, Fisk, Berkeley, and others were all founded by the churches in obedience to Christ's command to teach all nations and make disciples of men and women for God's universal kingdom, both in heaven and here on earth.

Subsequently, these universities and others have a moral obligation to provide godly education in order to increase the unconditional love for both God and human beings, everywhere, and subsequently, to facilitate global understanding, despite cultural and ideological pluralism, international cooperation, tolerance of diversity, a life of harmony, disarmament, and global peace. To do otherwise, would be tantamount to the negation of the essential teaching of Jesus, the true Church of Christ, and therefore, to negate both Christ's message of love and reconciliation, and as such to negate their own primary mission and the very reason for being there.

The Ancient Greek Education:
Knowledge for Virtue, a Good Life and Happiness

The Western intellectual tradition and education are heavily rooted within the ancient Greek intellectual tradition, particularly Athenian, which produced great philosophers, thinkers, scientists, and academicians like Socrates (469-399 BCE), Plato (427-347 BCE), and Aristotle (384-322 BCE). The other Greek city states, namely, militaristic Sparta, commerical Corinth, and Thebes were not intellectually inclined.

The latter mentioned Greek city-states were more interested in other things such as military and commercial power and domination of the region. This tension and rivalry led to the protracted, destructive, Peloponnesian wars beginning 431 and only ending in 404 BCE with the overthrow of the Athens by a coalition of Sparta, Corinth and Thebes, primarily, out of jealousy and fear of its growing moral intellectual military power and emperialistic expansionism in the region.

As we have already seen, Greek philosophy did not merge out of an intellectual vacuum since the intellectual traditions of both Egypt and the ancient Israel were readily accessible in the Mediterranean region.

However, the Greeks did a great job of systematizing the existing ideas into various intellectual disciplines, like metaphysics, ethics, logic, and natural sciences or geometry, as Plato referred to it, and required it of all his students.

It also is to be noted that for these Greeks the term "philosophia" which we translate as philosophy has the exclusive meaning which covers all branches of study and knowledge. It is literally and more correctly translated as "love of wisdom." This is why the highest degree that universities can offer is a PhD (Doctor of Philosophy), regardless of the field of study.

The Greek intellectual tradition, both before and after Socrates, the first greatest Greek philosopher,

thinker, and teacher, remains very diverse and pluralistic. For instance, the Ionians had primarily engaged
in what we would call natural science in trying to
determine the primary stuff or elements of which life
and things were constituted.

Thales had concluded that the world was made up of
water; Anaximader had said it was made up of fire
instead; and Anaxamines had disagreed and said it was
made up of air. Pythagoras (580-497 BCE), the great
mathematician and philosopher, had himself speculated
the universe was composed of numbers and ratios. His
religio-philosophical brotherhood and mystic community
had been established to live in accordance with his
philosophy.

Plato himself had also speculated on this problem
with the result of his famous doctrine of abstract
"Ideas" or "Forms," being the essence of reality and
the visible world being mere transitory phenomena or
appearance and illusory, whereas Ideas or Forms were
immutable, permanent, universal, perfect, and most
real.

For Plato, God (Demiurge) was the chief organizer of
these Forms so as to create the world of phenomena out
of them following the Idea or Form of the "good" which
is supposed to be the chief and most perfect as well as
inclusive of all these Forms. Subsequently, for Plato,
all human knowledge, choices, life, and will are required to be in line with the "good" in order to be
correct, acceptable, and satisfying to the community,
the doer, and God.

In other words, true human virtue, a good life, and
its coextensive happiness are only possible when the
human being discovers the "good," does it, and lives by
this knowledge and the doing of the "good" deeds. This
is "the good life" which is only made possible by a
state of virtue which is itself a result of correct
knowledge.

It is, therefore, in this understanding that Socrates
taught that "true knowledge was virtue" since it inevitably led to virtue, whereas ignorance and false

knowledge led to vice and an inauthentic form of existence, being unrelated to both truth or reality and the
good.

As a result, for Socrates and Plato, no ignorant
person would live a good life, and subsequently, no
ignorant or foolish person is able to live a life of
habitual virtue and correlatively to live a happy life.
It is very clear that this Greek form of education and
philosophy had supernatural salvation and human deification through both knowledge, correct moral life, and
good deeds as its primary function and chief priority
since to possess correct knowledge conferred a life of
virtue, self-control, satisfaction, and happiness on
the philosopher, thus becoming like God or the gods.

Before Socrates and his moral philosophy became important in Athens, along with his dialectics and ethical call to self-examination, search for the knowledge,
truth, the beautiful and virtue; as opposed to falsehood, ignorance, acceptance of the cultural moral norms
without question, and following one's base or lower
bodily sensuous desires without self-discipline and
self-control, blindly following corrupt moral teachers,
like some sophists like the famous Protagoras (481-411
BCE) who taught that "Man is the measure of all
things," regardless of whether they are good or bad,
"man" is the one that designifies them as such. Subsequently, he taught that whatever was good for "man"
was, therefore, also to be regarded as essentially and
intrinsically good. Conversely, that whatever was bad
for "man" was also essentially and intrinsically bad.

This is the kind of irresponsible, extreme relativism
that Socrates, Plato, and Aristotle had to fight a-
gainst. For instance, if the Society ever followed
Protagoras' extreme moral relativist theory, no human
being would ever judge anything as bad or evil since
there would not be any common moral law or even civil
laws for the lack of understanding and knowledge of
what is right and what is wrong in as much as there
were doers for each deed and claimed that it was good.

But even after Socrates, the Greeks still followed

different moral philosophies, such as Epicureanism, which tended to teach that pleasure as a countermeasure and cure of pain was the highest natural good to be aimed at as the principle and goal of living happily in the body and its pleasurable senses.

However, the extremists took this pleasure principle to its absurd limits by claiming that the good life was that of celebration of the body. This teaching could be summed up simply as "let us eat, drink, and have sex, for tomorrow we will die."

It should however, be noted that Epicurus (342-270 BCE) himself, never taught this kind of blatant hedonism, which is sometimes erroneously credited to him as its chief exponent. He even taught that too much pleasure could itself cause the pain that was the main evil to be avoided.

On the other hand, there were the contemplative, responsible, serene, and dignified tranquil Stoics. Zeno (336-263 BCE), the founder of Stoicism, being himself a Jew, combined the ethical principles of Judaism with these of the Hellenic culture to create this great philosophy that taught that the human being was a privileged creature which, though having an animal or earthly body filled with earthly requirements, needs, and desires, has also a divine soul which is part of the cosmic inclusive soul that is God.

This being the case, to be Stoic is to face life courageously and try to live a sober life filled and permeated with tranquility and transcendental peace for both the mind and the body, regardless of what the environment is and the earthly events which will happen according to pre-established laws.

Therefore, one has to learn these natural causal and involuntary laws, accept them, and live peacefully according to them. Consequently, one has to accept courageously, peacefully and willingly whatever comes in one's way, as essentially divinely predestined, and therefore, inevitable, definitive, essential, and as leading to the hidden ultimate destiny.

Nonetheless, this Stoic position was very different

from that of the naturalists like Diogenes (428-412 BCE), who taught that human beings should live simply, just like the rest of the other animals. He even suggested that human beings should be completely naked, if the weather allowed, and mate in public, just like the other creatures.

This kind of Stoic philosophy enables its adherents to view themselves as part of the irreversible, natural, and supernatural process to which they must surrender themselves if they are to live meaningfully in this world of historical events, human voluntary actions, disasters, pain, time, change, finitude and death. This position brings to mind the author of Psalm 23 who is ready to trust in God and leave the rest to God, including personal death itself.

We also find some kind of Stoicism in the Pauline Epistles and through Paul, Stoicism entered Christianity itself, but in a very modified manner. This would be mainly true for the mainline Churches, especially in Catholicism, Eastern Orthodox, and Anglicanism.

This should not be surprising since the early Church Fathers themselves deliberately studied Greek Philosophy, especially Neoplatonism, with its strong emphasis on the doctrine of the "Logos" which Christian philosophers and theologians most readily appropriated to teach the Christian doctrines of the pre-existence of Christ as the Logos or word of God through whom all things were made by God, and at the appropriate time, became incarnate in the world as a perfect human being to show all human beings what authentic humanity and authentic human life lived in complete daily openness and obedience to God is to be like (cf. John 1:1-18, 3:16-21).

We also know that the Protestant Christian tendency to fundamentalism and dualism, and subsequently, to view the body as evil since it expresses insatiable physical needs and sensuous desires and such, to be ascetically purged by the self-disciplined, self-denial of the bodily sensuous pleasure that comes with the fulfillment of these desires, in order to reach God

through intellectual contemplation and divine illumination is due to the Neoplatonic influences; especially
through St. Augustine of Africa (354-430) and his pro-
lific literature which has shaped the theology and
doctrines of the Western Church, particularly, in its
present Protestant expression.

However, the Catholic Church has preferred since the
thirteenth century to adopt Saint Thomas (1225-1274) as
its normative theologian, teacher, and philosopher. And
by so doing, the Catholic Church has strongly embraced
Aristotelian philosophy in which Thomas had grounded
his Christian works, both the logical and philosophical. In fact, the Summa Theologica and Contra Gentiles
are so steeped in Aristotelianism that one can hardly
understand them without the necessary background in
Aristotelian Logic, Metaphysics, and Ethics.

The works of Thomas seem to be more of a Christian
commentary on these Aristotelian works and their Christian appropriation for a new age and the Church than
anything else. This does not mean to deny that Thomas
was not one of the greatest original thinkers that the
world has ever known, but rather also to affirm that he
was one of the greatest Aristotelians and a Christian
Aristotelian teacher and systematizer.

Definitely, the main external, intellectual, ritual,
and expressive differences between Catholicism and
Protestantism can be mainly attributed to the great
differences between Platonism and Aristotelianism, both
in metaphysics and ethics, which these two Christian
traditions have inherited from these two main schools
of Greek philosophy.

The Evangelical and Protestant emphasis on heaven and
hell, sin and virtue, God and the devil, Spirit as
opposed to the evil desires of the body, death and
resurrection, and self-denial can all be said to be due
to this Platonic, dualistic influence with its teaching
on the two unequal and opposed worlds. The first being
regarded as good and ideal, being of the essences and
perfect and the other being imperfect, physical, and of
phenomena or becoming, and subsequently chacterized by

constant change. But for Catholicism, following Aristotelian philosophy, the world is an integrated whole composed of spirit, intellect, form or essence, and matter or substance.

In matters of Ethics, again, following Aristotle who taught that virtue and the good life in the middle of two opposing extremes, Catholicism advocates and teaches a life of moderation for most of its members, whereas, the Protestant emphasis is bodily negation, self-denial, and a life of ascetism rather than that of moderate Aristotelian self-indulgence, and a life of habitual virtue and goodness.

Therefore, the Greek influence on Western intellectual and religious life is very great and almost immeasurable. It extends beyond Hellenic Fraternities and Sororities on Western University campuses into the general education. It also grounds and underlies much of Western philosophy, and the Christian theological and dogmatic formulation and teachings, such as democracy, ethics, logic, and ideas like the Logos, Christology, the Incarnation, God's Perfection, Creation, Evil, Mind, Body, Heaven, Virtue, Morality, Truth, Eternity, and Immortality.

Subsequently, in the West, in order to study the classics, theology, and philosophy, one has also to learn ancient or Koine Greek in order to read the original texts and commentaries. Thus, dynamically perpetuating the ancient Greek intellectual life and traditions into the present, just like the Church and synagogues that have also preserved the Judeo-Christian intellectual and moral tradition, and reinterpreted it for today's modern generation that is more attuned to the future, space age and the wide cosmos than the past with its parochial and restrictive, rigid moralism.

Consequently, the modern generation needs modern moral and ethical codes and guidelines that are more modern, broad, global, flexible, pluralistic, scientifically based, inclusive, humane, and practical. The next section tries to deal with this specific problem.

Whereas it is positively affirmed that nobody can

make another person virtuous or morally responsible, regardless of threats, punishments, and pain, such as arrests, fines, and the imprisonment of the habitual criminals, it also generally recognized that just like cancerous cells contaminate, infect and destroy a previously healthy body, likewise, evil people also contaminate their friends and cause great harm to the community, if they are not removed society or adequately reformed.

In addition, it is also positively affirmed that good, wholistic education, early good correct child socializaiton, and instruction in good, humane, moral, ethical values and by providing a good moral and responsible role models, the young people will learn both the ethical moral codes and appropriate correlative ethical behavior, respect them, value them and live by them; there is the necessary moral support from the local community to which they belong as integral moral members and responsible social beings.

Consequently, ethics and morality are as much an individual affair as they are a collective and public affair. For in the good and harmonious community, what affects an individual, ultimately, affects the whole community, and conversely, what affects the community also affects the individual members of that community. For the two are mutually coextensively and correlatively intertwined, as well as being irrevocably and mutually interdependent.

Chapter Six

BASIC ETHICS AND MORAL EDUCATION

FOR A PLURALISTIC SOCIETY

Ethics is a branch of applied knowledge and critical moral education. It deals with human values, the norms of behavior, knowledge, experience, and other factors governing human moral judgements and choices, such as racial, color, religious, ideological, cultural, socio-economic, and class prejudice.

Therefore, ethics is for everyone who makes any value, moral judgements and choices. This is necessarily the case because all human beings are by nature called upon to be moral agents in the world, by the virtue of their superior brains and subsequent great mental capacity to think, to process information or data, memory and to possess knowledge.

Consequently, the human being is able to make appropriate judgments and decisions based on this knowledge or information. As a result of this most highly developed moral capacity and agency, the human being is able to become a true moral agent due to this superior intellect, and moral capacity to evaluate information, make judgements, and make consequential choices and decisions for which he or she is fully accountable and responsible for (as decisions or choices), as well as being also responsible for all the subsequent consequences resulting from these choices or decisions, and their corresponding actions.

All Human Beings are Called to Become
Voluntary Moral Agents

All normal human beings make moral decisions each day of their active, normal lives without first consulting an expert on ethics and morals. Consequently, each person is by essential nature, a voluntary moral agent, whose definitive, moral authority is the Holy God and a moral consequence to some degree an ethicist since he or she wills, intends, chooses, and acts one way or the other.

In addition, he or she makes these moral judgements constantly regarding what is right and what is wrong, what is true and what is false, what is beautiful and what is ugly, what is good and what is bad, what is appropriate and what is inappropriate, what is beneficial and what is harmful, what is important and what is trivial, what is moral and what is immoral, and what is just and what is unjust, and to do the right or the good voluntarily out of one's intrinsic, habitual, moral virtue and goodness.

These kinds of decisions are of great ethical and moral significance, not only for the individual person making these decisions, but also for the local human community, and in some cases, these individual moral decisions can have both national and global significance. For instance, an Arab's decision in Beirut or Tehran to take an American or a Soviet citizen hostage so as to prove his own loyalty to the fundamentalist and Jihadist Shi'ite Islamic teaching can cause actual global, military alertness, conflict, and serious destruction in terms of human life and material property.

However, the individual rarely receives the necessary wholistic education, information, and moral training in making these important, daily, ethical, and moral decisions which shape the lives of those making them, their community, their nation, and ultimately, the world.

Whereas it may well be true as Plato insightfully prophesied that "there will not be peace in the world until philosophers have become rulers, and rulers have, conversely, become philosophers," my own position is that there will not be peace on earth until all human beings have become not just philosophers, who have learned to respect each other's relatively different intellectual, cultural, and pluralistic religious positions, but also as people who respect and love each other without conditions.

As a result, human beings will be able to listen to each other with interest and to live with each other in mutual harmony and enjoyment of each other's differences and similarities as a source of intellectual, moral, religious, and cultural enrichment. Rather than avoiding the different, as either inferior or a threat, as is currently the prevailing, prejudiced tendency in the West, in respect to non-Western religions, cultures, philosophical systems, and the whole system of education.

This may be largely due to the exclusive nature of the Judeo-Christian tradition, which claims superiority over other traditions, and the finality of God's word, divine revelation, and supernatural salvation. Western modern technology tended to confirm this position until recently when Buddhist Japan and Communist Soviet Union began to catch up and even threaten to supercede the West. In this case, the claim of the East to be superior is merely based on mere prejudice, ethnocentrism, racism, and sin, rather than God's will and election.

Uunfortunately, this is as true in USA where there are different races and ethnic groups of people trying hard to live together, in equality and harmony, as it is still the case in South Africa where the Whites still claim to be the elect and chosen people of God and the Black people are still regarded and treated brutally and inhumanly as subhuman, inferior beings.

Therefore, it is extremely important that all human beings be required to take basic courses and training in ethics, moral judgement, and moral decision processes because all human beings make these important moral judgements and decisions and most people do it without proper knowledge, correct information, and training. As a result, today we have unnecessarily many harmful global problems which are made by well intentioned but ignorant people.

Ignorance is the worst enemy that our world has to face today. For instance, it is due to public ignorance that we have the deadly problem of ideological conflict and super power arms race funded by the ignorant tax paying masses who, in ignorance, believe that the other power is out there plotting to invade them and impose its own ideology on them by force of arms. And that nuclear arms build-up on land, water, and space provides protection and insurance for victory, rather than destruction.

In this respect, ignorance is two-fold: first, the mistaken belief by each group that the other is not peace-loving and planning a surprise attack. Secondly, the mistaken belief that nuclear arms build-up will ensure global stability and peace, rather than stimulating more military technological research to invent even more deadly weapons, and subsequently, leading to more and more military competition, and arms race.

Thus, esclating corresponding tension and real danger for nuclear confrontation, war, mutual annihilation, and global destruction, in the nuclear holocaust or the aftermath radiation and nuclear winter which would result from thick clouds of dark smoke that would block out the sun for a considerable period, to usher in a corresponding freezing period on earth, which Carl Sagan, the famous anti-nuclear war proponent, has called a "nuclear winter." This nuclear winter will be like another ice-age in which most of the earth's creatures froze to death and perished "en masse."

Mass Moral Education as a Prerequisite
for Democracy and Global Peace

For any democracy to work, the masses must be well educated. This is because in a democracy, the government is by the people, for the people, and for the common good of the people who elect and empower it. And in a great democracy like the USA, where the public vote is important for the elected public officials, including the president, the senators, and the members of Congress, these officials have to rule according to the will of those who elected them, otherwise they may be voted out of office.

As a result, even if the President was well qualified as the kind of Plato's Philosopher King, without an well educated and a moral citizenry to support him, in his noble programs of welfare and international cooperation and peace-making initiatives, he will become isolated, powerless, and ineffective.

This was undoubtedly the case with the former President James Carter, whose noble foreign policy of human rights and global peace-making initiatives were greatly applauded abroad, especially in Africa and the Middle East, but were never appreciated at home. And as we know, President Reagan's call for a stronger USA military so as to shift the USA foreign policy from peaceful, diplomatic, peace-making initiatives in the world to a superior military presence as the means to ensure that international peace got him elected into office, and President Carter, with his welfare and global peace-making programs, were rejected and consequently, Carter was voted out of office, largely, by the less sosphisticated voting masses who could not ethically and intellectually see the folly and great expense of militarism in this nuclear age.

International terrorism, American troops, jihadist bombardment, American hostages in Beirut, escalation of war in Central America, the bombardment of Libya, the invasion of Granada, "Star Wars", and the Iran Arms Scandal have been some of the results of this militarism, in addition to the record deficits, whereas the campaign promise was to balance the budget within the first few years in office.

Yet still, the masses cannot see that they have made a mistake to support a larger military budget expenditure at the expense of essential domestic welfare and educational programs; and that the nuclear arms buildup they have supported could only result in provocation and international military hostility and terrorism as a response to this renewal of American militarism, imperialism, and threat to the global military balance of power and peace, especially the so-called "moral majority."

Unfortunately, even some religious preachers have failed to see the danger of militarism and nuclear arms race, and have supported blindly the arms race, ironically doing so in the name of God. These preachers see communists not as men and women, created and loved by God, but as evil atheists, to be destroyed. Unfortunately, these preachers have forgotten that Jesus taught and commanded his followers to love everybody, including their own enemies.

Then, how can we as Christians morally support a government which spends too much money on military technological research and the refinement of nuclear arms, specifically designed to attack and indiscriminately kill God's people, of whom we are commanded to love in the same way we love ourselves? Since I would love to live a long, happy, and independent life, how can I support the government that tries to invade or support others to invade and subjugate other independent nations because they have chosen a different political or economic structure which suits them best and is most functional and meaningful for their own people in their own conditions and socio-economic context?

Since I value my own intellectual and religious beliefs, if I love others as I love myself, how can I then, clear conscience, despise their own and try to convert them to my own? Is this love or religious and intellectual imperialism? Can I love others without changing them first and creating them in my own image? And if I do convert others to be just like me, will I have done them any good, since I am myself imperfect and sinful?

If ever I had to convert someone, I would convert him or her in the name of Jesus Christ, my perfect example, and invite him or her to walk and follow Jesus with me in mutual love, faith, and sharing of each other's burden, in Christ, for I am no better than the person I have converted to Christ, and we are all fellow brothers and sisters, and fellow pilgrims and seekers of a good life, lasting happiness, harmony, and peace for ourselves and our fellow human beings, irrespective of color, gender, class, education, race, nationality, and creed, since they are all our neighbors, being God's children, created in his/her own very image, just like us.

In short, in whatever I do to my fellow human being, I must begin from an understanding that he or she is my own very brother or sister in God in whom we share a common origin, humanity, need, parenthood, neighborhood, purpose, meaning, and destiny.

In this beneficent, perspective, and starting point in relating to other human beings, there is the underlying, fundamental, vivid awareness, understanding, and unconditional, intellectual, practical, socio-economic and emotional acceptance that the other people are real human beings and persons just like me who need to be loved, valued, needed, and in need of personal well-being and protection from all manner of harm, whether bodily, mental, or socio-economic.

The Rejection of Jungle Ethics

Consequently, this Christian and humane starting point in respect to ethics and human interpersonal relationships, both in the local community as the microcosm of the macrocosmic national and global communities, and in creation as a whole, rejects the anachronistic and atavistic "jungle and beastly normative ethics" which are grounded in the natural norm of the survival of the fittest, where "might makes right," and weakness is regarded as a defeat and not tolerated.

As a result, life in the jungle is extremely dangerous for the small, the weak, the young, the slow, the old, and the infirm, who become easy prey for the strong. Subsequently, in "jungle ethics," virtues are composed of swiftness, strength, large body size, sharp horns, good sight, ability to camouflage and hide, ability to bite, stinging and injecting poison, foul smell to discourage predators, or body armor and spikes for self defense and protection against predators.

Nevertheless, each species rarely kills animals of its own kind, whether for food or for other rights, such as, a position in the hierarchy, for the purposes of supremacy and dominion, mating, territory, and food.

However, unlike the brotherhood and sisterhood of these animals of the same species, human beings seem to be slower in learning the most important natural lesson in survival than these less intelligent animals, in that any species of any creatures on this planet or another planet, that actively and indiscriminately kills or preys on its own kind would inevitably face extinction, sooner or later.

This is necessarily the case, because personal survival is intricately intertwined with the survival of others, most particularly, those of one's own family, community, and alternately, one's species.

This is also because nobody can survive meaningfully alone, for no human being is like an isolated island in the middle of the sea. Whereas an island may exist indifferently out in the sea far from another piece of land, no single human being could ever live and survive alone meaningfully on such an island. For to be human means to be social, humane, and interactive with others and therefore, to belong to the humankind and particularly, to belong to a family, a particular community, and a nation.

Yet, for many people today, the sense of belonging and being social or humane have been forgotten, and the results are tragic, inhumane, anti-social acts, such as violence, murder, theft, rape, unprovoked mass killings, vandalism, arson, suicide, sabotage, child abuse, aggression, and war.

These kinds of crimes and evil, malicious deeds do not only disturb the harmony and well being of the community, if not successfully checked, they can also threaten the very existence of the family and the community, the very institutions in which human life and that of the human species is firmly rooted, and without which the human species may become another extinct species just like the dinasaurs or pre-historic man.

Today's unchecked, suicidal, nuclear arms race and foolish militarism may actually lead our naively divided and warfaring, unloving, unforgiving, and careless human species into global nuclear war, massive radiation, and total extinction of the human species due to global radiation contamination that would make normal human life on this planet impossible for thousands of years to come.

Therefore, some of us, just like the Hebrew prophets of old feel like shouting just like shouting in the streets: "let those with ears to hear God's word of warning of the impending doom, and act appropriately to check this evil and global threat to life lest, we all live together disharmoniously and also perish together just like fools in a tragic nuclear holocaust of our own making."

214

Obedience to God's Commandment of Love
and Justice for All

In order to avoid this foolish, tragic self-destruction, we must obey God's commandment through Jesus' teaching and requirement of unconditional love for God and our fellow human beings regardless of whether they are already friends or enemies, whom we would have naturally preferred to fight and destroy, instead of loving.

This commandment of universal, unconditional love of the neighbor has to become our imperative starting place and grounding of our ethics of life and normative measure of what is morally right and what is wrong, what is just and what is unjust, what is good and what is bad, what is appropriate and what is inappropriate, and what is godly and what is evil and sinful. The ethical norm and rule here, is do to others the good that one would seek for oneself, in order to enhance maximum personal worth, maximize a good life, and realize true happiness.

This ethical normative rule is required in order to banish the evil of personal greed, malice, selfishness, exploitation, or oppression of others for personal gain and profit at the expense of others as unchecked, extreme capitalism tends to do, thus creating two opposed extremes of the privileged few, rich individuals, who get even richer, at the expense of the poor masses, who tend to get even poorer, in correlative proportion to the rich exclusive class which is morally insensitized against the poor masses; a smooth buffer zone of the middle class whose elitist members enjoy to keep the status quo because they benefit most from being the "middlemen" of the flow of wealth from the lower class to the small, upper rich class that controls everything by its vast resources and wealth in "immoral" economies where "money speaks" and people just listen!

Who then is the master, the money or the people? What is the good end or the good life? Is money the end, or a mere means to some end? Is technology the means for those who possess it to create more wealth for themselves by exploiting those who are technologically not yet developed? Or is technology the human tool for the advancement of knowledge, the improvement of industrial and agricultural production so as to meet the needs of the world's people, so as to improve their quality of life, the standards of living, the provision of medical and health-care? And therefore, enhance global, human, general well-being, health-filled longevity, peace of both body and mind, and as such, the attainment of good life and happiness.

But if technology and money are viewed not as the means to this noble end, but rather as the destiny in themselves, then surely, humanity faces an inevitable doom since it will have abdicated its position as master, to be replaced by money for which they become the slaves and the worshippers, having replaced the true God with this idol of the love of money found in extreme godless capitalism where "money makes right" and a good life and the lack of money is considered by the majority a curse to be avoided at all cost, including fraud, theft, cheating, smuggling illegal trade in currency and drugs, murder, pornography, and prostitution.

This is the kind of inevitable moral depravity and rampant vice prevailing in the kind of society whose "God" is money and pleasure. The end of such a godless, materialistic, immoral society is lawlessness, crime, immorality, misery, hate, murder, and self-destruction; for human beings can only be as good as the God they admire, worship, and seek to imitate in order to be like him, her, or it.

Therefore, the ethical and moral ideals, and the values of each individual human being are closely correlated and intertwined with the individual's ideas of God, the good, justice, love, forgiveness, happiness, the neighbor, sin, and oppression.

Faith alone without Good Deeds of Love
and Justice is Worthless

We have always to remember that it was because Christianity had failed to live to its calling as the religion of justice and unconditional love for the neighbor
that led Karl Marx to denounce it in the last century
as an "opium of the people." The church had failed to
respond to the immense problems created by the in-
dustrialization in Europe and the creation of the land-
less, urban, poor masses whose livelihood and plight
were tied to the availability of work in the factories
where they worked long hours in unhealthy and hazardous
conditions for very little pay.

Karl Marx's solution was the unification of the workers and revolutionary seizure of the factories which
they would collectively win and control. Since then,
Russia, China, and Cuba have undergone this communist
revolution and others may soon follow suit if the West
does not come to terms with both God and the unconditional love of the neighbor that ensures impartial
treatment and justice for all human beings, and the
correlative, equitable distribution of natural resources according to need, and not according to color,
race, military strength or superior technology as it is
the unfortunate case at the moment with the people of
color, and those without modern technology being either
cheated or given the leftovers and cast-offs.

Subsequently, these two groups are viable candidates
for communism unless the West changes its socio-economic structure so as to include them fully as equal
partners in whatever ventures, advances, planning,
successes, and losses that happen to be of importance.

In addition, the church cannot afford to keep quiet
about the important issues today, such as nuclear arms
race, wars, injustice, sexism, racism, poverty, hunger,
and disease, for this would be to make the same kind of
mistake like the church has made over the previous
hundreds of years, by siding with the rich, kings,

rulers, imperialists, slave traders, and other kinds of
oppressors, and by so doing, not just neglecting its
prophetic and redemptive mission in the world, but also
becoming an accomplice with evildoers, and therefore,
partners with the devil itself.

Therefore, if there is to be meaningful peace in the
world, Christians and the church must become its van-
guard, for it is the church which has God's explicit
commandment given to it and all its members to love
each other unconditionally and all human beings, including enemies; to turn the other cheek in place of
retaliation; to walk the extra mile; to become the salt
and light of God in the dark world of sin and injustice; to become the apostles of the good news of God's
salvation; and to become the peace-makers in the world
of strife.

The Christian's divine mission in the world is probably best summed up in the words of the famous prayer
of Saint Francis of Asissi (1182-1226) which reads as
follows:

Lord make us instrument of your peace:

Where there is hatred, let us sow love;
Where there is injury, pardon;
Where there is discord, harmony;
Where there is doubt, faith;
Where there is despair, hope;
Where there is darkness, light;
Where there is sadness, joy.

Grant that we may so much seek to be as consoled
    as to console;
To be understood as to understand;
    to be loved as to love.

For it is in giving that we receive;
    it is in pardoning that we are pardoned;
And it is in dying that we are born to eternal
    life.

It is self-evident that St. Francis is praying for a Christian practical life and the faithful manner in which it is to be lived out daily in the world. It further illustrates our own failure to live by the Gospel, God's commandments, and Christ's teaching. For Jesus taught us to pray that "God should forgive us in the same way we forgive others" and that judgement will be according to how we respond to the need of the poor, the hungry, the oppressed, the sick, the homeless, the naked, and the falsely imprisoned (cf. Matt. 25:31-46). St. James puts it drastically as follows:

My brother, what good is it for someone to say that he has faith if his actions do not prove it? Can that faith save him? Suppose there are brothers or sisters who need clothes and don't have enough to eat. What good is there in your saying to them, "God bless you! Keep warm and eat well!" - if you don't give them the necessities of life? So it is with faith: if it is alone and includes no good action, then, it is dead.

But someone will say, "One person has faith and another has actions." My answer is, "show me how anyone can have faith without action. I will show you my faith by my actions...." You fool! Do you want to be shown that faith with actions is useless? (James 2:14-20).

Indeed, the Christian problem is that, unlike St. James, we have concentrated on the preaching and requirement of faith as the necessary prerequisite for Christian adult baptism and supernatural salvation. Subsequently, we have tragically tended to ignore and neglect to emphasize that faith alone without corresponding personal discipline of good, just, godly, loving, and charitable deeds is dead and worthless, just like a fruit tree which never yields any fruits is worthless.

It is therefore, mere unfruitful faith is neither holy nor redemptive. Such a faith, is a mere empty, hypocritical confession of Jesus Christ as Lord while ignoring his essential requisite commandment to love God and one's fellow human beings without any conditions, and to minister to the needy, the hungry, the weak, the poor, the homeless, the sick and the oppressed.

As a result, most Western Christians have most ironically and sinfully identified themselves, their values and style of living with those of the rich, the greedy materialists, and subsequently, have become evil partners with the imperialists, slave-traders, the colonialists, the exploiters, and the oppressors. They have tragically succumbed to this dehumanizing moral evil mainly because of their uncontrolled greed and avarice. Fatefully, their love for money, power and supremacy have sadly outweighted their love for God and Jesus Christ's call to the way of justice, honesty, simple living, suffering for God's righteousness sake.

Ultimately, these kinds of greedy and egocentric people have in essence most tragically rejected God's free redemptive call in Christ which is ever inviting all human beings everywhere, to hear, respond and become God's own essential and authentic temporal representatives in the world, and as such, active instruments of God's unconditional love, salvation, caring, fellowship, peace, and happiness in this world of self-centeredness, sin, selfishness, greed, strife, division, hatred, unhappiness and self-destruction.

220

Basic Contemporary Issues
in Ethics

The extreme moral relativists have tended like Protagoras to teach that morality is a personal and a private
affair which can not be legitemately legislated one way
or the other since there is no meaningful agreement on
what is morally good and what is bad, what is morally
right and what is wrong since what is considered morally good and right by one person may be viewed as moraly
wrong and harmful by another depending on one's background, gender, age, upbringing, socialization, intelligence, education, socio-economic, class, creed race
and culure.

For instance, whereas some Northern Whites in this
country saw slavery as morally wrong and mobilized
others of goodwill and moral conscience to oppose it,
at the same time, it was being religiously and morally
vigorously defended in the South as both divinely ordained, moral and economically beneficial, and therefore, desirable and justified enough to be forcefully
defended by resorting to war and secession. As a result, this moral dilemma, disagreement on racism, slavery, segregation, and oppression led to the historic
American moral and military civil war and the aftermath
moral issues relating to the newly emancipated slaves
who also happened to be racially African and also being
black to be readily identifiable.

These are academically very interesting moral issues
and moral dilemmas to analyze for ethical normative
judgements and moral values. It is very clear that for
some people, slavery was viewed as morally wrong, re-
pugnant and not to be tolerated since it meant the
brutal degradation, and material possession of one
human being by another, which effected both the master
by brutalizing him/her while dehumanizing the slave
into some kind of thing or object by virtue of being
material property.

Slavery is morally and ethically viewed as one of the

greatest forms of human degradation and hence, an extreme evil. Slavery led human beings to be abused by other fellow humans by enslaving them out of greed for the selfish evil motive and purpose of exploiting them, and utilizing and reducing them to the status of beasts of burden. Slavery became a great temptation for the rich and the powerful because it provided a physical means of cheap labor and production in the fields, factories and at home "in lieu" of other appropirate cheap animals of burden and machines.

In addition, the slaves were most often physically mistreated, overworked, and not paid for their labor or allowed to share in the profits of what they produced for their idle parasitic masters. This illustrates the problem of moral theory of experience and pleasure for the majority.

From this extremely dehumanizing moral problem of slavery which is the worst moral act one group of people can do to another, apart from senseless war, destruction of both life and property, and in some case, real genocide, one can deduce that regardless of the scriptures normal moral human beings view life as sacred and as such, not to be abused either by slavery, arbitrary arrest, confinement, discrimination, violence, lawlessness and murder. This is not only true for human beings, but also to a certain extent to the rest of life in creation.

In this respect the environmentalists seek to protect animals, plants, air, rivers and lakes from human careless abuse, misuse, pollution and destruction. These questions of how to view God's creation, nature and the environment are, indeed, very much moral issues, as are murder, rape, greed, stealing, abortion and capital punishment. For all these deal with both life and property on which this life is based. If killing is morally wrong and evil since it eliminates life, instead of ehancing it, then pollution of the environment is also morally wrong and evil, since it destroys the very environment that enables life forms to exist on this unique planet, unlike Venus, which is too hot to support life, and Mars which is too cold to support any life forms.

But without proper moral and legal controls, the human beings may just concentrate on making money with the factories and products while ignoring the problem of increased emission of carbon dioxide, carbon monoxide and sulphur oxide which are responsible for the air pollution, acid rain and destruction of vegetation, as well as warming the atmosphere and creating destructive seasonal changes like the recent failure of rains and fatal droughts in Africa and India.

If carbon dioxide increases drastically due to uncontrolled factory and car emissions in the atmosphere, whereas forest and vegetation got destroyed, this planet may warm up and lose its water into the air and become a hot and lifeless planet just like Venus.

This environmental issue is fundamental, and therefore, as morally important as nuclear arms race, which are similarly, capable of destroying life on this planet in either a direct immediate nuclear holocaust or the aftermath massive radiation and thick smoke clouds which would turn the earth into another lifeless iced up planet, like Mars through human bigotry, belligerence and stupidity.

Consequently, in view the unprecedented global dangers and threats to life as we know it today in this fragile planet, we have to reject traditional ethical theories such as those based on Stuart Mill's utilitarianism, which advocates the maximization of pleasure for the maximum number, and shift the emphasis back to axiological ethics which insists on the value goodness and good results of an action if it is to be regarded as morally sound. This theory also compels all moral agents not to only avoid harming the other people, but also to act voluntarily in moral goodness to prevent harm from befalling others whether they know it or not.

Personal intrinsic moral authority is a result of correct knowledge, personal goodness and virtue and rewards are realized in doing the right thing and not in monetary terms or praise and glory to be received

from others. In this understanding, Kant's moral imperative for doing the morally right as a divine duty out
of love and moral obligation, is the best expansion of
this theory. This Kantian categorical moral imperative
to moral duty provides a necessary ideal corrective and
radical negation to the recklessness of the pleasure
principle and moral expediency.

In other words, what is morally right and just is not
what is necessarily the most pleasurable or the most
expedient. In fact, very often, the reverse is the case
and that is why there is always a moral crisis for most
people because what is morally correct and just is
always unattractive, unpleasurable, and less profitable
in terms of money, wealth, fame and prestige. It is
probably for this very reason that for many people, it
has appeared that politics and morality, and commerce
and morality do not mix and that they are diametrically
opposed.

However, it would be very tragic for any just, democratic, moral and responsible people and society to
separate morality from economics and to separate morality from politics. For this would create a monster for
government that cares less about the human rights of
its citizens and those of others in the international
community. Therefore, the politicians and legislatures
are to be the good public examples and ideal role
models of good, moral, responsible, law abiding and
caring citizenry so as to emulate, and not to be the
law-breakers, robbers, public scandals and terrorists
of the public.

Public and elected national officials have the moral
obligation, duty, responsiblity and chance to be the
moral guiding shining stars of their own generation,
nations, and the global community which is shaped by
their significant moral or immoral decisions and actions.

Therefore, it is imperative that nations should seek
to elect into key public offices and support the most
educated moral, caring and responsible people among
them. For it is a great tragedy when people elect the

immoral and the unjust to lead them just because they
are either rich or great public speakers, manipulative,
unscrupulous and shrewd political actors.

This is the kind of tragic situation which Jesus
denounced as "blind guides of the blind" who will lead
themselves and their blind followers into the pit or
over the cliff and destruction.

It is also in this context that Plato called for a
Philosopher King or ruler if there was to be global
enlightenment, good will and lasting peace, instead of
ignorance, prejudice, poor judgement, strife and wars
which characterize our untutored world which is still
heavily steeped in barbaric and naive mutual ignorance,
suspicion injustice, hostility, strife hatred and war.
In this respect, Socrates' teaching that "virtue is
knowledge" and ignorance the curse of evil ravaging
human beings and the world has proved to be true.

Therefore, in order to reduce human evil in the world
and facilitate peaceful interpersonal and international
communication and cooperation, good international and
moral education are essential prerequisites. Jesus'
commandment of mutual unconditional love and acceptance
is the necessary bedrock which this global system of
education communication and cooperation must be grounded, otherwise, very little will be accomplished as in
the past, and tragic global consequences will inevitably follow.

If human species have to continue to survive on this
increasingly "shrinking" plant, human beings have got
to learn to live together in harmony and peace as
loving, caring, responsible, sharing, moral agents, and
as brothers and sisters in the one global family of
God.

Therefore, prejudice, racism, slavery, imperialism,
ethnic or religious bigotry, fraud, exploitation, deceit, poverty, disease, injustice and warfare have all
to go because they do not enhance global mutual life
nor do they create the ideal conditions conducive to
mutual trust, justice, mutual acceptance in unconditional love, a good life, happiness and peace for which

the human being deeply yearns and strives constantly to
achieve in whatever he or she does, regardless of
whether it is noble, good, just or selfish, evil and
unjust.

Even in doing evil, the evil-doer sees in it some
desirable good and personal fulfillment. However, due
to ignorance and lack of goodwill, the evil-doer is an
evil and dangerous to himself or herself and the society because of this hazardous ignorance and malevolent
lack of goodwill to do the good where it is clearly
known. This option for the evil doer to do the less
good instead of the better alternative, commulatively
and ultimately, threatens to overwhelm human affairs
with human evil and its consequent misery and pain to
both the doers and community.

This is why it is both an individual and collective
moral obligation for human beings of moral conscience
and goodwill to act both alone and together to fight
evil, especially sadism, discrimination, ignorance,
sexism, oppression, dictatorship, abuse of human
rights, crime, poverty, exploitation, militarism, violence and war wherever they exist on this globe. To
this end, the United Nations Declaration of Human
Rights and Amnesty International have been very helpful.

This is why it is important for the USA not to with-
draw its membership from some UN educational and other
programs in protest against the so-called communist
infiltration. This would amount to cupitulation to
communism, and therefore, an unwise and unconstructive
move regardless of the funds that would be missed.
Beneficience is of greater global moral significance
than either holding the world hostage with military,
nuclear and economic threats and sanctions.

Furthermore, nations, just like individuals have a
right of speech, freedom of self-determination, self-
governing and self-development without reference either
to the systems of the USA or the Soviet Union. The
superpowers have to learn to live together in mutual
peace and have to accept that military, economic, ideo-

logical an religious or cultural imperialism in the modern world, is not favorably viewed as a moral thing to do.

In addition, for the individual, national and global responsible freedom, harmony and peace are the highest and most valued virtues and the main objectives of all morally, ethically and critically thinking of all good willed godly, moral and peace-loving people everywhere on this most blessed living planet. Unfortunately, many of its inhabitants have not yet discovered how unique, and most blessed they are.

Subsequently, we all still need to learn to live together lovingly in godly peace in order to enjoy most fully God's special beauty in creation life and its unique heavenly blessings to be seen and enjoyed on this planet and nowhere else in this wide, but largely lifeless, cosmos.

The Moral Requisites for a Good
Human Community

For any human community to exist and continue in this existence, it must necessarily become a moral community which encourages its members to become ideal voluntary moral agents, desiring, willing, and aspiring to do their best and to achieve the best in whatever they do, whether in public or in private, whether personal or for the public. And therefore, legislate against and proscribe evil deeds which are motivated by extreme self-love, self-interest, selfishness, self-centred-ness, greed, ignorance, prejudice, individualism, envy, malice and hate.

For these evil deeds and evil expressions are not motivated by the unitive goodly spirit of mutual uncon-ditional love, acceptance, togetherness, goodwill, justice, sharing and cooperation, which are the basic essential moral requisites for the existence of any viable moral, just, harmonious and peaceful human fami-ly and the wider macrocosmic community of which the family is the basic foundation and microcosm.

Consequently, the moral foundation of the viable local community as well as the larger human community both national and internaional is the good and morally sound human family. It is in the human family that all individuals are born, raised, socialized, educated, humanized and enculturalated as human beings, and as members of the human race which is the larger global human community, of which the local human community is an essential and integral constitutive member or part both at local and global levels.

Subsequently, it is quite clear that no individuals and no human community can be either moral or healthy unless the human family itself is healthy since it is the primary societal foundation. And as such, the human family is the human "co-creator" with God, protector, educator, socio-economic safeguard of the individuals

created into the world through it and the community
based on it.

Therefore, a weak and morally unhealthy family is a
great societal tragedy. This is particularly true for
some families where proper sex behavior and sex roles
are absent, where incest, adultery and fornication are
rampant, and where most children are born out of wedlock without ever knowing their real biological fathers, where most children are brought up by young poor,
uneducated, unmarried, promiscuous, single mothers on
public welfare, living in crowded public housing projects with their parents or alone, as it is currently
unfortunately the case with most USA Black poor families in the inner city communities.

These kinds of families represent a multitude of past
and present socio-economic and political evils of slavery, oppression, discrimination and dehumanization.
They are the victims of the prejudice, oppression,
poverty and crime.

Therefore, these families represent divine judgement
and a societal hazard for which both the local community and the nation will pay a very heavy socio-economic
and political price for having allow such inhumane and
immoral conditions of poverty and moral degradation to
exist within its boarders.

The community and nation that permits such economic
and educational injustice and moral degradation to
occur among its own members will inevitably pay heavily
for this evil in terms of increase in crime, particularly, theft, rape, burgarlies, robberies, arson, lar-
cenary, fraud, assault and vandalism.

For these kinds of crimes are usually committed by
people who have been wronged by society either economically or socially through parental neglect, abuse,
hunger and poverty as they were growing up, and subsequently as adults these people sometimes turn to a life
of crime because of psychological problems, negative
values programming, revenge, sadism, indifference,
poverty, lack of marketable job skills, survival com-
pulsiveness and habit.

As a matter of fact, some of these homeless, poor
habitual criminals are sometimes better off in jail
than on the unfriendly streets with no home or caring
family and relatives to come back to, since in jail
they are sure of a free roof over their heads, free
utilities and daily food right on time.*

However, this is in no way to suggest that all criminals should be kept locked up in prison in order to
protect the community from moral and physical harm. But
the real care for criminals and crime prevention is not
jail long sentences and nor is it barbaric capital
punishment, since capital punishment does nothing to
reform the criminal and nor does it essentially reduce
the crimes and homecides of passion.

On the contrary, a more meaningful and effective
Christian means for a lasting crime prevention, is the
global eradication or drastic reduction of poverty by a
more moral, loving, just, Christian unconditional and
beneficent equitable redistribution of natural resources, wealth and property so that nobody is forced
to resort to a life of crime or stealing in order to
live, the provision of a more wholistic liberal arts
education which cultivates the free mind and ability to
think more analytically and critically about life,
existence and to make informed sound moral choices and
decisions with responsibility for the consequences.

Nevertheless, since the family remains the basic
foundation of the community, if the community is to
thrive and endure in a meaningful and peaceful manner,
it has to ensure the healthy endurance, moral well-
being and socio-economic integrity of the family. As a
result, the society must assist families to stay intact
both morally and socio-economically.

---

* See Appendix D for Mr. Malcolm Dean's Freshman class
  paper dealing with the problem of morality, poverty
  and crime within a USA inner city Black Community in
  which he grew up.

To this end casual sex, teenage pregnancies, single parentage, causal marriages and divorces must be strongly discouraged. The sanctity of sex, the seriousness of sexual relationship, the sanctity and permanence of vows and the marriage bond must be reaffirmed by the Church and the community.

Today's threat of deadly sexually transmitted diseases may be God's way of warning and punishing us for our irresponsible sexual practices which reject God's laws of the sanctity of sex, marriage, monogamy and the subsequent proscription of adultery, fornication, homosexuality and beastiality as as immoral and social and medical hazardous practices, which both injure the perpetrators and the community.

Consequently, if the ancient divine warning against sexual aberration, promiscuity and immorality is not seriously heeded in good time, in the face of new deadly sexual diseases like AIDS, we can easily become another Sodom and Gomorrah which were destroyed because of their sins of disobedience and rampant homosexuality (Gen. 18:16-19:29; cf. Rom. 1:18-32).

Unfortunately, many people have erroneously thought that since these days many people engage in pre-marital sexual relations or live together in trial marriages, commit adultery, commit homosexuality, abort or have children out of wedlock, and divorce in large numbers, that therefore, these practices should be subsequently, viewed as being morally acceptable for our generation!

The illogical presupposition and moral theory in this kind of argument is the mistaken extreme moral relativistic view that whatever the majority do is morally right and that whatever feels good and expedient is in fact good and morally acceptable. For this kind of crooked moral thinking, the majority is alaways right and their will is thought to constitute the common good and whatever moral and ethical! Undoubtedly, this is the kind of "mass gate" that leads to immorality, oppression and destruction.

This kind of moral teaching can only come from an evil or sinful desire to commit evil without being

morally sanctioned either by personal moral conscience
or the community.

However, the fact remains that right and wrong, moral
and immoral, sin and evil are not grounded in the
"maximum number theory" of moral utilitarianism and
pragmatism. Instead, they are grounded in God's eternal
truths, natural laws and moral laws as found outlined
in the decalogue and Jesus' teaching and commandment on
the imperative unconditional love for both God and
one's fellow human beings or the neighbor.

Therefore, even if everybody cheated, committed adultery or fornicated, and even if many people become
homosexuals or found beastiality more appealing, it
would never make it ethically and morally correct or
right. For instance, the fact that at one time most
Christians saw nothing wrong with slavery, did not make
it morrally correct, though athey found it morally
acceptable; for rightness corresponds to the good,
truth, reality, and God's Moral Law as both revealed in
nature and moral consciousness, in addition to the
various scritures.

It can therefore, be axiologically urgued that it was
for this reason that God sent the prophets into ancient
Israel to denounce its prevailing immorality, lawlessness, idolatry, greed, exploitation, injustice, oppression of the poor, corruption and pervasion of justice
for a bribe, and the rich people's excessive greed for
money and property, at the expense of the poor who were
becoming increasingly disposed. Prophets like Amos,
Habakkuk, Hosea and Isaiah vividly addressed these
moral issues and promised God's severe punishment to
the nation due to these sins.

It is to be noted that God and the prophets never
accepted these sins and evil deeds as moral and acceptable just "because everybody did them." Instead,
"because everybody did them," therefore everybody was
to be punished, including both the religious and political leaders who out of love for popularity and material wealth did nothing to stop these evils being
committed in their nation.

Subsequently, what we need most today are more dedicated prophets of God who will speak out boldly in the name of the most holy, loving, redemptive, and righteous God who will only tolerate our sins only to a certain point without punishing us.

These kinds of prophets should be above the temptation of money and material wealth for church leaders and religious ministers have been already largely silenced by the world and evil through corrupting them by bribery of money, cars, property and sex, and then effectively holding them hostage with the threats of blackmail, scandal and public disgrace.

Nevertheless, the family being the primary foundation of society remains with the primary "creation" of human beings, socializing them into the ethical values of living most meaningfully and peacefully together with others in community. And that the community and its well-being are possible by each individual's moral duty and obligation to protect the other members so as to be protected, especially the young and the weak, with all one's ability and strength, reliability to keep promises and vows made to one another in public or private, honesty, loyalty, truth telling and not telling lies or gossip about other people since it harms them and the welfare of the community; responsibility not to steal but rather to share one's property freely with others in need; to observe all the rules both written and customary on the right behavior and social interaction so as to facilitate harmony and peace within the community.

It is clear that the paradigm for this kind of socialization and ethical mutual beneficent moral imperative duty follows that of the Good Samaritan. The idea here is to be conditioned through correct socialization to the habitual state of personal moral virtue and beneficent goodness. So that each human being as an adult member of the community is truly an authentic moral agent who knows, desires and seeks to do what is good, just, and morally correct without any conditions or expectation for personal reward apart from the per-

sonal intrinsic moral satisfaction that is derived from
doing well one's moral duty and obligation.

This this concept of categorical moral obligation to
duty and work is similar to the Hindu concept of both
"Karma Yoga" which is the path to God through doing
one's work dutifully, and also "Jnina Yoga" which is
the path to God through correct knowledge and the
virtuous life that it makes possible as explictly expressed in both word and deed.

However, since many parents are ignorant and poorly
educated, and subsequently not able to socialize well
their young ones without help from the community and
larger society, and since many parents are also poor
moral agents, and therefore, poor moral role models for
their children, it is my view that the community should
use the school classroom opportunity to impart the
necessary essential universal social and ethical values
and skills required to work, cooperate, and live together with others in harmony and peace, regardless of
the inevitable differences of gender, color, race,
creed and nationality.

These global human moral values cannot be left out
nor can we entrust families to impart them to their
young during the socialization process because they
require a well informed, trained objective and sensitive teacher to teach them, as well as the essential
exposure to the different people of different races and
ideas just like the way it is in real life in this
pluralistic world.

But the community and the family working together
will do an excellent job in children's essential education as an intellectual, moral and social equipment
for living most meaningfully, morally, productively,
socially, peacefully and happily in this pluralistic
world of interpersonal relationships and potential for
strife and breakdown.

The well socialized, educated and integrated moral
agent or well humanized person, should also be able to
love, honor, forgive, accept himself or herself, so as
to freely love, honor, forgive, and accept others un-

conditionally as he or she does himself or herself in unconditional redemptive love that makes authentic personal and collective life with the neighbor a possible fulfilling reality.

In short, it is a human moral obligation to love oneself as God's good creation unconditionally in order to love others divinely in the same manner we love ourselves, and do this cheerfully in full obedience to the Lord Jesus Christ's teaching and commandment of gratuitous redemptive love for all human beings as God's own beloved children.

Finally, it must be always remembered that just like we reap what we sow, namely, that if we sow rice we reap boutiful rice, if the weather and soil are right, similarly, if in relating to others we sow the seeds of hate, we will also reap the violent fruits of hate and if we sow the seeds of unconditional love, harmony and peace, likewise, we will reap the fruits of love, harmony, peace.

Subsequently, we will be able to realize the true fruits of a good life and its coextensively correlative true human happiness which all thinking human normal beings crave and yearn for as their most desired divine fulfillment and ultimate destiny, in God's divinizing eternal presence.

This ultimate divine and happy destiny is also traditionally described as both "heaven" and God's Kingdom." It is typically characterized by divine unconditional love, fellowship, forgiveness, righteousness, holiness, beauty, glory, eternity, peace and happiness, which are also the very moral virtues and universal ethical values and moral requisites for a viable, strong, moral, healthy, harmonious, peaceful and happy human community here on earth.

Consequently, the true peace, joy and happinness of heaven is accessible here in the present and can truly be enjoyed here on earth at this very moment if we faithfully obey Jesus Christ's call and commandment of unconditional, consequential love for both God and all fellow human beings as our neighbors.

Chapter Seven

PEDAGOGICAL PROBLEMS

AND A CONSTRUCTIVE APPROACH TO ETHICS

AND MORAL EDUCATION

The problems of moral eduction, ethics, partisan religious values, and public education in a pluralistic
society are so great and almost overwhelming.
   Ever since the trial, conviction and execution of
Socrates, the great moral philosopher, in 399 BC, in
Athens, moral philosophers, teachers and writers everywhere, have had to contend with the mass public outcry
of crimes like "heresy," "treason," "atheism," "blasphemy," "communism," "revolution," and the like which
incite the public into an irrational frenzy, denounci-
ation and rejection of new ethical values, even if they
are godly and based on God's eternal moral laws in
nature and deductive intellectual eternal truths which
transcend all finite barriers of era, time, culture,
established religious and moral beliefs and practices.
   Jesus himself was another great example of a religious and moral teacher whose moral teaching was rejected, not because it was wrong, but because it was true,
right, just, and threatened the relative moral, religious and social complacency along with the material
comfort and wealth robbed from the defenceless and the
poor masses who are constantly cheated and exploited by
the rich to grow even richer, whereas the poor grow
poorer and desparate.

236

Hence, Jesus' uncompromising denouncement of these rich priestly groups and the self-righteous Pharisees who were so legalistic that they shunned mixing with the rest of the people for fear of moral, spiritual and ritual contamination.

As we also know Jesus' teaching of nonviolence and commandment of unconditional love which was extended even to enemies did little to endear him with a sinful people whose moral philosophy and ethics were grounded in the Mosaic Law which strongly commended the morality of equal retaliation for equal offense (lex talionis), summed up as "life for a life," an eye for an eye and a tooth for a tooth" (Exod. 21:24).

Subsequently, the religious leaders, Mosaic Law and the moral teachers (Scribes and Rabbis) and the Pharisees banded together in a coalition against the new moral teachings of Jesus, accused him of blasphemy against God, and impiety, condemned him and got the ignorant masses to agitate for his death.

As a result, Jesus who was the most innocent God-fearing, nonviolent moral teacher of imperative unconditional love for both God and all one's fellow human beings, was ironically executed on the cross having been convicted of the same evil crimes of hate and violence he had denounced and negated by his life of unconditional love and forgiveness for all human beings, irrespecive of their sins, socio-economic status, creed, race and nationality.

However, Jesus had warned his followers to take up the cross if they wanted to follow him and had also warned them, that since a disciple is not greater than the master, they too would be persecuted and would also be killed like he was if they remained faithful to his teaching, since "the world hates love," truth and justice; and instead prefers, suffering the choas of hate, falsehood and injustice, and the exploitation and oppression of the weak and the defenceless.

Subsequently, Gandhi and King's moral teachings of unconditional love and nonviolencce have been, likewise, rejected, their teachers violently killed, just like Jesus.

In modern times, we have also seen that the world still prefers ignorance and falsehood, to truth, if the truth does not confirm the traditionally held religious, scientific and moral beliefs.

Such was the case with Galileo who was forced by the Church to recant his scientifically well researched teachings. For instance, Galileo had proved that the sun was the stationary center of the universe, and not the orbiting earth, and the Church had instead refused to examine his evidence and proofs.

On the contrary, the Church, instead, threatened Galileo with torture and execution for his scientific findings and teachings which had been theologically judged to be dangerously secular, irreverent to the Bible, and therefore, irreligious.

Similarly, three centuries later Darwin's theory of evolution would be rejected outright by the Christian Church, just because it contradited the ancient and prescientific "mythical accounts" of creation found in the book of Genesis which simply stated that God created heaven and earth through a period of six calender days, of which, three days are said to have actually occurred before the actual creation of the sun itself.

Just several decades ago (July 10 to 21, 1925), John Thomas Scopes was tried in Dayton, Rhea, county for teaching the theory of evolution during a biology class and just two years ago Tennesses's Hawkin's County Board of Education was sued unsuccessfully by "fundamentalist" parents composed of three families on the grounds that the public school had violated their religious and moral values by teaching their children the unchristian theory of evolution, feminist values, witchcraft through literture which mentions witches and wizards, religious relativism, namely, the view that all religious are equally valid and true for the people who practice them; globalism and international interdependence, and the essential need and moral obli-

gation for richer nations to aid the underdeveloped
poor ones, rather than, encouraging parochial patriot-
ism, ethnocentric nationalism and aggressive militarism.

These Tennessee infamous religious law suits against
science and "secular humanism" in the public school
system, and the subsequent frenzied trials, do indicate
that the USA educational system is still democratic and
flexible enough to recognize the role of parents and
families as the primary educators and role models of
their young children, and as such, the primary determi-
nants of the kind of moral, religious, social, and
educational values as well as skills that are most
appropriate for their own children.

Nevertheless, the recent State intervention in a
family situation in Christian County of Kentucky, where
the State took the ten children away from parents that
never allowed their children to leave their home or go
to school is also evidence that the community and the
State are also equally concerned about the moral and
educational values of the growing children since these
are the leaders and adult citizens of tomorrow. And as
such, to educate and shape them well in the right
values and responsibilities is to educate and shape the
moral values and course of the world tomorrow.

Therefore, if we want a better world, we have to
create it today by our own resolute and moral dedication to the wholistic liberal arts education, correct
moral education and training for today's formative and
receptive young generation that will become tomorrow's
leaders and active responsible citizenry. If we train
them well today, they will do a good job tomorrow out
of good moral habit or conditioning as well as critical
moral thinking and moral intellectual creativity.

The Family and Moral Education

As it has been already well discussed, moral education and moral training begins at home in the family setting. But since the traditional family moral value units of father and mother have been eroded and largely broken up, immorality, socio-economic hardships, poverty, divorce, feminism as changing sex roles, with the tragic result of a high increase in sigle parents and children born to unwed teenage uneducated mothers, society has to take an increasing role in the moral education and training of the children in a formal classroom set-up, irrespective of some protest from some parents, especially when it comes to sex education and moral family values, property, rights and gender roles. If the school must do it, then the teachers must become the ideal moral role models in place of irresponsible or non-existent parents, particularly the male role of father for children who come from female-headed single parent homes.

However, sex or family education teachers* should always be mature, well informed, sensitive, moral and responsible adults since this role has been traditionally reserved for responsible parents, ministers and marriage counselors. Good moral sex and family education should include the traditional moral values and rationale for insistence on abstention from sexual intercourse until marriage, the biology of the reproductive system, the proper function of these organs, how children are created, child spacing, child adoption

---

* See Appendix C where Dr. Henry Ponder, as President of Fisk University addressing these issues in his speech to a freshmen class. This is a good example of what educators can do in order to constructively deal with moral and ethical problems and issues in a college or university setting.

contraceptives and how they function, moral problems of abortion, sexually transmitted diseases, the sanctify of marriage as an honorable covenant and the importance of waiting until one is emotionally, physically and financially ready in order to be sexually active in a monogamous relationship under the protection of the marriage bond and covenant of mutual obligations for each other and the offspring.

The main objective of sex education is, therefore, to bring about moral sexual awareness and responsibility for ones moral choices, decisions and alternatives for one's sexual encounter can reduce the high incidence of unplanned teenage pregnancies, school drop-out, prevent or reduce sexually transmitted diseases, particularly, now the deadly AIDS, and facilitate moral responsibility for one's moral decision when tempted to engage in premarital sex. Correct information and good moral training are important in all moral decision making processes including those involving personal, social and sexual relationships. Subsequently, ignorance, trial and error, and the hazards correlated with them, will be greatly reduced if not entirely banished.

However, when it comes to religious values, public schools should never try to present one religious system as superior to another. For this would be to favor and establish one religion over the others which is expressly prohibited in this country by the constitution. Moreover, apart from prejudice and subjectivism, there is no scientific or objective basis on which such a determination could be made.

Therefore, the public school can only offer and teach religion and philosophy from a strictly academic, non-partisan and comparative point of view which seeks critical understanding and not moral judgement, propagation of indoctrination in respect to any one religion.

Subsequently, Christians, Muslims, Hindus and Atheists can all sit together in the same religious course and do well in it merely as an intellectual exercise and an open academic analysis of the religious material as religious literature and philosophy.

This neutral academic approach in the study of world religions is essential if all people have to learn to live together in harmony and peace as one family of God.

Schools, Colleges and Universities: The Problem of Moral Education

All effective education and knowledge lead to behavioral visible and measurable effect and modification in behavior, values, concepts, beliefs and practices. Great scholars and moral teachers like Socrates, Plato, Aristotle, Jesus, Augustine, Thomas, Luther, Descartes, Calvin, Hume, Locke, Kant, Rosseau, Jefferson, Marx, Freud, Jung, Kierkegaard, Tillich, Barth, and Whitehead, Skinner and Piaget have all taught that good education and correct knowledge are important in making the knower whole, integrated, virtuous, moral, self-confident, dutiful, skilled, peace-loving and happy.

Since all human beings are born without any rational knowledge and experience, therefore all moral values, knowledge and beliefs are learned after birth through the unconscious, unthematic and conscious cognitive processes of both structured formal and unstructured informal education and socialization.

Informal and unstructured education as a main form of socialization and humanization takes place all the time everywhere, unlike the formal one which takes place in planned settings and pre-planned curricula in schools, colleges, universities and churches.

Whereas the former takes place anywhere and anytime, some settings are most ideal for it, particularly, at home and within the social and cultural interaction within the family context. Here, parents, siblings, grandparents, neighborhood peers and playmates play a key role as the informal teachers and role models.

In addition, these days the mass media, particularly

television, has also taken a very significant role in this educational and socialization process, the cartoons and other actors being the ideal new role models presented to the children by the mass media. Unfortunately, these new mass media role models are often immoral violent characters who cheat each other and fight each other violently most of the time.

But whereas, cartoons do not die even after being pushed over high cliffs or after being shot at several times at close range, real human beings will die if pushed off a clift or shot. Yet children are not taught this moral message, whereas, they are being conditioned to view strife, rivalry and violence as a normal acceptable way of human life.

Subsequently, parents, schools and other good willed people need to protest to the mass media so as to make sure that more moral characters are created for the young television audience viewing the cartoons and other children's programs. The public education network channels are already doing a good job and setting a good example for the commercial networks.

Sesame Street and the Muppets are excellent programs for the children to view. They are educational and provide good moral role models for all children to see and seek to emulate. And it is good that many pre-school as well as elementary schools utilize these programs in formal classroom conditions in the day to day formal process of eduction. Character animation of the story and the book being read is a valuable and great eductional method of teaching the young.

Whereas, the private shcools and colleges have no legal constraint in what subjects they teach, including religious education, Bible knowledge, moral education, ethics and moral philosophy, the public schools and colleges are legally bounded and constrained from teaching religion and partisan sectarian moral values. This would amount to the breach of the USA Constitution which prohibits the favor and government establishment of any religion or denomination.

Therefore, teaching moral values in public schools

and colleges is a more tricky and complex task. Yet it
is to be done. However, it must be done in a non-
sectarian and non-partisan manner if it is to succeed
and if it has to go unchallenged by both parents and
law courts for constitutional legality and conformity.
To this end, the schools can introduce Civics and
Ethics courses whose basic texts can be the Decalogue,
Sharia, the USA Declaration of Independence, the USA
Constitution, and the UN Declarationof Human Rights.*

The documents can be studied for their view of humanity, God, human rights, moral values, and obligations
of individuals to the State and the obligation of the
State for the citizens such as protection, law enforce-
ment, material welfare, the provision of basic education, medical and economic services.

The study could involve debates, semminars, workshops
and outside speakers on current moral issues such as
AIDS, capital punishment, abortion, genetic engineering, organ transplant, euthanasia, suicide, nuclear
war, international terrorism, world hunger, poverty,
disease, Darwinism or evolution, nuclear winter, and
pollution, creationism, homosexuality, marriage, divorce, the ordination of women to the ministry, inclusive language, sexism, the problems of institutional
racism and color prejudice in South Africa and divest-
ment. The experts should be asked to lead the discus-
sions, give lectures, provide reading and research
data, answer questions, chair and moderate debates.

However, the students should always be allowed to
make up their own minds on what is moral for them on
the basis of the data and presentation. They should
never be compelled or coerced to change their moral
views except on the basis and level of moral logical
critical reasoning based on objective data, and accumulated experiences and facts.

Any form of indoctrination is not part of any good

---

* See Appendix A for the fuller Charter of Human Rights
passed by the United Nations in 1948.

education and should never be tolerated in a public
education system. For it turns students into irresponsible social and moral robots unable to think ethically
and critically for themselves on important moral issues
of life.

A good liberal art education and moral critical thinking are the essential cures to this problem because
ignorance and lack of a free thinking mind, the absence
of positive moral role models and reinforcement for
good moral actions and habits are the greatest dangers
for a community's and the world's welbeing,
harmony, peace and happiness.

This is necessarily the case because it is easier and
also because very often, it is more immediately reward-
ing to do the wrong thing than the right thing which
most people find embarrassing just because they are
themselves evildoers who hate both good and the morally
upright who are just and do good to negate these evil
deeds of the evildoers.

That is the main reason why good people and the vocal
advocates of justice and morality get violently hated
and subsequently killed by bad and evil people. Evil
cannot afford to stand against the contrast and opposition of the good without being exposed for what it
truly is, namely, evil and ugly.

Therefore, it tries to corrupt the good and if this
move fails, then it resorts to the total elimination of
the good. Subsequently, uncompromising great moral
teachers like Socrates, Jesus, Gandhi and King; and the
prophets of justice and divine holiness were all killed
by sinful and hateful evil men.

As a result, the students have to learn the real
truth that being moral and virtuous requires courage to
face riducule, temptation, suffering, rejection and
even death. This can be taught virtually and comparati-
vely in terms of the trial and execution of Socrates
and Jesus; the violent assassinations of Ghandhi and
King.

Excellent educational films and books exist on the
lives, work, death and significance of these great

moral teachers whose teachings have irreversibly changed the world from barbaric hate, retaliation and violence to the moral universal requirement of moral knowledge, mutual acceptance, unconditional love, forgiveness, nonviolence and peace.

To bring some of the moral issues to life, the teacher should devise actual moral dilemma simulations, such as a UN mock debate on the USA military action in Lybia in order to punish Khadafi for his role in international terrorism. For instance, a forum can be created to discuss and debate the problem of nuclear arms race and nuclear war; and have half of the panel representing the Soviet Union's view whether they agree with it or not.

The same can be done about other controversal issues, such as abortion as a legitimate woman's moral right on demand, the right to die in dignity and euthanasia, the moral imperative to disclose confidential information when human life is endangered or when injustice is about to be committed, refusal to undergo medical treatment, the moral value dilemma of truth telling and self-incrimination or self-endagerment should be discussed and debated, in classroom structured setting.

This kind of approach is important because it confronts the individual with real life moral conditions and moral choices and decisions to be made. Consequently, the students' moral awareness is greatly aroused and the ability and skills to make moral evaluation of available data, weigh alternative choices and their consequences, and ability to arrive at the most appropriate choice and to make the relevant decision and to accept responsibility for it are all invaluable essential stages in all moral judgements and moral decision making process which characterize human life since all human beings are by nature essentially moral agents.

This is the "a priori" moral condition which is the essential moral requisite for being human. It cannot be otherwise, although the human being can rebel against his or her essential nature and in ignorance and self-negation and self-destruction live an immoral life of vice in the ever present torment of daily guilt for failure to do the good and the right when it is clearly known.

Consequently, authentic humanity is essentially constituted by moral uprightness or virtue, love, justice and humane kindness which are moral requirements for personal integrity, wholeness, general well-being, peace and happiness.

The Role of the Church
in Moral Education

All churches and religious institutions have a moral obligation to educate their members in ideal religious moral values, such as justice, unconditional love for all human beings, charity and concern for the poor, the homeless, the oppressed, the hungry, and the sick and dying.*

Ideally, education in this religious context should not be by the methods of preaching, indoctrination and intimidation. But rather, the members should be carefully taught why the church teaches the very values and commandments it teaches. Moral education for all people is essential because people will become better and more responsible moral agents when they know the reason why they believe certain moral beliefs and hold certain religious values.

Then, they will not be easily tempted and swayed or threatened when they meet and live with other people who do not share their own moral values or religious beliefs. This is the main reason why religious fundamentalists tend to feel very insecure with their moral values and religious beliefs when they are exposed to the academic challenges and scrutiny of the sciences,

---

* See Appendix B for the Biblical Essay and Suggestions for Workshop by Margaret Shafer of the NCCC Education in the Social Unit.

especially, the theory of evolution as opposed to the literal, interpretation of the Genesis mythical accounts of creation.

Therefore, in a pluralistic society such as ours (here in the USA), the safeguard for religious values and ethics based on Church doctrinal teachings and rigid dogmas, cannot be the pressing for legislation, since this would be an unconstitutional request. But rather, to establish Sunday School, Church related schools, colleges and universities, and therefore, teach all the doctrinal, moral, ethical and religious teaching needed and in the manner most desired by the particular Church.

However, this should never be expected or asked of the public school system and institutions of higher learning. As a result, public prayer in these public school systms would be very unconstitutional and religiously divisive, since public institutions are open to the people of all creeds, religions, philosophies, and to those who are either agnostic or self-confessed atheists.

Therefore, Christians should never use force, deceit, legislation or threat to compel anyone to become converted to Christ for Jesus himself rejected and overcame the very temptations of the use of power, force and miracles at the beginning of his ministry, in order to convert people to God.

Instead, Jesus chose to employ the humble but humane and loving method of moral teaching and persuation of men and women to hear, understand and make a personal moral choice and consequential decision to obey his call and teaching, and to follow him even if this obedience might lead to personal rejection, suffering and death at the hands of hateful and sinful men. But it is also his promise that all those who would obey and follow him would become immortal since God would raise them to eternal life if they got killed for righteousness and for Christ's and the Gospel's sake.

Consequently, all those people of good will who do good works in the name of God, and who love their fellow human beings unconditionally and seek to become God's moral ambassadors of love, reconciliation, non-violence, harmony, unity, peace and happiness, even if they get killed because of their message, will be raised by God to eternal life, and their legacy will continue to live forever shaping men and women and the world, long after they have gone.

Therefore, let all men and women of moral virtue and goodwill rise and carry forward the shining torch of moral welbeing and the divine unconditional love which we are to express to all our fellow human beings and the world which is already tired of hate and evil, and therefore, eagerly waiting for the Gospel of unconditional love, mutual acceptance, forgiveness, unity co-operation, and peace.

May God make us his effective representatives and ambassadors in the world torn with the human moral evil of greed, self-centeredness, selfishness, strife, hate and war so as to bring God's own unconditional re-demptive love, harmony, peace and happiness.

Let the peace loving people of God and all those peace loving people of goodwill, everywhere, answer in a resounding, "Amen!" And let them go out in God's name to love and serve their fellow human beings to accomplish the loving works of charity and justice; let them become the concrete God's representatives in the world by becoming willing and active peace makers everywhere, on earth where there is constant strife, conflict or war. Jesus himself commended peace making as a divine mission when he declared: "Blessed are the peace-makers for the Kingdom of God is theirs" (cf. Matt. 5:8).

Appendix A

THE UNITED NATIONS

UNIVERSAL DECLARATION OF HUMAN RIGHTS

1948

PREAMBLE

Whereas recognition of the inherent dignity and of the equal and inalienable rights of all members of the human family is the foundation of freedom, justice and peace in the world,

Whereas disregard and contempt for human rights have resulted in barbarous acts which have outraged the concience of mankind, and the advent of a world in which human beings shall enjoy freedom of speech and belief and freedom from fear and want has been proclaimed as the highest aspiration of the common people,

Whereas it is essential, if man is to be compelled to have recourse, as a last resort, to rebellion against tyranny and oppression, that human rights should be protected by the rule of law,

Whereas it is essential to promote the development of friendly relations between nations,

Whereas the peoples of the United Nations have in the Charter reaffirmed their faith in fundumental human rights, in the dignity and worth of the human person and in the equal rights of men and women and have determined to promote social progress and better standards of life in larger freedom,

Whereas Member States have pledged themslves to achieve, in co-operation with the United Nations, the promotion of universal respect for and observance of human rights and fundamental freedoms,

Whereas a common understanding of these rights and freedoms is of the greatest importance for the full realization of this pledge,

Now, therefore,

The General Assembly

Proclaims this Universal Declaration of Human Rights as a common stand of achievement for all peoples and all nations, to the end that every individual and every organ of society, keeping this Declaration constantly in mind, shall strive by teaching and education to promote respect for these rights and freedoms and by progressive measures, national and international, to secure their universal and effective recognition and observance, both among the peoples of Member States themselves and among the peoples of territories under their jurisdiction.

ARTICLE 1

All human beings are born free and equal in dignity and rights. They are endowed with reason and conscience and should act towards one another in a spirit of brotherhood.

ARTICLE 2

Everyone is entitled to all the rights and freedoms set forth in this Declaration, without distinction of any kind, such as race, colour, sex, language, religion, political or other opinion, national or social origin, property, birth or other status.

ARTICLE 3

Everyone has the right to life, liberty and the security of person.

ARTICLE 4

No one will be held in slavery or servitude, slavery and the slave trade shall be prohibited in all forms.

ARTICLE 5

No one shall be subjected to torture or cruel, inhuman or degrading treatment or punishment.

ARTICLE 6

Everyone has the right to recognition everywhere as a person before the law.

ARTICLE 7

All are equal before the law and are entitled without any discrimination to equal protectin of the law. All are entitled to equal protection against any discrimination in violation of this Declaration and against any incitement of such discrimination.

ARTICLE 8

Everyone has the right to an effective remedy by the competent national tribunals for acts violating the fundamental rights granted him by the constitution or by law.

ARTICLE 9

No one shall be subjected to arbitrary arrest, detention or exile.

ARTICLE 10

Everyone is entitled in full equality to a fair and public hearing by an independent and impartial tribu-

nal, in the determination of his rights and obligations
and of any criminal charge against him.

ARTICLE 11

1. Everyone charged with a penal offense has the
right to be presumed innocent until proved guilty according to law in a public trial at which he has had
all the guarantees necessary for his defense.

2. No one shall be held guilty of any penal offence
on account of any act or omission which did not constitute a penal offence, under national or international
law, at the time when it was committed. Nor shall a
heavier penalty be imposed than the one that was appli-
cable at the time the penal offence was committed.

ARTICLE 12

No one shall be subjected to arbitrary interference
with his privacy, family, home or correspondence, nor
to attacks upon his honour and reputation. Everyone has
the right to the protection of the law against such
interference or attacks.

ARTICLE 13

1. Everyone has the right to freedom of movement
and residence within the borders of each State.

2. Everyone has the right to leave any country,
including his own, and to return to his country.

ARTICLE 14

1. Everyone has the right to seek and enjoy in
other countries asylum from persecution.

2. This right may not be invoked in the case of
prosecutions genuinely arising from nonpolitical crimes

or from acts contrary to the purpose and principles of the United Nations.

ARTTICLE 15

1. Everyone has a right to a nationality.

2. No one shall be arbitrarily be deprived of his nationality nor denied the right to change his nationality.

ARTICLE 16

1. Men and women of full age, without any limitation due to race, nationality or religion, have the right to marry and to found a family. They are entitled to equal rights as to a marriage, during marriage and at its dissolution.

2. Marriage shall be entered into only with the free and full consent of the intending spouses.

3. The family is the natural and fundamental group unit of society and is entitled to protection by society and the State.

ARTICLE 17

1. Everyone has the right to own property alone as well as in association with others.

2. No one shall be arbitrarily deprived of his property.

ARTICLE 18

Everyone has the right to freedom of thought, conscience and religion, this right includes freedom to change his religion or belief, and freedom, either alone or in community with others and in public or private, to manifest his religion or belief in teaching, practice, worship and observance.

ARTICLE 19

Everyone has the right to freedom of opinion and expression; this right includes freedom to hold opinions without interference and to seek, receive and impart information and ideas through any media and regardless of frontiers.

ARTICLE 20

1. Everyone has the right to freedom of peaceful assembly and association.

2. No one may be compelled to belong to an association.

ARTICLE 21

1. Everyone has the right to take part in the government of his country, directly or through freely chosen representatives.

2. Everyone has the right of equal accesss to public service in his country.

3. The will of the people shall be the basis of the authority of government; this will shall be expressed in periodic and genuine elections which shall be by universal and equal suffrage and shall be held by secret vote or by equivalent free voting procedures.

ARTICLE 22

Everyone, as a member of society, has the right to social security and is entitled to realization, through national effort and international co-operation and in accordance with the organization and resources of each

state, of the economic, social and cultural rights
indispensable for his dignity and the free development
of his personality.

ARTICLE 23

1. Everyone has the right to work, to free choice
of employment, to just and favourable conditions of
work and to protection against unemployment.

2. Everyone, without any discrimination, has the
right to equal pay for equal work.

3. Everyone who works has the right to just and
favourable remuneration ensuring for himself and his
family an existence worthy of human dignity, and sup-
plemented, if necessary, by other means of social protection.

4. Everyone has the right to form and to join trade
unions for the protection of his interests.

ARTICLE 24

Everyone has the right to rest and leisure, including reasonable limitation of working hours and periodic
holidays with pay.

ARTICLE 25

1. Everyone has the right to a standard of living
adequate for the health and well-being of himself and
of his family, including food, clothing, housing and
medical care and necessary social services, and the
right to security in the event of unemployment, sick-
ness, disability, widowhood, old age or other lack of
livelihood in circumstances beyond his control.

2. Motherhood and childhood are entitled to special
care and assistance. All children, whether born in or

out of wedlock, shall enjoy the same social protection.

ARTICLE 26

1. Everyone has the right to education. Education shall be free, at least in the elementary and fundamental stages. Elementary education shall be compulsory. Technical and professional education shall be made generally available and higher education shall be equally accessible to all on the basis of merit.

2. Education shall be directed to the full development of the human personality and to the strengthening of respect for human rights and fundamental freedoms. It shall promote understanding, tolerance and friendship among all nations, racial or religious groups, and shall further the activities of the United Nations for the maintenance of peace.

3. Parents have a prior right to choose the kind of education that shall be given to their children.

ARTICLE 27

1. Everyone has the right to participate in the cultural life of the community and its benefits.

2. Everyone has the right to the protection of the moral and material interests resulting from any scientific, literary or artistic production of which he is the author.

ARTICLE 28

Everyone is entiled to a social and international order in which the rights and freedoms set forth in this Declaration can be fully realized.

ARTICLE 29

1. Everyone has duties to the community in which alone the free and full development of his personality is possible.

2. In the exercise of his rights and freedoms, everyone shall be subject only to such limitations as are determined by law solely for the purpose of securing due recognition and respect for the rights and freedoms of others and of meeting the just requirements of morality, public order and the general welfare in a democratic society.

3. These rights and freedoms may in no case be exercised contrary to the purposes and principles of the United Nations.

ARTICLE 30

Nothing in this Declaration may be interpreted as implying for any State, group or person any right to engage in any activity or to perform any act aimed at the destruction of any of the rights and freedoms set forth herein.

Appendix B

A BIBLICAL ESSAY ON JUSTICE

AND WORKSHOP

UNITED CHURCH OF CHRIST BOARD FOR HOMELAND MINISTRIES

132 West 31st Street
New York, NY 10001
September, 1986

Dear Pastor, friend of Public Education, and/or Ecumenical Colleague:

General Synod XV adopted a Pronouncement on Public Education which affirmed the importance of public education for church and society. It asked the entire church to "develop strategies for making public education at all levels (elementary, secondary, higher, adult, and continuing) a major concern for the United Church of Christ..."

With this mailing we are making available materials which will help you respond to that affirmation. Here are resources to assist you in celebrating AMERICAN EDUCATION WEEK, November 16-22, 1986, or at any other time you might wish to do so. Here you will find a BIBLICAL ESSAY ON PUBLIC EDUCATION, a BIBLE STUDY, and other aids for your efforts. The impressive LITANY can be xeroxed as is or adapted for your use.

This mailing represents the work of many talented and concerned people: the Biblical Essay and Study come from Margaret Shafer of the NCCC: the Litany and Suggested Worship Resources were adapted from the work of the Revs. Fidelia Lane and Davida Foy Crabtree, who created them in consultation with the Connecticut Conference Task Force on Public Education.

Our public schools are, as never before, in need of that responsible and caring support which our church has traditionally given them. Indeed, as they become increasingly the hope for full empowerment of the children of the poor and the marginalized in our society, the public schools can clearly be seen as an essential tool in the search for social justice and peace.

There are many ways for us to manifest our support for public education as a contributor toward a just, participatory, and harmonious society. Please let me know if these materials -- or adaptations of them -- were helpful to you, or if you found other ways to respond to the General Synod pronouncement; your responses will appear in our report to General Synod XVI. Thank you, and please know that we are available to help you in any way we can.

Grace and peace and courage to you all,

NANATTE M. ROBERTS, Ph.D.,

Secretary, Public Issues in Education
Division of the American Missionary Association: UCBHM

BIBLICAL ESSAY ON PUBLIC EDUCATION

(Prepared as a background statement to the "Policy
Statement on Elementary and Secondary Public Education
in the Society" for the Governing Board of the National
Council of Churches of Christ in the USA, May 1986.)

"The National Council of Churches of Christ in the
United States of America is a community of christian
communions which, in response to the gospel as revealed
in the Scriptures, confess Jesus Christ... (and) re-
lying upon the transforming power of the Holy Spirit,
bring these communions into common mission."

It is the nature of a Council to bring together
differing views; thus the work of the National Council
of Churches of Christ is based on a shared conviction
that within our diverse theological orientations and
interpretations of scripture we are called to a common
commitment to the public good. Always our wholeness
requires us to try to be sure our activity in the
public arena arises out of the traditions of our faith.

The contemporary Christian community always confronts the difficulty of relevantly interpreting the
ancient Biblical word for today. In considering issues
of public education, for example, the gap between modern structures and the social institutions of the Biblical period can be disconcerting. As with many current
concerns there are no direct experiences or parallels
which make the interpreter's task easy.

Biblical writers have nothing resembling public
schools on which to comment. There are no Biblical
models from which to work, no proof texts to cite. We
are forced to dig deeper into both Old and New Testaments to find the great truths which will guide us as
we relate our faith to public education in 20th-century
America.

We believe the following five principles emerge
from the biblical witness as relevant standards for
actions of the Christian community on matters related

to education. Each attempt to translate a Biblical truth into terms which may be acceptable to those in the larger public as well.

"All people are created by God and are therefore to be highly valued." The creation accounts of Genesis and Psalm 8:4-8 remind us how highly God values humanity as part of creation. Amos 9:7 and the stories of Jonah, Ruth, and the Good Samaritan all make clear the worth of peoples of all nations, not just Israel. The New Testament, especially the missionary thrust of Paul, accepts a cultural pluralism (need not become a Jew to be a Christian--see Acts 10 and Galatians 2) and assures us that in God's eyes there are no limits on who is worthy of God's grace.

The Christian community models a society in which "There is neither Jew nor Greek, slave nor free, male nor female" (Gal 3:25-29). The incarnation itself sets aside social class: God's own son reaffirmed the value of humanity, coming in flesh and blood and in poverty. He gave his life so that all through him might be saved. ALL PEOPLE ARE HIGHLY VALUED.

"Persons are nurtured to maturity in community with God and one another." God's activity through history is a continuation of God's creative activity. Israel was a corporate personality. God held the society, as well as its individual members, responsible for fulfilling the purposes of creation (Amos 3).

Just as God called the people of Israel into community, so Jesus called persons--men, women, poor and rich, righteous and sinners, princes and outcasts--into relationship with one another and with God (Matt. 22:37-39, John 13:34). Jesus himself, who grew in wisdom and in stature, and in favor with God and humanity (Lk. 2:52, cf I Sam. 2:26), is the full measure of mature personhood (Eph. 4:13). PEOPLE NEED COMMUNITY TO GROW.

Wisdom and knowledge are among the ways God empowers people for freedom and promotes their growth toward full humanity. The Lord gives wisdom; from God's mouth comes knowledge and understanding; ... you will

understand righteousness and justice and equity" (Prov.
2:6-10). Knowledge means to go beyond appearances;
wisdom is insight into the mysteries of the universe.
In a sinful world, the wisdom given by God empowers
people because it sees more than the status quo and
conventional wisdom.

The prophetic tradition continually reminds us that
to understand the history of Israel is to challenge
accepted notions of worldly wisdom, of power and wealth
and status. In the Wisdom tradition, such books as Job
and Ecclesiastes ran counter to the common wisdom of
their time and place and encouraged inquiry and debate.
Jesus used parables to raise incongruities and expose
shallow, short-range and self-serving conventional
wisdom. Jesus' teaching express the Truth which confounds and enlightens. In the Old and New Testaments we
experience the true function of education: to move
first-hand experience to a larger perspective and deeper understanding. Thus we grow into a fuller humanity.
PEOPLE ARE IMPROVED THROUGH LEARNING.

"The concerns of God expressed by the prophets for
justice and equity must be at the heart of education."
Consciousness of God's concern for justice and righteousness begins for the people of Israel with the Call
of Abraham, "I have chosen him, that he may charge his
children and his household after him to keep the way of
the Lord by doing righteousness and justice" (Gen
18:19). From Moses (Deut 18:15-22) to Malachi, the
prophets are God's spokespersons, God's teachers,
charging the people with their covenant obligations and
social responsibilities. In the years of Israel's monarchy, kings were charged with the responsibility to
remind both king and people of the Covenant.

Isaiah and Ezekiel envision a ruler coming to sit
upon the throne of David and establishing a just kingdom (Isa 9:6-7, Ezek 37:24-28). And Micah: "He has
showed you what is good....to do justice, and to love
kindness, and to walk humbly with your God" (Micah
6:8). In Matt 22:37-40, Jesus reminds us that we must
love our neighbor as ourselves. Justice and equity are

God's intention for society and are to be both its
means and its end.   These are the values which must be
passed on from generation to generation.   PEOPLE MUST
LEARN JUSTICE.

The Teacher is Central
to the Development of Persons.

Jesus exemplified the finest of teachers. One of the
most frequent titles by which people addressed Jesus
was Rabbi, teacher. The role of teacher comes out of a
rich tradition. From the earliest Biblical times, even
when there was no office of teacher, there was emphasis
on the importance of teaching (Deut. 4:10). The wisdom
tradition emphasizes teaching. The book of Proverbs is
a compendium of moral and religious instructions for
Jewish youth.

The Pharisees were a lay movement dedicated to the
teaching of the law and understanding of the covenant.
Their work culminated in the setting up of academies
for religious instruction parallel to the Greek academies for secular learning.

Both Christianity and Judaism have been shaped by
great teachers.   Jesus the Rabbi, was seen to be "a
teacher come from God" (John 3:2). Through the integrity of his personhood, the caring for his pupils, the
clarity of his message, and the passion of his procla-
mation he profoundly affected the lives of all who
heard him. Moreover, he charged the community of believers to live out the truth to which he witnessed,
providing a living lesson that has been learned and
relearned in succeeding generations. The church focuses the conceptual understandings of the Creator and the
world into interpersonal relationships.   Thereby education can be instrumental in helping transform us into
a just society in tune with the whole creation. TEACH-
ERS CHANGE LIVES.

BIBLE   STUDY: THE CHURCH AND PUBLIC EDUCATION
(The Leader's Guide)

Prepared by Margaret L.   Shafer, Education in the
Society Unit, National Council of Churches in the
USA

Use "A Biblical Essay on Public Education" (above) as a
study paper with your group.   In introducing the subject,   you will   need to begin with the ideas   in   the
second paragraph,   which discusses the relevance of the
ancient Biblical word for modern social institutions.

If   your time is limited,   you will want to choose
only one or two of the five themes for your discussion.
Which   ones you choose will depend on the interests   of
your   group and the current issues in   your   community.
For   example,   if   you have new immigrants of a   multi-
cultural   consciousness in your community,   use   I;   if
people   are particularly interested in the   growth   and
development   of children,   use II;   if the intellectual
and academic aspects of public education are of   utmost
concern,   use III;   if justice issues and minority concerns catch the attention of your congregation, use IV;
if teachers and teaching are on people's minds,   use V.
Whichever   theme(s)   you select,   you may use   the
following suggestions to develop a Bible Study session:

I. CREATED BY GOD, ALL PEOPLE ARE HIGHLY VALUED.

Read Acts 10 and Gal.   2.   Discuss the parallel between
the   debate in the early Church about the necessity   of
becoming   a   Jew   in order to be a   Christian   and   the
contemporary debate about becoming "Americanized" to be
considered a person of worth.   (What does it say to bi-
lingualism,   to desegregation, to a curriculum centered
on our European heritage and western democracy?)
Extend the discussion to the model community   Paul
describes in Gal. 3:25-29. Do we accept this same   goal

for our society? If so, what does it say to the objectives for and support of public education? What does it say to issues of segregation, sexual bias, classism?

Ask someone familiar with state education funding formulas to outline efforts to deal with inequities. Close with the question of what Jesus might say in addressing the state legislature on this subject.

II.   IN COMMUNITY WITH GOD AND ONE ANOTHER,
      PERSONS ARE NURTURED TO MATURITY.

Ask people to list the essential ingredients for the wholesome growth of a child. Read Ephesians 4, seeking for a Christian understanding of what it means to grow into mature personhood. Discuss what aspects of this nurturing process can appropriately be asked of the public schools.

Christians have a highly developed sense of the importance of relationships within a group of mutual support and of ministry to one another. How can we translate this quality for application in public schools? How can we enlarge our ministry to include care for the growth and maturity of the institutions of public schooling and for the people involved in those institutions?

III.   WISDOM AND KNOWLEDGE ARE AMONG THE WAYS GOD
       EMPOWERS PEOPLE FOR FREEDOM AND PROMOTES
       GROWTH OF PERSONS TOWARD FULL HUMANITY.

For your own background and understanding of the special Old Testament understanding of Wisdom, try to read the article on "Wisdom" in the Interpreter's dictionary of the Bible. Then take a familiar parable like the Prodigal Son (Lk. 15:11-38), or a teaching of Jesus' like the widow's offering (Lk. 21:1-4), and show how God's ways cut through the commonly accepted values.

Discuss the sentences, "Jesus' teaching expresses the Truth which confounds and enlightens. In the Old and New Testaments we experience the true function of education: to move first-hand experience to a larger perspective and deeper understanding."

What is the first-hand experience of a 6-year-old, a 12-year-old, an 18-year-old? How does a "larger perspective and deeper understanding" empower them? What are the implications for society if children are empowered or not empowered? What are the implications when some children are more empowered than other children?

Are there contradictions between God's wisdom and society's wisdom? How do we help children to understand these differences? What does this say about church/state issues? Whose point of view should be represented by government and taught in government (i.e., public) schools? What does this say about the teachings of other cultures and religions? How should Christians make sure their children learn our understanding of God's wisdom?

IV. THE CONCERNS OF GOD EXPRESSED BY THE PROPHETS
     FOR JUSTICE AND EQUITY MUST BE AT THE HEART
     OF EDUCATION.

The role of the prophets was continually to remind both king and people of their Covenant. Discuss this role, citing such passages as Isaiah 9, Micah 6:8, Amos 5:10-15, and Obadiah 1:15. In Matt. 22:37-40, Jesus reminds us that we must love our neighbors as ourselves. Is justice a uniquely Christian concern, or are the principles of justice held in common by all religions?

Raise the question, how do children learn justice and injustice? Can church people encourage school people in the task of teaching children justice? Can a child learn justice if he or she doesn't experience it? What does our discussion tell us about what we, the church, should be doing in our community about public education?

V. THE TEACHER IS CENTRAL TO THE DEVELOPMENT
OF PERSONS.

Use a concordance to check the times Jesus was addressed as "Rabbi." Use a Bible Dictionary to learn the
significance and usage of the words, "rabbi" and
"teacher."   Then go back and see how teaching is described at various periods of biblical history:
Deut. 4:10; Prov. 1:2-6 (Read the introduction to
Proverbs in the Oxford Annotated Bible); Luke
2:46;

Using John 3:2 and gospel accounts of Jesus' life
and ministry with which group members are familiar,
draw up a list of characteristics Jesus evidences as a
teacher.

Ask people to remember the best teacher they ever
had. Do any of the characteristics from the list about
Jesus correspond to their personal memories? What qualities do we have a right to expect of all teachers?
What resources does the church have to support and help
teachers?   (If the group wishes to pursue these ideas,
a most helpful book about the christian vocation of
teaching is Who Will Be My Teacher?, Marti Garlett,
Word Books: Waco, TX, 1985.)

THE LITANY FOR PEACE

LEADER: Faithful and ever-present God, we lift to you this morning our concern for public education, its people and its future. We raise for your blessing and guidance all who work and learn in the public schools and colleges of this state. We bring to you our hopes and expectations that they may be made one with Your Will.

PEOPLE: NOW HEAR OUR PRAYER, O GOD.

LEADER: We pray for our public schools and colleges, where generations have gathered for learning, where knowledge is advanced, where individuals grow.

PEOPLE: MAY THEY BE EVER STRENGTHENED AND EVER FAITHFUL.

LEADER: We pray for teachers, administrators, and all who work in education.

PEOPLE: MAY THEY KNOW THEIR OWN CREATIVITY, OUR GRATITUDE, AND OUR CARING.

LEADER: We pray for students of all ages, who are the future, yet have no assurance of what the future will bring.

PEOPLE: MAY THEY KNOW COURAGE, FAITH, AND THE JOY OF LEARNING.

LEADER: We pray for legislators and school board members, who spend long hours to shape the policies that guide education.

PEOPLE: MAY THEY SEEK YOUR GUIDANCE AND DO YOUR WILL.

LEADER: We pray for those who advocate, for parents' groups and special interest groups, for professional and student organizations.

PEOPLE: MAY THEIR EFFORTS RESULT IN EDUCATION WHICH IS RESPONSIVE, EFFECTIVE, AND DIVERSE.

LEADER: We pray for families who yearn for involvement, but find institutions and systems distant and specialized.

PEOPLE: MAY THEY OVERCOME THAT DISTANCE AND FULFILL THEIR YEARNING.

UNISON: HOLY GOD, WE ASK FOR ALL OF US YOUR BLESSING AND PRESENCE AS WE STRIVE TO DO YOUR WILL IN THIS COMMUNITY. KEEP US EVER FAITHFUL IN OUR CARING, READY TO SUPPORT AND TO CHALLENGE. VISIT YOUR LOVING KINDNESS UPON ALL THOSE FOR WHOM PUBLIC EDUCATION IS A WAY TO A FULLER LIFE IN A JUST SOCIETY.

GRANT THESE PRAYERS IN THE NAME OF JESUS CHRIST, THAT GREAT STUDENT AND TEACHER WHO DIED THAT WE MIGHT ALL HAVE LIFE ABUNDANT. AMEN.

AMERICAN EDUCATION SUNDAY

(Suggested Worship Resources)

Scripture Passages:

Deuteronomy 6:1-9	Jeremiah 31:31-34
Proverbs 1:1-9	Psalm 119:33-45
2:1-10	John 21:15-18
3:13-27	I Timothy 4:11-16
4:1-8, 11-13	

Hymns: (Pilgrim Hymnal)

Awake, Awake to Love & Work	# 34
Our God, to whom We Turn	# 86
Life of Ages, Richly Poured	#236
We Limit Not the Truth of God	#259
Strong Son of God, Immortal Love	
(Language may need some changes)	#357
Lord, Speak to Me	#397
These Things Shall Be	#450

OTHER POSSIBILITIES FOR CELEBRATION

-- Recognize persons in your congregation who are involved in Public Education as teachers, administrators, school board members, students, etc.; list their names in your bulletin;

-- Ask the congregation to hold them in special prayer that Sunday and during the week;

-- Learn about your school's programs by talking with principals, parents, and students; inform your congregation;

-- Note accomplishments of students and teachers, and hold them up to the congregation;

-- Involve children wherever possible: Junior High students could write a group litany giving thanks for things they learn in or like about their schools, or they could write prayers for students and teachers;

-- Primary and Kindergarten children could make pictures of things they like about school or would like to learn about;

-- Where possible, display these materials in the church, and inform the school of what you have done.

Appendix C

"TAKE THE ROAD LESS TRAVELED"

by

Dr. Henry Ponder
(An Address at a Freshmen Banquet
on
Sunday, August 24, 1986
Fisk University, Nashville, Tennessee, USA)

Thank you for that gracious introduction. Please be assured that what we have tried to do here has been made possible by all segments of Fisk and the larger community.

To the Board of Trustees, Alumni, Faculty, Staff, Returning Students, Class of 1990, and Friends of Fisk University - I greet you as we move into our 121st year of existence as a leader in Higher Education.

First, I want to express sincere appreciation to our Board, which has been responsible for propelling Fisk into the forefront of higher education. You, our Trustees, have been special friends to Fisk and to its President.

Actually, I know of no university in America to-day, where there has been a more harmonious relation-ship among the sectors of the institution, including Trustees, Alumni, Administration, Faculty, Staff, and Students, as there has been at Fisk these last two (2) years. I thank you very much.

To our Faculty, Staff and Students, I thank you for your continuing commitment, dedication, interest and special concern both to the University as a whole, and for me personally. I assure you that I sleep, pray, think and work for Fisk, figuratively, twenty-four hours a day. Aside from my wife, Eunice, and daughters, Cheryl and Anna, the University is my most consuming possession. Sometimes, I think my family believes it is my most consuming.

My friends, we begin this, our One Hundred Twenty-first (121st) year on a high note of optimism. Recently, June 30th, we closed out our second consecutive year with a balanced budget - in "Black"; furthermore, we have reduced our debt to $450,000.

I recently returned from the Annual Convention of the United Church of Christ and I am pleased to inform you that this body voted to increase funding to Fisk from $18,000 to $100,050 per year into the future. I am also pleased to tell you that your class, based on various data, is a very bright and alert one, as well as the largest freshman class we have had in recent years. My challenge to you is: "To whom much is given, much is expected." Your class numbers 171, who represent some 27 states and two foreign countries.

Furthermore, I am pleased that we have an alumnus who recen- tly established a $50,000 endowed scholarship fund here at Fisk. Let me hasten to add that he is not a wealthy person, but one who worked hard, was frugal and wanted to help someone else, because someone had helped him financially to get through Fisk.

Now, if I were to stop with the good news and not tell you some of the obvious problems, that would be dishonest, deceptive and misleading. There is some unpleasant news and I want to share that with you, also.

First, the dormitories are not what they should be. I simply want you to know that we are aware of this condition and hope you will bear with us awhile longer. Renovations have begun on Jubilee Hall and others will follow.

Secondly, and very regretfully, and yet understandably, we found it necessary to deny admission to sixty (60) high school graduates who wanted to attend Fisk. They just did not meet our admission standards. You are, indeed, fortunate to be here.

Thirdly, we had to drop thirty-four (34) students because of poor grades. This pains me, but I do hope it says to you that we are not just engaging in meaningless rhetoric when we speak about raising our academic standards. We are "dead serious."

Lastly, there were those students whom we had to refuse admission, because we simply did not have sufficient Financial Aid or Scholarships to provide for them....

Robert Frost, in his poem, "The Road Not Taken." tells of his choice in life:

Two roads diverged in woods, and I. . .
I took the road less traveled by,
And that has made all the difference."

In history, it has been those who have taken "The Road Less Traveled" who have made the difference in the lives of people, or a nation. W.E.B. DuBois, a Fiskite, Class of 1888, took "The Road Less Traveled" when he headed the "Niagara Movement" that led to the founding of the NAACP.

There will always be those who will say, "What can one person do?" You are only knocking your head against a brick wall." But Rosa Parks ignored the skeptics, she took "The Road Less Traveled" when she refused to give up her seat on the bus to a white man. She is the mother of the Civil Rights Movement.

All of us must be alert to the forces of evil wherever we find them. Sometimes these evil forces invade our personal lives, and it is during these times that I would urge you young people to have the courage to take "The Road Less Traveled." I would urge you to listen to Michael Jackson, and say, "Beat It!" to your peers who may offer you drugs by telling you how great it is to get high. My guess is that when Michael was growing up in Gary, he had the guts to say, "No" and "Beat It!" to the gangs with whom he probably came in daily contact. He took "The Road Less Traveled."

Today's acceptance of some social or moral freedoms necessitates that we take "The Road Less Traveled." Our country, the most advanced in the world, has an enormously high infant mortality rate. Our rate is on par with some of the undeveloped countries. How can that be? The primary reason is due to the large number of underweight infants born to teenagers. More likely than not, the pregnant teenager gets little or no prenatal care, thus her child is poorly nourished and has less chance of survival in its first year of life.

There is another corollary to this statistic. The single mother and her child are the greatest source of the increase in poverty in this country. This burden increases the welfare roles which the taxpayers are called upon to bear. This pattern is something which young people themselves can do something about, if they will take "The Road Less Traveled."

According to Harold L. Hodgkinson, teenagers give birth to more than half a million children each year - 10,000 to mothers under 15 - children giving birth to children. About 800,000 teens face unwanted pregnancies each year for which there are no good solutions. Sixty (60) percent abort, while of the 40 percent who give birth, more than half will raise their children themselves. These children will be "at risk."

Nearly half of all births to unmarried teenagers are to Black mothers. The adolescent single mother was the exception in the 1950's and has become the rule in the Black community in the 1980's. The White rate of teenage births, while not as high as the Black rate, is still twice as high as any other Western nation (Hodgkinson). Our teenagers must take "The Road Less Traveled."

My young friends, believe me when I tell you, there are all kinds of "roads" out there. There is the shuck and jive "road," there is the eat, drink and be merry "road," there is let's just do enough to get by "road," there is the "road" that teaches, blame it all on race, discrimination and color, there is the drug "road," there is the "road" that teaches aim for the tree tops; the order is blood, sweat and tears - and one that teaches, work hard, burn the mid-night oil; a man's reach should exceed his grasp or what's the heaven for?

My young friends there are roads that are saying - do not register and vote - your vote will not make a difference. I hope the students, faculty and staff of Fisk Univeristy will follow "The Road Less Traveled" and register here in Nashville and vote in the November elections. We can make a difference if we vote here.

The political system is the oil that makes the government receptive to the need of the masses. Seldom, if ever, do those in power voluntarily bestow upon others a share in the power without a struggle. The great Abolitionist Frederick Douglass put it this way:

If there is no struggle there is no progress. Those who profess to favor freedom and yet depreci- ate agitation are men who want crops without plow- ing up the ground. They want rain without thunder and lightning, they want the ocean without the awful roar of its waters.

Despite this gloomy picture my young friends, you are still free to make choices, and to listen to the drumbeat which motivates you to "hitch your wagon to a star" and to "Plant your feet on higher ground." You are still free to "choose to be the best that you can be," and to help make this world a better place, just as many who have gone before you have done, and have opened many doors which have led to greater opportuni- ties for you to enjoy. They have given generously of themselves, and of their funds, to improve the quality of life for all of us.

Today, I salute them also, because they have beaten a path so that you might see a light in the clearing. Because of them, and of all those who have gone before, who dared to fight and even lay down their life for justice and equality, you have "promises to keep." So,

I would say to you, do not tread the "road" of medioc-
rity, inertia, and self-satisfaction; but, rather the
"road" which leads you to the persuit of excellence. No
mountain is too high for you to climb, no task too
difficult to tackle.

May I remind you that there are "roads" today that
sell numerous myths - and I must say that all myths are
not bad - much depends upon how they are interprered as
giving positive meaning to life and destiny. Most myths
are based on actual group experience. For example,
racism in this country by any standard is a reality.
Despite racism, and it abounds a plenty, young Blacks
need to see themselves as members of a special group
capable of overcoming most odds.

Therefore, what we need, among other things, is a
myth that is constructive and evokes a sense of pride,
self-esteem, identity, and energy to move ahead. If we
give up trying, we lose.

Friday night we had a "Block Party" on campus. I
hope you enjoyed it. Saturday morning I walked the
campus and was amazed at the amount of debris, beer
cans and bottles lying around. Mrs. Ponder and I
picked up many of them!

What was needed, and is needed, are students with
"too much pride" to allow this campus to be littered
with debris. One student could have initiated a "clean-
up" after the party. Here clearly was an opportunity
for students to take "The Road Less Traveled."

Yes, you as one person, can make a difference, if
you "Take The Road Less Traveled."

Finally, I am sure that many of you saw the "The
Wiz," and will recall Dorothy was told to follow the
yellow brick road. On that road there were no sign
posts, nothing to tell her to go right, or left. In
many ways we might compare the yellow brick road to the
path we take in life.

The directions we get in following it are acquired
along the way: the lessons of integrity, of responsibility, of common sense, of faith, of confidence in one's
self which helps set goals, of concern for one's fellow

man, of appreciation to those who lend a helping hand, and many others. We learn to make choices along the way. Sometimes we make the wrong choices, but we must not be defeated by our mistakes. We must learn from our mistakes.

You are now a part of FISK UNIVERSITY.* May your contributions add to her fame!

---

* Dr. Henry Ponder is the President of Fisk University. If every educator and administrator in education, followed his noble example of addressing key moral issues, in a constructive manner, our educational systems would improve greatly, and educated people would truly be more moral, ethical, productive and responsible citizens they were meant to be.

This is true because, education without a moral emphasis is almost a worthless and costly hazardous venture which does little good to anyone; but instead, might actually threaten the very safety and existence of the community. This is the case with nuclear technology without strong moral and ethical norms and regulations to restrain its misuse and the subsequent resulting global nuclear deadly threat to both human and terrestrial life.

Appendix D

THE PROBLEM OF MORALITY AND CRIME

IN A BLACK INNER CITY COMMUNITY

by

Malcolm X Dean

There is a widespread problem of crime in the nation's
lower class black neighborhoods. Why is there such a
problem with crime in the urban black community? The
answer may be given in several reasons: lack of food,
money, decent housing, and lack of opportunity all
contribute to the plight of the urban black community.

Since we already know that there are various
causes for crime in the black community, how can we
take effective steps in reducing some of these problems
that plague the black community? Someone might say,
give them decent housing, good schools, hospitals, and
public services and the black community will have a
different outlook in life. Whether or not this outlook
will be more positive or negative remains the question.

But, if the black community will work together, it
can really improve it's present condition of poverty
followed by crime and provide a peaceful life for all
blacks regardless of financial status.

First of all let us examine the types of people
that live in the urban black community. When one thinks
of the urban black neighborhood, what comes to mind? Is
it the pimp, drug pusher, car thief, housing project,
or the unambitious hoodlum walking the street that
comes to mind first. In some cities, these conditions

are a reality. The drug pusher is just as much a common
sight as the pimp.

These types of people project a negative image to
the average black child growing up in the urban black
community. Black children in these communities idolize
these people because of the fast, easy money that can
be made. More and more today, young black children are
becoming involved in crimes that were once reserved for
older people. For instance, in Detroit, there was a
notorious drug ring entitled "Young Boy Incorporated"
which used children as young as 10 or 11 years of age
to sell drugs on the street.

These children could make $300 or $400 a week or
more. They do not worry about being caught because of a
juvenile system that seemingly "protects" these young
people. Once one of these young "runners" is picked up
by the police, he is usually back on the street within
the course of a week because the laws protect these
children from any serious punishment.

Then you have your typical black teenage male that
walks the streets or stands outside of party stores on
the street corner. These teenagers stand out waiting
for some innocent victim to come along so they can
harrass them of their possessions. There are the different youth gangs representing various neighborhoods
that fight against each other for no apparent reason
but to prove how tough they are. It seems that there
has never been a greater pressure on the black male
than the pressure to impress his friends or peers.

The black teenager feels as though it will impress
his friends if he steals a car or snatches a purse.
These teenagers feel as though they have not "gotten
around" unless they have done something to break the
law.

These types of people as well as a lot of other
types make up most of the urban black community. In
some ways one might understand why a black teen-ager
living in a low income housing project in a lower class
black neighborhood will trun to a life of crime instead
of finishing school, going to college and living a

"respectable" life.

To the young black child in low income neighborhoods, it is the criminal that lives the respectable
life. Let's face it, the shiny luxury car, fur coats,
fancy jewelry are appealing but is it worth all of the
trouble that comes with it? These black children stand
in awe of the money that these neighborhood crime
figures make and immediately they decide that they want
fast and easy money also.

A seat in the Senate seems far off to the neglected
teenager in the urban community. Usually, the parent is
not bringing in enough money to support the family and
some children feel that they must find a way to help
support the household. Then suddenly, crime does not
seem too bad.

In fact, this life of crime can be neccessary. It
also seems hard to attain a decent education on an
empty stomach. In some families where food may be
scarce, a younster may also be tempted to snatch a few
purses to get money for food. Females are also involved
in crime within the urban black community. First of all
there is the common prostitute on the street. These
women could work for a pimp or they could be self
employed for extra money.

Female gangs are also part of the crime scene.
Although the females are less apt to be as violent as
males, they may occasionally get involved in theft.
There are also other sights in the urban black neighborhoods such as the drug addict who may run to a life
of crime to support a bad habit.

There is also the street bum who may do the same
to support a habit of drinking. These people and more
are the types of people that may be found in the urban
black community.

Now that we know the types of people that live in
the lower income black neighborhoods, let us examine
the different types of crimes that they commit and
possibly why these people may commit these crimes. In
spite of any negative influences to the black community, there will always be some positive influence. The

Black Church has been a source of peace and serenity
for the people of a neglected black neighborhood.

As stated before, some crimes are not committed
for no reason. There are several factors that shape the
existence of blacks in the urban community. For instance, there is the type of morality that exists in
the black urban community.

What may be perceived to be right in a suburban
society may not be percieved the same way by those in a
urban community setting. Morally, stealing is considered wrong but when a person is used to living without
good housing and eating, stealing may be viewed as a
means for survival.

It is sad that one should have to resort to crime
as a means for survival but, everyone wants clothing to
wear, a house to live in, and food to eat. These are
neccessities for twentieth century life but as wealthy
as this nation is, there are still those who live far
below the standards of American life; particularly the
people occupying the neighborhoods of the black slums
where this low standard of living is a way of life for
some who have to struggle for survival.

Growing up in a slum certainly does have a different effect on a person's outlook on life than growing
up in an upper-middle class society. Many of the blacks
living in these slums do not have the skills to get
successful jobs so they do not have as much to live for
as does the upper class society.

Lack of public services also contribute to the
development of crime in the black urban community. Many
teenagers may get involved with projects or activities
to help boost the morale of the people and influence
them in a more positive way. There are not many who
care about the needs of the urban community, so in
turn, neither does the urban community care about itself.

As a result, we have all of the murders, stealing,
vandalism, and other criminal acts that are associated
with urban life. A vandal paints obscenities on a wall
because he or she does not have the same values as

person of the upper class.

Within the urban society, there is always something to be desired whereas, within the suburbs there is little or nothing to be desired. In turn, the person living in an urban community has a different set of goals.

The life of a person in the urban society is centered around getting the neccessities of life while the person in the upper class seeks to add to what is already required. It is also believed that a person's behavior is influenced to a certain extent by friends or associates. A black teenager may rob a party-store in order to impress friends or to keep from being called a chicken.

A teenager in the urban community may turn to drug dealing because the minimum wage jobs at different fast food resturaunts do not pay enough money to satisfy his desires. Why work at Mac- Donalds restaurant for $80 a week when you can make more than that amount in a day on the streets selling drugs. This is the brand of mentality displayed in the urban black community.

Also, as a result of extensive boredom, rape occurs in the urban environment. Usually, those who commit such acts of sexual violence are thought of as being mentally impaired. Black youths may also be tempted to commit various acts of crime because of a bad family life. Because a black teenager is unable to get along with parents, he or she may turn to crime as a sort of punishment for the parents. As for the females, pregnancy may result.

There is always the temptation to break the law in the urban community. Some break the law in order to gain respect from others. This is probably common among street gangs. Street gangs fight in order to defend their turf and gain respect from the other kids in the neighborhood. In turn, the young children, out of admiration for the older gang members, want to grow up and join a gang also. Joining a gang could enhance a young man's relations with the opposite sex.

After a while, these teenage delinquents drop out of school and move on to the bigger crimes. Why it is so hard for some youths in the black slums to stay in school is also a major question. It seems that streets have more to offer than a good education. They feel that if they can not succeed in their school studies, they can drop out and turn to something that they feel they can succeed in.

Later on in life, they realize that they made a wrong turn. But, now it is either make some fast money or continue the "cycle of poverty." Although it is almost neccessary these days to have a college education in order to get a well paying job, many of the families in the urban black community cannot afford to send their children to college and when the child does not perform well and misses a chance at a possible scholarship, the door to opportunity is shut. Then, there is a young person with dreams like everyone else but with no visible means of making these dreams a reality.

Now that different reasons have been discussed on why a person in the urban society may turn to crime, how can we prevent a child who dreams of being a drug pusher from taking a wrong turn in life? How can we keep the crime rate down in the black urban society? Is the death penalty a good solution or do we find something for these people to do to prevent them from turning to crime. Surely, we all want to walk our neighborhood streets without the fear of being robbed.

In Detroit, there have been so many shootings on the street, that one wonders whether he will return if he left home. The ages of these criminals are becoming younger and younger and it is up to the parents to educated their children on the dangers of the street. In spite of any instruction given from parents, there will always be the temptation to turn to crime because the parents can not watch their children all of the time.

Somewhere, someone will offer them an opportunity to make some "fast money." Another effective means of curving a relatively high crime rate would be for the members of the neighborhood to get to know each other well. If everyone on the block knows each other, they can look out for each other. Various neighborhood watch programs have been started. Crime will never decrease unless the citizens get involved.

Too many people have been killed on the streets but no one saw what happened or who committed the crime. If there is no-body to testify against the criminals, there is no way that they can be punished. Soon they are back on the street. Citizens need to stand up against crime and not be afraid or we will never solve the problem of crime in our urban black communities.

It has been said that "an idle mind is a devil's workshop." If we do not find any programs or activities for our black youths to participate in, someone on the streets will instead. Various churches have excellent youth programs that can give the black youth something to do in the spare time. Even the worst hoodlum walking the street would enjoy a good game of basketball sometimes.

If the leaders of the community would show more interest in the youths by providing various activities, the youth will have a healthier outlook on life. So far, methods for preventing probable criminals from getting into trouble have been discussed but, what do we do about the select few that do not heed warnings. Sure, we could stand to make the laws governing young hoodlums stricter.

If a youngster was sure without a doubt that he would be severely punished for selling drugs or stealing, he would probably think twice before turning to crime. The problem today is that many criminals know that they would not be punished severely or they feel that they would not be caught.

There will always be someone out there destined to be a law breaker. But if the community will work together to provide more positive role models for the youths, it may curve their appetites for crime. Everyone is entitled to live a happy life free from fear and with some work, we can help clean up the black neighborhoods, and live a happy life. Most importantly, Black people as a whole have to learn to live together and stop fighting each other.

If we look closely, we will find that we are our own worst enemy. Most of the crimes committed, in this country, involve a Black person against another Black person. If we as black people would learn to work and live together in peace, that would solve many of our crime problems that we have, and face today, in our urban black communities.

Appendix E

TWESIGYE'S COMMANDMENTS

FOR

CREATIVE GLOBAL PROBLEM SOLVING

1. Thou shalt not create a problem where one does not exist.

2. Thou shalt not create a greater problem in the process of solving a simpler one.

3. Thou shalt not attempt to solve a problem which has not yet been clearly identified and carefully studied for all possible causes and possible alternative solutions.

4. Thou shalt not point a gun at what you do not intend to shoot or kill.

5. Thou shalt not argue on anything of which you are ignorant, for it can be a source of great evil and self-damnation.

6. Thou shalt not assume that it is true beause somebody says it is true or because it is written down in a book or a newspaper, unless it can be proved by objective evidence.

7. Thou shalt not appeal to the infallible authority of your religion or holy religious book(s) to establish scientific, imperical, and historical truths, for this is to misuse both religion and

its sacred gods, unless the gods are able to speak for themselves during the debate.

8. Thou shalt not invoke the sacred name of God, in order to validate your argument and its truth, for God is the same one Creator who gave you the mind and intellect so that you could verify the truth through the sacred activity of the mind in vigorous, orderly, creative and critical thinking processes.

9. Thou shalt not assume that what you say and intend to be heard is what is actually said, heard and understood by your audience. Therefore, always repeat it in various ways and in different words and seek an honest feedback, in order to ensure effective mutual communication or else speak to the trees and the sky.

10. Thou shalt not assume that difference denotes something bad or inferior, for variety and contrast are the spices of life. Therefore, learn to appreciate the differences as God's valuable gifts to break the boring monotony of life.

11. Thou shalt learn to recognize thine own ignorance, prejudice, and limitations, so as to be able to avoid them or change them.

12. Thou shalt learn to recognize thine own ethnocentricism, prejudice and bigotry in dealing with other people, particularly, those of another nation, religion, class, race, color and gender.

13. Thou shalt learn to listen to others in order to hear, learn, understand, become wise, and in order to facilitate effective mutual communications, for nobody can communicate to anybody when everybody is talking, with nobody listening to anybody.

14. Thou shalt not speak in a language that is foreign to your audience, unless there a capable interpreter available.

15. Thou shalt not assume that other people see the same "world" and the same "reality" that you see, for our perception of both the world and reality are very personal and very different. In other words, what is visible and sensible to us is subjective reality, and the objective reality is never fully available to our subjective experience, for it is infinite and transcendent.

    Therefore, avoid debates about the nature of the world, for they tend to be analogous to debates about the nature of the shapes of clouds.

16. Thou shalt not fight a war or kill your opponent because of a verbal or an intellectual disagreement, for physical violence is not an appropriate response to an intellectual threat or inferiority. Moreover, violence only provokes more violence, and counter violence, and therefore, violence never solves any problems since it creates more problems than it solves.

    However, in the absence of good willed great creative minds to provide creative and humane global problem solving skills, violence remains a viable solution to global problems, since it appeals to the ignorant masses who lack the capability to see the real nature of human problems and their true constructive political and economic solutions.

17. Thou shalt not argue with a fool, for it is mere waste of valuable time.

18. Thou shalt not assume that one race or religion is superior to another, for it is the major source of many serious global human problems, and great evils in the human world.

19. Thou shalt not do to others what you do not want done to you, for this is the only true earthly practical measure of love and justice.

20. Thou shalt not love thy self and others in the same way, if it is not wholesome; for free unconditional love for the self and others is the key to both happiness and meaningful global harmony, peaceful human coexsistence and mutual fulfillment.

21. Thou shalt always remember to smile, for it costs less energy than frowning, yet, it is the sunshine of love in a gloomy world starving for free love and forgiveness. Besides, a smile is the best weapon and means to win over enemies, permanently, without firing a single shot!

22. Thou shalt not abuse or oppress the weak and the defenseless, for human strength is only measured in goodness and not in evil accomplishments.

23. Thou shalt not desire to be another person, for God made you to become a unique and a special person in the world, and therefore, you can only be truly happy when you find and like the authentic self or person that you were created to become.

24. Thou shalt not confuse religion with science, for it is the source of many evils and great human misery in the world today.

25. Thou shalt not accept a bribe, for it is the perfect conventional disguised blindfold for unsuspecting foolish greedy victims, being "set up" for an eventual terrible day of destruction.
    Remember, the true worth of a human being is not measured in material goods, wealth and material possessions, but rather, in the individual's

personal moral values and responsibility as a thinking moral agent capable of acting in a manner that will enhance goodness, beauty, justice, love and tender care, in the indifferent world.

26. Thou shalt not entertain sexual temptations for self-gratification, for sex has been the human problematic broad gate leading to both unhappiness and destruction. Besides, AIDS has no mercy on those who have no room for self-control.

27. Thou shalt not postpone to tomorrow what can be done today.

28. Thou shalt not take love or friendship for granted, for that is the sure way to abuse and lose it.

29. Thou shalt not say anything in private about any person, that you cannot say in the presence of that person.

30. Thou shalt not do evil in order to bring about the good, for evil only produces evil, and only the good is capable of producing a greater common good.

31. Thou shalt not solve a political problem with military violence for a political problem requires a political solution just like a medical problem requires a medical solution and not a military one.
However, most human and major global problems can easily be solved through love and constructive politics.

32. Thou shalt not forget that many deadly and savage wars have always been ironically fought in the name of the Loving Almighty God, superiority, freedom and liberation.

Thou shalt not forget that the victorious liberators soon become themselves corrupt evil oppressors to be overthrown for having succumbed to the evil temptations of power, wealth, sex, technology and superiority complex.

Therefore, thou shalt remember that true human liberation will not come until the liberators learn that true lasting human liberation, global freedom and peace consist in the dual liberation of the oppressor and the oppressed from mutual fear, distrust, prejudice and hatred; as well as a being freed from the other invisible evil chains of ignorance, selfishness, pride, ethnocentricism, racism, color-prejudice, discrimination, sexism, class consciousness, materialism, idolatry, violence, hate, injustice, greed, oppression, malice, envy, sadism and both religious and ideological bigotry.

A SELECTED BIBLIOGRAPHY AND SUGGESTIONS

FOR FURTHER READING

Abelson, Raziel and Friquegnon Marie-Louise. Ethics for Modern Life. New York: St. Martin's Press, Third Edition, 1987.

Bahm, Archie, J. Comparative Philosophy: Western, Indian and Chinese Philosophies Compared. Abaquque: World Books, 1977.

Barret, William. The Irrational Man. New York: Anchor Books, 1962.

Beach, Waldo and Niebuhr, Richard, H. Christian Ethics: Sources of the Living Tradition. New York: John Wiley & Sons, Second Edition, 1973.

Brunner, Emil. Man in Revolt. Philadelphia: Westminister Press, 1948.

------------. Moral Man and Immoral Society. New York: Scribners, 1960.

Buber, Martin. I and Thou. Translated by Walter Kaufmann, New York: Scribners, 1970.

De Chardin, Teilhard. The PHENOMENON of MAN. New York and London: Harper & Row, 1975.

Farley, Edward. The Ecclesial Man. Philadelphia: Fortress, 1975.

Foucalt, Michael. The Order of Things: An Archaeologi-
cal of Human Sciences. New York: Vintage Books, 1970.

French, Peter, A. and Brown Curtis, eds. Puzzles,
Paradoxes and Problems: A Reader for Introductory
Philosophy. New York: St. Martin's Press, 1987.

Guthrie, W.K.C. The Greek Philosophers: From Thales
to Aristole. New York: Harper & Row Publishers, 1950.

Harrelson, Walter. The Ten Commandments and Human
Rights. Philadelphia: Fortress Press, 1980.

Hawley, Robert, C. & Hawley, Isabel L. Human Values in
the Classroom: A Handbook for Teachers. New York:
Hart Publishing Co. Inc. 1975.

Heidegger, Martin. The Question Concerning Technology
and Other Essays. New York/London: Harper & Row,
1977.

Moltmann, Jurgen. Man: Christian Anthropology in the
Conflict of the Present. Translated by John Study.
Philadelphia: Fortress Press, 1979.

Moore/McCann/McCann. Creative and Critical Thinking.
Boston: Houghton Mifflin Co., Second Edition, 1985.

Niebuhr, Reinhold. Moral Man and Immoral Society.
New York: Charles Scribner's Sons, 1960.

----------. The Nature and Destiny of Man. (2 Vols.)
New York: Scribners, 1964.

Niebur, Richard H. Christ and Culture. New York: Harper
& Row Publishers, 1951.

Pannenberg, Wolfhart. Human Nature, Election and History. Philadelphia: The Westminister Press, 1977.

----------. What is Man? Philadelphia: Fortress, 1970

Parker, William R. and Aldwell, Enid. Man: Animal and Divine. Los Angeles: Scrivener & Co., Third Edition, 1970.

Perkins, Hugh V. Human Development and Learning. Belmont, Ca.: Wadsworth Publishing Co., Second Edition, 1974.

Pittenger, Norman W. The Christian Understanding of Human Nature. Philadelphia: The Westminster Press: 1964.

Rahner, Karl. The Evolutionary Origin of Man as a Theological Problem. New York: Herder & Herder, 1965.

----------. Foundations of the Christian Faith. New York: Seabury Press, 1978.

----------. Spirit in the World. New York: Herder & Herder, 1968.

----------. The Hearers of the Word. New York: Herder & Herder, 1966.

----------. Grace in Freedom. New York: Herder & Herder, 1969.

Reale, Giovanni. The Systems of Hellenistic Age: A History of Ancient Philosophy. Edited and Translated by John R. Catan. Albany: State University of New York, 1985.

Ring, Merrill. Beginning with the Pre-Socratics. Palo Alto: Mayfield, 1987.

Stegenga, James A and Axline, Andrew W. The Global Community: A Brief Introduction to International

Relations. New York & London: Harper & Row, Publishers, Second Edition, 1982.

Tillich, Paul. Systematic Theology. 3 Vols. Chicago: Chicago University Press, 1960.

----------. The New Being. New York: Scribners, 1955. Twesigye, Emmanuel K. Common Ground: Christianity, African Religion and Philosophy. New York: Peter Lang, 1987.

Werkmeister, W. H. Historical Spectrum of Values Theories. Lincoln: Johnson Publishing Co., 1970.

Whitehead, Alfred North. Adventures of Ideas. New York: MacMillan Publishing Co., 1983.

--------. Science and the Mordern World. New York: MacMillan, 1925.

--------. Religion in the Making. New York: MacMillan, 1926.

--------. Process and Reality. New York: MacMillan, 1978.

Wicks, Robert J., Parsons, Richard D. and Capps, Donald E. eds. Clinical Handbook of Pastoral Counseling. New York: Paulist Press, 1987.

Wittgenstein, Ludwig. Philosophical Investigations. Third Ed. Translated by G.E.M. Anscombe, New York: Macmillan, 1968.

INDEX

Anthony J. Blasi

MORAL CONFLICT AND
CHRISTIAN RELIGION

American University Studies: Series VII (Theology and Religion). Vol. 35
ISBN 0-8204-0497-7   190 pages   hardback US $ 33.50*

*Recommended price – alterations reserved

This work takes up the problem of moral conflict, wherein a person must choose between two or more evils. The problem lies behind such issues as the defensive war, therapeutic abortion, and contraception. It becomes a religious question because, as the author argues, religion elicits the same kind of openness to values as is needed for addressing moral dilemmas. After culling insights out of the history of Christian ethics, Blasi presents phenomenologies of both moral decision making and religion, and uses the results to address the variety of moral dilemmas.

"This is an original and enlightening study of a timely and important subject."

> *Leslie Dewart*
> *St. Michael's College*
> *University of Toronto*

"Conflict situations will always exist. And therefore so will the need for thoughtful precision in dealing with them. Blasi's book is a significant contribution to that precision."

> *Richard A. McCormick, S. J.*
> *University of Notre Dame*

PETER LANG PUBLISHING, INC.
62 West 45th Street
USA – New York, NY 10036

Emmanuel K. Twesigye

COMMON GROUND

Christianity, African Religion and Philosophy

American University Studies: Series VII (Theology and Religion). Vol. 25
ISBN 0-8204-0408-X   241 pages   hardback US $ 31.00*

*Recommended price – alterations reserved

Common Ground: Christianity, African Religion and Philosophy is a result of many years of research and reflection on the problem of human existence or «the human problematic» as dealt with in the philosophical-theological traditions of both Africa and the Christian West. With the help of Karl Rahner's philosophical-theological framework, the author finds that both traditions are concerned with the same universal problems facing the human being arising out of finitude, sin and guilt. Subsequently, the author shows how in each tradition, the preoccupation of both philosophy and religion is that of soterilogy and salvation. It is also shown how both traditions are concerned with how to live a Good Life, and that the Good Life is correlative with the free human obedience to God as the Holy Creator and perfect fulfillment of all obedient human beings, everywhere.

PETER LANG PUBLISHING, INC.
62 West 45th Street
USA – New York, NY 10036